CHARACTER EVIDENCE

Argumentation Library

Volume 11

CHARACTER EVIDENCE

An Abductive Theory

DOUGLAS WALTON
University of Winnipeg, Canada

Springer

A C.I.P. Catalogue record for this book is available from the Library of Congress.

ISBN 10: 1-4020-4942-0 (HB)
ISBN 13: 978-1-4020-4942-2 (HB)
ISBN 10: 1-4020-4943-9 (e-book)
ISBN 13: 978-1-4020-4943-9 (e-book)

Published by Springer,
P.O. Box 17, 3300 AA Dordrecht, The Netherlands.

www.springer.com

Printed on acid-free paper

For Karen, with love

CONTENTS

Acknowledgements xi

Introduction xiii

1

The Problem of Character Evidence 1

1.1 Individual Worth and Respect for Character 2

1.2 Ruling on Relevance of Character Evidence in Trials 5

1.3 Problem of the Two-sided Nature of Character Evidence in Law 9

1.4 Innuendo and Attacks on Character 15

1.5 Character Assassination and Panegyric Discourse 17

1.6 Reputation and Character 20

1.7 Character Attacks and *Ad Hominem* Arguments 24

1.8 A Problem of Reasoning and Evidence 27

1.9 Character Properties in Law and Ethics 29

1.10 Character Evidence in Law and Artificial Intelligence 33

2

Defining and Judging Character 39

2.1 Bias and Character 40

2.2 Habit, Propensity and Motive 43

2.3 Agents, Practical Reasoning and Character 46

2.4 Character as the Property of an Agent 49

2.5 Evaluating Witness Testimony 52

2.6 The Structure of Abductive Reasoning 56

2.7 Character as an Interpersonal Notion 61

2.8 Evidence for Character Judgments 64
2.9 Drawing Conclusions by Abductive Reasoning from Given Data 67
2.10 Differentiating Character, Motive and Bias 74

3
Integrity and Hypocrisy 79
3.1 The Three Central Characteristics of Integrity 80
3.2 Judging a Person's Integrity 82
3.3 Commitment and Integrity 84
3.4 A Case Where a Person's Integrity is in Doubt 87
3.5 Living Up to a Commitment 88
3.6 Integrity and Living Up to a Commitment 90
3.7 Character Attack Based on Alleged Hypocrisy 94
3.8 Evaluation of the Alleged Hypocrisy Case 98
3.9 Evidence for Judgments of Integrity and Hypocrisy 101
3.10 The Defeasibility of Character Judgments 105

4
Simulative Reasoning and Plan Recognition 109
4.1 Collingwood's Theory of Reenactment 110
4.2 Simulative and Autoepistemic Reasoning 112
4.3 Strategic Use of Simulative Reasoning 116
4.4 Scripts and Stories 119
4.5 Simulative Practical Reasoning 123
4.6 Plan Recognition 125
4.7 Characteristics of Simulative Practical Reasoning 128
4.8 Combination of Simulative and Abductive Reasoning 130
4.9 Abstraction and Chaining 133
4.10 Defeasible Reasoning 135

5
Multi-Agent Dialogue 139
5.1 Plausible Reasoning 140
5.2 Plan Recognition and Dialogue 146
5.3 Sources of Dialogue Evidence 149
5.4 Commitment in Dialogue 153
5.5 Legal Evidence and Examination Dialogue 155
5.6 Examination Dialogue and Conversational Postulates 159
5.7 A Dialectical Theory of Explanation 162
5.8 A Dialectical Argumentation Scheme for Abduction 165

5.9 Abductive Evidence for Courage Judgments 170
5.10 Abductive Evidence for Integrity Judgments 174

6
A Multi-Agent System for Character Evidence 177
6.1 Character-Based Inferences 178
6.2 Inferences Linking Evidence to Character 181
6.3 Generalizations and Fallacies 185
6.4 Character-Based Evidence Contrasted to Other Evidence 189
6.5 Argumentation Schemes 192
6.6 *Ad Hominem* Arguments 196
6.7 Plan Recognition and Practical Inconsistency 200
6.8 Simulative Reasoning in *Ad Hominem* Arguments 204
6.9 The PFARD Multi-Agent Dialogue System 207
6.10 Summary of the Method 214

Bibliography 221

Index 231

ACKNOWLEDGEMENTS

The first rough draft of this book was written during the spring term of 1999 while I was Visiting Professor in the Communication Department at Northwestern University. My research during this period was also supported by a Fulbright Senior Fellowship. I was unable to do much further work on the manuscript until my research and study leave in the spring term of 2001, spent as Visiting Professor in the Communication Department of the University of Arizona. During that period I was able to get access to Lexis-Nexis and to the Law Library at the University of Arizona, and collect more of the legal material I needed for the book. Towards the end of that visit, I was able to get a second draft of the manuscript ready. I would like to thank my colleagues in both departments who, through many discussions on allied matters, enabled me to learn more about various aspects of subjects treated in the book. I would especially like to thank Mike Leff, Jean Goodwin, David Zarefsky and Tom Goodnight of Northwestern University, and Michael Dues, Scott Jacobs and Sally Jackson at the University of Arizona. My collaboration on other projects with Chris Reed and Henry Prakken has also helped me to gain insights on argumentation schemes and legal reasoning that were useful in parts of this book.

I would like to thank Craig Callen for organizing and chairing the conference "Visions of Rationality in Evidence Law", held at the Michigan State University College of Law, April 3–6, 2003, and for discussions after the conference. The book has also benefited a good deal from discussions with other participants in the conference, both during the conference itself and afterwards by e-mail: especially I would like to thank Richard Friedman, Erica Beecher-Monas, Mike Redmayne, Greg Mitchell, Kevin Saunders, Michael Risinger, Michael Saks, Roger Park, Ron Allen, Myrna Raeder, Eleanor Swift and Bruce Burns. I would like to thank John Zeleznikow for inviting me to take part in the Second Joseph Bell Centre Workshop on the

Evaluation of Evidence at the University of Edinburgh in June–July 2003. I would like to thank John Zeleznikow, as well as Gary Davis, Philip Dawid, Jeroen Keppens, Sacha Iskovic, Moshe Koppel, Uri Schild, and Burkhard Schafer for discussions at the workshop that turned out to be helpful. Discussion with Eveline Feteris, Jose Plug, Bart Verheij, Tom Gordon, Trevor Bench-Capon and Arno Lodder has proved valuable, and it is obvious that the book has benefited from their written works as well.

I would like to thank Terry Anderson and William Twining for discussions on evidence during a visit to the University of Miami in December, 2003. I would like to thank the program committee of the Seventeenth Annual Conference on Legal Knowledge and Information Systems (JURIX 2004) held in Berlin, December 8–10, 2004 for inviting me as keynote speaker. For helpful discussions during and after my talk I would particularly like to thank Trevor Bench-Capon, Floris Bex, Wolfgang Bibel, Alison Chorley, Tom Gordon, Henry Prakken, Bram Roth, Burkhard Schafer, Bart Verheij, and Radboud Winkels.

Some of the research in this book derives from recent collaborative research on AI and law undertaken with Henry Prakken and Chris Reed. Their strong support has been very important for the continuation of my work on AI and law. Throughout the development of the project, my work was supported by a series of research grants from the Social Sciences and Humanities Research Council of Canada. I would like to thank Bill Dray, my former professor at the University of Toronto, who read through the whole manuscript and made many corrections and stylistic improvements. Special thanks are due to Roger Park for reading a previous draft, and making many corrections and suggested refinements of formulation. As well, he has provided a good deal of legal information that helped the book immensely.

I would like to thank the Social Sciences and Humanities Research Council of Canada for a research grant that supported the final work on this book, and to thank Katie Atkinson for discussion after my paper on practical reasoning was read at The Norms, Reasoning and Knowledge in Technology Conference, June 3–4, 2005, Boxmeer, Holland. These comments helped me to make some key improvements. A revised version was read as an invited lecture for the department of philosophy at the University of Siena in Italy on June 13, 2005. I would like to thank Christoph Lumer and Sandro Nannini for questions and comments that turned out to be useful.

I would like to thank Rita Campbell for making the index, and Fabrizio Macagno and Anahid Melikian for proof-reading.

INTRODUCTION

The theory in the book is based on the latest research in argumentation theory, and especially on new applications of artificial intelligence (AI) to legal argumentation. The methodology of the book derives from recent work in argumentation theory and AI in which forms of reasoning other than deductive and inductive have been the focus of much investigation. The aim is not just to show how character judgments are made, but to show how they should properly be made based on sound reasoning, in order to avoid certain fallacies, errors and superficial judgments of a kind that are common. The book is about character judgments, but centrally about the kind of logical reasoning and evidence that should properly be used to support or question such judgments. According to the new theory put forward in this book, such evidence is based on a kind of multi-agent simulative reasoning in which one agent is able to explain the actions of another by understanding the situation confronted by the other, and recreating the plan adopted by the other. According to the theory, one agent can reach reasoned conclusions about the presumed character properties of another, using plan recognition and argumentation schemes representing stereotypical forms of reasoning.

We use character evidence every day in reasoning, as in the inference, "He has a certain character trait, so that is evidence he is the one who carried out this particular action". This kind of character-based inference has probative value in everyday reasoning, for otherwise it would not usually be worthwhile for employers to ask for references for potential employees (Friedman, 2003, p. 979). Similarly, the typical kind of inference based on circumstantial evidence, like "His shoe matches the shoe-print found at the crime scene, therefore he must have been the one who committed the crime" has probative value. In both instances, if the premise is accepted as a fact, the inference from it gives some evidence to support the conclusion. Why is it then that the latter kind of inference is generally considered relevant evidence in our evidence rules in law while the former kind, the character-based inference, is generally considered not to be (subject to several important kinds of exceptions)? The answer, expressed very clearly in the Federal Rules of Evidence, is that character evidence might tend to prejudice a jury. Character evidence is treated in law as on a razor's edge. It is both probative and prejudicial. It is a kind of evidence that we often need to use in trials, for example, for cross-examining a witness. But its proclivity to mislead has required drawing strict and often complex boundaries around how it can be used.

Judging another person's character is necessary for activities like writing a biography, writing history, or evaluating legal and ethical arguments about a person's actions. But trying to determine the evidence on which character judgments should be based is filled with all kinds of problems and limitations, often leading to errors, wrong judgments, bias, and even allegations of slander. Character judgment is often abused, resulting in extremes. At one extreme are cases of character assassination and vicious attacks based on dubious evidence. At the other extreme are idealized, flattering portrayals of role models in propaganda whose worst qualities of character are hidden or minimized while their supposedly good qualities are puffed up. This book examines both abuses and reasonable uses of character judgment, answering key questions about how such judgments are and should be supported or refuted by verifiable evidence. What data are relevant to supporting character judgments? When one person makes a judgment about the character of another person, what kind of inference is drawn from the data, and how should such an inference properly be drawn? What kind of evidence should be used to support or question the conclusion drawn? For example, if I claim that some particular person is courageous or has integrity, what kind of data can be used to support or refute the claim? And once a conclusion is drawn from the given premises, what kind of evidence should be used to support that inference from the premises to the conclusion?

This book offers a new way of judging character evidence based on a set of argumentation schemes, or forms of argument, for reasoning about character. One of the most important of these schemes represents abductive reasoning from given data to a hypothesis that explains the data, a form of reasoning that is very common in forensic evidence (Walton, 2004). For example, if pieces of a knife blade are found in the window frame of a house where a burglary occurred, the best explanation may be that entry took place by someone's prying open the window with a knife. Abductive inference has been recognized as centrally important in AI (Josephson and Josephson, 1994; Walton, 2004), where it is seen as an important kind of reasoning used at the discovery stage of scientific hypothesis formation and testing. Abductive argumentation, based on a balance of considerations in a case, is deployed using a multi-agent dialogue model to represent the arguments for and against a claim. Abductive inferences are defeasible, meaning that they can be defeated or revised as new facts enter in. According to the new theory, such abductive character evidence arguments are fallible, but can be accepted as reasonable under the right conditions. They can also be unreasonable, as shown by the examples of character assassination in the book. The book shows how to use character evidence to support or refute character arguments, based on a computational model of argument for legal reasoning support systems.

Many of the kinds of character judgments studied in the book arise from legal cases in which arguments about character are used in trials, or are barred from use in trials on ground of relevance or irrelevance. Other character judgments arise from controversial cases in history or ethics that concern ethical qualities of character like honesty, courage and integrity. Many will read the book because they are concerned about character evidence in law or history, because they have been concerned about whether character judgments can be supported by verifiable evidence, as opposed to purely subjective opinion. But merely to state this aspect of the book is to indicate that it is also an original work in cognitive science and argumentation that presents a theory concerning the evidential support for inferences drawn by one person about the thoughts and actions of another. Thus the findings of the book have significant implications not only for law and history, but as well for argumentation theory generally as a basis for evidence. The book is written in a clear style, and explains all new terms and concepts. It can be widely read by anyone with no special training in law or computing. It can be used in courses where character evidence is a topic of interest, like courses on law (evidence law, legal reasoning, criminal law), philosophy (ethics, philosophy of history, philosophy of law and philosophy of mind), artificial intelligence, cognitive science, argumentation, speech communication, rhetoric, linguistics, political science and sociology.

Chapter 1

THE PROBLEM OF CHARACTER EVIDENCE

Character evidence is regarded as so powerful in law that its use in trials is carefully circumscribed by the Federal Rules of Evidence. In criminal law, for example, the argument "The defendant is a bad person (perhaps as shown by previous convictions), therefore he is guilty of the crime he is charged with" is ruled inadmissible. And yet where it is allowed in a trial, for example in attacking the honesty of a witness in cross-examination, character evidence can be the deciding factor. It is perhaps for these reasons that character evidence has recently become so controversial in law, and why, even at the pretrial stage attorneys will argue strenuously about its admissibility. But character argumentation is not confined to law. It is a potent tool of political rhetoric, as used in negative campaign tactics. It is also significant in history and philosophy. One only has to cite the examples of Francis Bacon and Friedrich Nietzsche to realize how a famous philosopher, many years after his death, can have his work discredited by attacks on his character. Of course, not all character-based arguments are negative. As Aristotle pointed out, positive *ethos*, or character of a speaker, can greatly enhance the persuasive power of arguments put forward in a speech. If character evidence is so important in all these areas, why is it we seem to know so little about its structure as a form of argument? How can we overcome this ignorance, and provide an objective basis for identifying, analyzing and evaluating this kind of argument?

The central problem posed is to determine the kind of evidence that is, or should be used, to support or criticize judgments of the kind that are made every day about a person's character. The problem is to come to understand how such claims can be justified, when they are true, or acceptable on the basis of the evidence, and how they can be refuted when they are false, or not acceptable on the basis of the evidence. The subject of the investigation then is one of evidence. It has to do with how we can properly support or refute claims made about a person's character using logical reasoning and argument. The best route to solving the problem, it will be argued in this book, lies in recent findings in two other fields, artificial intelligence and argumentation theory (informal logic). This subject falls within cognitive science and the study of rational argumentation as applied to human thinking, because the aim is to find the kind of evidence and the structure of argumentation that should properly be used to support judgments about a person's character. But the viewpoint is not primarily one of psychology, at least insofar as psychology is the empirical science of human behavior. The viewpoint is better seen having a strong ethical component, since judgments about a person's character are based on how ethical qualities of character should be defined in virtue ethics. It also has a strong legal component, because character evidence is a centrally important part of evidence law. Law has developed specific methods and procedures for processing and evaluating character, and these methods and procedures are very useful for coming to understand reasoning about character. The viewpoint also has a logical component, because the kind of reasoning used in the justification of character judgments is at the heart of the problems posed by the uses of character evidence. So this chapter will introduce various logical matters of reasoning and evidence, as well as matters of ethical and legal argumentation about character.

1.1 Individual Worth and Respect for Character

The traditional framework for judging a person's character was built around the notions of respect, individual worth, and reputation. The framework supports three kinds of judgments about a person's worth and character. One is that we have respect for someone who has proved that they have excellence of character. A second is that we have less respect for someone who does not have excellence of character. For example, when we first meet someone, and know nothing about them, then we neither respect nor disrespect that person. Third, we have no respect for someone who is "worthless", and has shown they do not deserve our respect, because they have exhibited some weakness of character like dishonesty. A person's reputation will affect which of these three evaluations will be appropriate in a given case. But as well as reputation, the evidence of a person's actions, including what they say as well as what they do, will count in such evaluations. Much historical evidence of the importance of such moral evaluations of character can be found. Benedict Arnold is categorized as a traitor, for example, while the many moral qualities of character of Abraham Lincoln have been extolled in historical writings.

Respect for worth is also identified in the social science literature with "face", in the sense of "saving face". Respect is also associated with dignity.

A dignified person deserves our respect and, presumably, has done something to deserve it in the past. A person who deserves our respect is worthy of it because they have exhibited admirable qualities of character, and presumably will continue to do so. This traditional view of character even has an aristocratic flavor at times, for example, when someone is said to have shown a "noble" character. This traditional framework of judging the worth of a person's character could perhaps be called the respect model. In light of recent emphasis on self-esteem, it may seem that respect for the respect model has eroded considerably. It could perhaps be that many object to, or feel uneasy about the apparent implication that respect implies that one person is better than another. This implication may even seem offensive today to many people, somehow seeming to imply a traditional aristocratic class system that fosters inequality. But that is not necessarily so. It depends on how you judge what is better.

In fact, we make judgments about character all the time. Such judgments might even show excellence of character of a kind that goes against a traditional aristocratic class system. One small incident can reveal a lot about a person's character, as the following story about Abraham Lincoln (Wecter, 1947, p. 90) illustrates.

> A story, told with many variations, ran that at a levee the President had interrupted a young English peer a moment after his introduction: "Excuse me, my lord, there's an old friend of mine," and stepped over to greet a bent Illinois farmer and his sunbonneted wife, come to see their wounded son in a Washington hospital.

This small story relates a relatively insignificant incident, but it tells a lot about Lincoln's character. Many conclusions can be drawn from it about Lincoln's values. It shows his loyalty to his friends, even if they were people that would not be considered important, glamorous, or influential. It shows Lincoln acting in a certain perspective that reveals what was evidently important to him. It is hard to say in words just exactly what it shows, but it makes me, and I am sure many others, have great admiration and respect for Lincoln as a person. This incident shows how respect for a person's character does not at all imply any kind of inequality, or favor of an aristocratic class system.

Another possible implication of the respect model is that judging anyone's character implies a kind of God-like stance. The question that will be asked is: how can anyone think that he or she has the right to judge another person? This rhetorical question implies that anyone who judges the worth of the character of another person is putting themselves on a higher plane than the person they are judging. This inequality, it is suggested, is a bad thing, because, in the end, both parties are human beings. The "us-them" judgment implied in such an act of judging is equated with "looking down" on another person. This criticism does pose a genuine problem for the project of attempting to judge character. How can it be done in an objective way if both the judged and the judge are persons who share the same character faults as well as virtues? This problem is a hard one. It may be that character judgments are fallible and prone to bias and error. But suppose that underlying the fallible nature of such judgments we can find an objective structure of reasoning. This structure could be useful in helping us to recognize and avoid errors and misconceptions of superficial character judgment.

We make character judgments all the time anyway. Such judgments are inherently imperfect and fallible, but they are vitally important in business decision-making, especially in hiring. In politics, much of the basis of voting for a candidate, particularly in presidential elections, is character judgment. These are judgments that large numbers of people make routinely. The problem is to gain insight into how they are made, and how they should be made, and to carry out this task not in any arbitrary or God-like way, but by understanding the kind of reasoning we already use, and learning more about its structure. Some empirical evidence suggests that evidence of past crimes tells us something about a person's character. Redmayne (2002, pp. 693–695) has examined statistical evidence suggesting that previous convictions have considerable probative value in relation to the conclusion that an individual is more or less likely to commit the same type of crime. The statistics vary with type of crime involved. For example, the likelihood of committing robbery is much higher than that of a drug offense. These statistics suggest that character evidence does have some value as evidence in predicting certain types of crimes, but statistics are notoriously slippery (Redmayne, 2002, p. 700). Even though its use is restricted in law, character judgment is often vitally important as evidence when witnesses are cross-examined in court.

Why is it important or useful to study judgments of character? The applicability of the subject is wider than just the field of ethical theory. Recent trends highlight why judgments of character are vitally important in both legal and political argumentation. Because of recent political developments in which character attack arguments have been prominent in negative campaign tactics and political attack argumentation generally, it has been made quite evident how important judgments of character are in a democratic political system. One might also cite the recent trial for the impeachment of the president of the US. In the Anglo-American system of legal argumentation, judgments of the character of a witness are vitally important evidence in a trial. Character evidence can be so influential on a jury in criminal trial that it is often ruled inadmissible. It is well known, for example, that the sexual history of the victim is deemed irrelevant in a rape trial. In other criminal cases, the argument, "This person has a bad character therefore he must be guilty of the crime", would have such a powerful impact on the jury that it is not generally allowed as relevant evidence to be introduced in court. Character is also vitally important in witness testimony, as mentioned above. Witness testimony is based on the credibility of the witness, which is in turn based on the perceived character of the witness. A witness who is perceived as being honest, and of good moral character generally, will be taken as credible. Hence the testimony of this type of witness will be taken as highly plausible, other things being equal. However, if a witness is judged by the jury or the judge to be a dishonest person, or otherwise to have bad moral character, his or her testimony will be found to be much less plausible. The character of the witness may even be attacked when he or she is impeached. Since witness testimony is such a vitally important kind of evidence in legal cases, the study of judgments of character is fundamentally important in law. Few would contest that judgments of character are also vital in ethics and politics. But as shown below, they are important, as well, in history as an academic discipline, and even, more surprisingly, as will be shown below, in computer science

1.2 Ruling on Relevance of Character Evidence in Trials

The televised criminal trial in the O. J. Simpson case provided an example of the importance of character issues in legal argumentation. The Simpson trial was by no means a typical case, but it showed up some of the problems of ruling on the relevance of character evidence in a spectacular way. One question that had to be resolved by Judge Ito concerned the evidence of Simpson's abuse of his wife. There were photographs as well as other evidence of Simpson's having stalked and beaten Nicole Brown Simpson. The teams of attorneys on both sides put forward arguments on the relevance of this character evidence and whether it should be admitted in the trial (Park, 1996, p. 748). The defense cited the rule against character evidence, a California rule that is similar to Rule 404 of the Federal Rules of Evidence[1] as the basis of their argument that character was not a relevant issue to be raised. The prosecution cited a California law ruling that domestic violence evidence is in general relevant, even when it is character evidence. They also argued it was relevant because it showed that Simpson had a motive of controlling and dominating Nicole Brown Simpson (Park, 1996, p. 749). Judge Ito admitted some but not all of the spousal abuse evidence on the ground that it showed motive. Thus the case shows that in

[1]See the presentation of these rules in Section 3 below.

matters of legal evidence, motive is treated as distinct from character. Motive can be relevant, even if character is treated as not relevant under the current federal rules of evidence used in American trials. What effect did the spousal abuse evidence have on the jury in the Simpson case? It is hard to say. It must have had some effect, but in the end whatever persuasive effect it had was outweighed by other evidence.

An important part of this other evidence was the alleged racism of Detective Mark Fuhrman, whose testimony turned out to have an important impact in the case. Fuhrman was the first police officer to find the bloody glove at the crime scene and he testified to this effect in the trial. But the defense had found that Fuhrman had made racist statements in the past that could be documented. They argued that this evidence should be considered relevant on the grounds that bias is an important and legitimate issue when raising doubts about the testimony of a witness. They argued that Fuhrman's recorded racist declarations showed that he had a bias against black persons. The key point to be noted about this line of argument is that it postulates an important legal distinction between character evidence and evidence of the bias of a witness. Character is held to be a general disposition of an ethical nature in law[2], whereas bias is something different. It is hard to say exactly what bias is, but it seems to be an inability or reluctance to fairly look at both sides of an issue in an open way. The recorded statements attributed to Fuhrman certainly showed a racial bias. Fuhrman used the "N-word" 41 times in the tapes and transcriptions of tapes cited as evidence of his racial bias (Mueller, 1996, p. 733). Not only that, but statements made by Fuhrman in the tapes seemed to suggest that all kinds of unfair police tactics, like covering up evidence, could be regarded as legitimate methods for the police to use in dealing with blacks (Park, 1996, p. 758). The jury was predominantly made up of blacks, and this evidence, if admitted, would be sure to have a considerable emotional impact on them. What happened was that Judge Ito did not admit all this evidence, but he admitted enough of it to have the impact the defense hoped for. The "race card", by all accounts, was an important factor in the argumentation leading to a finding of "not guilty" by the jury. Although this evidence was admitted on the ground that it showed a bias in the testimony of a witness, at the same time it also functioned as a kind of character evidence. It made Fuhrman appear to the kind of person who has a bad ethical character generally, and especially bad for a police officer who is supposed to treat people fairly.

Another bloody glove matching the one found at the crime scene was discovered behind Simpson's house. This glove, along with other evidence, made Simpson appear guilty of having killed his wife. The argument that

[2]It is shown in the next section how character is defined in Rule 404 of the Federal Rules of Evidence.

Fuhrman may have planted the second glove at Simpson's house seems in itself not very plausible. But the evidence of his bad character, conveyed by his recorded racist remarks, may have made the scenario of a plot by racially motivated police officers seem plausible. Or even if not, it may have created such an atmosphere of hostility and distrust that the jury came to feel somehow that the police were in the wrong and that doubts about Simpson's guilt were therefore possible. At any rate, the character evidence appeared to be important in determining how the trial turned out. This case shows the potential volatility of character evidence in a criminal trial. It also shows the judge struggling with complex decisions about whether to admit character evidence as relevant or not. And it illustrates the complexity of the rules of evidence in dealing with character evidence, and the difficulties of dealing with the various possible exceptions to the general rule that does not allow character evidence as relevant in considering a single action.

It is quite common for character evidence to be banned from a trial on the ground that it is irrelevant. In law, even if character evidence may be considered relevant, it can be banned if it might tend to prejudice the jury. Such a rule seems to presuppose a distinction between logical relevance and legal admissibility. Something could be logically relevant even if it is not legally admissible as evidence in a trial, by the rules of evidence. Cases of this sort, where character evidence is ruled inadmissible in a trial, are very common in Anglo-American law. The kind of problem of concern to the public arising from current trial rules governing the admission of character evidence can be indicated by the following case.

> In 1991 William Kennedy Smith stood trial for the rape of Patty Bowman. Bowman testified that Smith had raped her on the lawn near his house. Smith acknowledged that he and Bowman had sexual intercourse, but he maintained it was consensual. Though three women separately came forward and told of being raped or sexually assaulted by Smith, the judge refused to allow them to testify at trial. The reason for this refusal was the propensity rule or "character rule", and Smith was subsequently acquitted (Colb, 2001, 940–941). The Smith case appears to have played a role in motivating some legal reforms that allow for exceptions to the character rule in cases of rape and child molestation (Colb, 2001, p. 941). However, the character rule remains as a general rule of evidence in all federal and most state courts in the U.S.

The character rule referred to in the last line of the passage quoted above is the rule that character is not generally admissible as evidence. The Federal Rules of Evidence, the most significant set of rules concerning character evidence and relevance, do not really attempt to define what character is; all that is said in the official commentary on rule 404, is that character is a habit or general trait or disposition, like honesty or peacefulness. As Park *et al.* commented (1998, p. 132), this description "only begins to explain the meaning of character, but does not complete the story". This omission is an unfortunate gap in the law, but an understandable one, for character is more than merely habit or a statistical propensity to perform certain kinds of actions. It is an ethical concept that expresses the moral qualities of a person. Thus the gap that is found here can only be filled by a philosophical analysis of the concept of the character of a person that takes its ethical nature into account. Defining character is a philosophical problem of some stature, and also a kind of logical problem about evidence of some difficulty, because it is far from obvious how factual evidence can properly be used to support or refute generalizations and allegations about a person's character. As Park *et al.* commented (1998, p. 133), "unfortunately, the drafters of the Federal Rules did not attempt to define character, and the legal literature reflects little effort to do so". Still, if some theory were brought forward that would show how character evidence should be collected and evaluated, and how it should be used as evidence in an inquiry or trial, that theory could be very valuable in helping legal practitioners to devise evidence rules appropriate for this kind of reasoning.

Character evidence is tricky and problematic in certain respects, and how it is used in law is a fairly subtle matter. Assertions about character are generalizations, or hypotheses about a person's thinking and conduct. Thus they are not subject to proof or disproof in any direct way by factual evidence about single actions or incidents. The single action needs to be interpreted or evaluated in a certain way. For example, the very same action could be described as courageous by one observer and cowardly by another, depending on how the act was taken or interpreted, and what motives it supposedly revealed. The character ban only prohibits broad generalizations about character, like saying a person is lawless, a liar, a rapist, an embezzler, intemperate, cruel, lazy, and so forth (Park, 1998, pp. 718–719). Thus it cannot be argued that a defendant committed a crime because he committed a previous crime of the same type. The ban does not prohibit propensities that are linked to specific actions, however. It would not exclude evidence of a propensity to do things like abuse a particular spouse, or rob banks using poetic threats (p. 719). Such habits or propensities could be ruled relevant as evidence in a trial. The specific wording of the character rule, and related rules in the Federal Rules of Evidence, will be presented and discussed in the next section.

The issue of relevance or irrelevance of character evidence in evidence law is subtle. For example, some alleged facts about a person's character or past acts could be judged relevant if they are being used to prove something like motive. And yet the same facts could be judged irrelevant if merely used as character evidence. The problem posed by the William Kennedy Smith case above, and many other cases like it, is that the jury is not hearing the whole truth. Whether the evidence concerns good character or bad, such evidence does seem to be logically relevant. It may be hard for someone not trained in current trial practice to understand why laws are the way they are. In the case of the laws of evidence, they have evolved from earlier cases in common law at a time when character evidence was allowed. This sort of evidence was seen as highly relevant, and was often the deciding factor in a trial. If a defendant is obviously an unsavory character, and has committed serious crimes in the past, a jury surely will take these findings, once presented to them, as evidence of the defendant's guilt in the crime he is now charged with. Presumably then, in order to prevent juries from being overwhelmed by the power of the personal character attack argument, exclusionary rules had to be devised. In the next section, some background to how the present system developed is presented, and an account is given of how the current legal rules treat character evidence.

1.3 Problem of the Two-sided Nature of Character Evidence in Law

In Roman law, the whole body of argumentation in a criminal trial was centered on the issue of the defendant's moral character. One of the strongest arguments for the defense was the argument that the defendant was a person of good character. One of the strongest arguments for the prosecution was to attack the ethical character of the defendant and portray him as a bad person. Wigmore also noted that character evidence was "resorted to without limitation" in early English law. But at some point in legal history, trial by character began to be prohibited. According to Leonard (1998, p. 10), the rule excluding character evidence to prove a person's conduct was "well settled" by the first decade of the nineteenth century.

What is needed here is a quick review of what the Federal Rules of Evidence say about character evidence.[3] Rule 401 defines relevant evidence as evidence having any tendency to make the existence of any fact "that is of consequence to the determination of the action more probable or less probable than it would be without the evidence".[4] But what does this mean? It means that in a trial there is a conflict of opinions, and the purpose of the trial is to resolve this conflict by means of rational argumentation. By "conflict of opinions" is meant that each side has a thesis or particular proposition to prove. This is called burden of proof. In criminal cases, the prosecution has to prove that the accused is guilty of the crime alleged, while the defense only has to prove that the prosecution's argumentation in

[3]The latest version of these rules can be found on the web at www.uscourts.gov/rules/newrules4.html.

[4]According to Redmayne (2002, p. 685), English law does not have a single definition of relevance. However, he suggested that rule 401 of the U.S. federal rules of evidence provides a definition of relevance that can provide a guideline for judgments of relevance in trials.

the trial is inadequate to prove her thesis. Relevance according to the account given in the Federal Rules of Evidence is defined in terms of what is called probative weight or probative value. An argument is relevant in a trial only if it makes the thesis of one side or the other more probable or less probable. However, "probability" is not to be understood here in the sense of statistical probability, although that sometimes enters into it. It is meant rather in the sense that factual evidence can combine with logical reasoning to make a conclusion carry more probative weight than it did without such evidence. What is actually meant by relevant evidence in this sense will not become apparent until the last chapter of this book.

Rule 403 is also very important. According to it, evidence, even if it is relevant according to Rule 401, may be excluded if its probative value "is substantially outweighed by the danger of unfair prejudice, confusion of the issues, or misleading the jury, or by considerations of undue delay, waste of time, or needless presentation of cumulative evidence". Even if some claim put forward is evidence that is relevant, perhaps only slightly so, it may be excluded if it might tend to prejudice the jury. What is important to note here is that character evidence is not being excluded on the ground of relevance, or not on the ground of relevance exclusively, but on grounds that it might tend to prejudice the jury (Park, 1998, p. 720). This leads us to Rule 404, which flatly states that character evidence is generally not admissible for the purpose of proving conduct. In other words, what Rule 404 says is that you cannot use the argument that this person is guilty because he has a bad character.

The exclusion of character evidence is set into place as a general principle by the first sentence of Rule 404. Several subsidiary rules define exceptions to the exclusion of character. One exception is that if character evidence is introduced by the defense, the gate is opened for the prosecution to use character evidence in rebuttal (Rule 404a). For example, if the defendant puts in testimony about a trait of his own character or of the character of the victim, the prosecution is allowed to retaliate by attacking the defendant's character or bolstering the victim's character. Rules 608 and 609 also allow the credibility of a witness to be attacked or supported by character evidence in the form of opinion or reputation (though witness character may be supported only if it has been attacked), or in the form of evidence that the witness has been convicted of certain crimes. This is clearly a very important exception.

Evidence of crimes or bad acts may also be admitted if the evidence is offered, not to show character, but for some narrower purpose such as showing motive, opportunity, intention, preparation, plan, knowledge, identity, or absence of mistake, as provided in Rule 404(b):

> Evidence of other crime, wrongs, or acts is not admissible to prove the character of a person in order to show action in conformity therewith. It may, however, be admissible for

> other purposes, such as proof of motive, opportunity, intent, preparation plan, knowledge, identity, or absence of mistake or accident, provided that upon request by the accused, the prosecution in a criminal case shall provide reasonable notice in advance of trial, or during trial if the court excuses pretrial notice on good cause shown, of the general nature of such evidence it intends to introduce at trial.

If a trait of character is an essential element of a charge or defense, character evidence is also admissible (Rule 405b). This rule is rarely pertinent in criminal cases, because in modern law it is not a crime to have a bad character trait, and hence evidence of character is usually offered in order to invite a further inference about conduct, and not as an end in itself. However, the "essential element" concept still occasionally applies, for example when the defendant raises the defense of entrapment, which requires a judgment about whether the defendant had the character of being predisposed to commit the crime. Another example of the application of Rule 405(b) is a civil case in which the issue is negligent hiring or negligent entrustment. In this kind of case, the character of the person would be relevant to the issue of whether the defendant was negligent in hiring or entrusting property to an unfit person (Landon, 1997, p. 584).

Under Rule 406, the habit of a person or the routine practice of an organization is admissible to prove that the conduct of the person or organization was in conformity with that habit or routine practice. Habit evidence is considered not to be character evidence because it is evidence of a narrow, situationally specific propensity rather than of a broad character trait.[5]

Why is character excluded as evidence in law? As Landon points out, there is a history behind this rule in Anglo-American law. It was found that

---

[5]Rape shield legislation, for example, Fed. R. Evid. 412, precludes character evidence about the sexual predisposition of the complainant in a rape case. However, according to some notes given to me by Roger Park, this particular restriction on character evidence is outweighed by subsequent developments that open the door for greater use of character evidence. Character evidence may be admitted to show the propensity of a defendant to be a rapist or a child molester under a 1995 amendment, see Fed. R. Evid, pp. 413–415, and the 2000 amendments to the Federal Rules of Evidence give the prosecution greater power to fight back with character evidence when the defendant attacks the character of a victim. See Fed. R. Evid. 4040(a) (as amended 2000). Moreover, the passage of substantive statutes that enhance crimes that are committed as part of gang-related or organized-crime activity, and that require proof of other criminal activity as a predicate for the enhancement, lets in evidence of criminal acts that previously would have been excluded as character evidence. See, for example, People v. Gardeley, 927 P.2d 713 (Supreme Court of California, 1996). The expert testimony explosion has resulted in some types of testimony, for example, battered woman's syndrome, that borders on character evidence. Finally, anticrime or victim's rights initiatives in states like California and (more recently) Oregon have made it easier for the prosecution to put in evidence of prior convictions to impeach a criminal defendant. See California Constitution Art. 1, sec. 28 (initiative measure approved by the people June 8, 1982, known as "The Victims' Bill of Rights") (providing that any prior felony conviction may be used without limit for purposes of impeachment; the California Supreme court later construed the provision to allow admission only of felonies of moral turpitude, but this still represented a substantial expansion of the amount of character evidence admissible to impeach a criminal defendant).

character attack was so successful that in order to get a fair trial judges had to keep hemming it in on grounds of irrelevance. As Landon (1997, p. 584) put it, "Rule 404 is the sum of hundreds of years of court wrestling with the question of what is the appropriate place of evidence as to the defendant's character in a criminal or civil trial". But the other side of it is that character is often relevant in a trial, and needs to be seen as such in certain specific instances. Hence the list of exceptions to Rule 404 noted above. According to Leonard (1998, p. 21), it is hard to answer this question. But one especially important reason for the exclusion appears to be not failure of relevance but worries about prejudice. As noted above, Rule 403 allows relevant evidence to be excluded "if its probative value is substantially outweighed by the danger of unfair prejudice, confusion of the issues, or misleading the jury, or by considerations of undue delay, waste of time, or needless presentation of cumulative evidence". The worry about character evidence under this heading is that it may be too powerfully persuasive in its impact on a jury, leading it to give it too much weight, and give other evidence too little weight. Basically the rationale behind this rule is that character attack is such a powerful form of argument that it can too easily be used to argue, "He is a bad person, therefore he must be guilty". This worry about misuse of character evidence expresses the implicit assumption that the jury may be influenced by prejudicial judgment.[6] One function of the rules of evidence, so conceived, is to try to prevent prejudice from arising in the jury of a kind that could bias its thinking, leading it to make a wrong decision or to engage in wrong thinking.

The fallible nature of character evidence was well brought out by Uviller (1996) when he contrasted it with other kinds of evidence used in trials. Character evidence is based on the propensity of a person to carry out a certain kind of action. But just because someone has such a propensity, it may not follow that he ever actually carried out a certain kind of action in some instance. Thus character evidence is an inherently weaker form of argumentation than many other kinds of evidence commonly used in court. For example, take the argument that the fact that the victim's blood was on the defendant's glove is evidence that supports the conclusion that the defendant stabbed the victim. This kind of argumentation may not be conclusive, but it represents a rational way of supporting a claim that we accept as relevant evidence. If the premise is true, then the argument is very definitely relevant evidence supporting the conclusion. As Uviller pointed out (p. 219), if a lawyer stood

[6]It is clear however that the rule against character evidence also has other purposes. Preventing the jury from punishing someone for prior acts even though he is known to be innocent is one (Park, 1996). Preventing procedural unfairness caused by the surprise need to defend multiple accusations is another (1A Wigmore, Evidence 216, at 1870 (Tillers rev. 1983)). Still another is avoiding the cost of trying mini-cases based on multiple accusations of bad character (Park, 1996).

up in court and objected to the admission of this kind of evidence as irrelevant in a criminal trial the objection would be laughable. But contrast such a case with one involving propensity evidence. Suppose it is argued in court that the defendant coerced a contract because he's a racketeer. Uviller (1996, p. 220) put this argument in the form of a syllogism.

Major Premise: Racketeers coerce contracts.
Minor Premise: Delta is a racketeer.
Conclusion: Delta coerced the contract at issue.

This argument is not as compelling as the example of the blood evidence. The problem is that it could be wrong. Many racketeers do not coerce contracts, and many contracts are coerced by racketeers other than Delta (p. 220). This argument from character evidence could be relevant in a criminal case, however. It makes it somewhat more likely that Delta coerced the contract than if he had been an honest citizen and not a racketeer. But it is such a fallible argument that the danger is that it may induce a jury to take it for a stronger argument than it really is.

The general problem posed by propensity arguments in law arises from their two-sided nature. They can be relevant, but they can also be misleading, because they may appear a lot stronger than they really are; so how do we separate evidence that is relevant, and also probative in the sense that it provides some reasonable weight of evidence to support a conclusion, from evidence that is prejudicial, meaning that it's only weak at best and could easily lead a jury to a wrong conclusion. Because of this possibility of fallacy, arguing on the basis of propensity can lead to serious injustice. Uviller (1996, p. 218) puts the point this way.

> There are lots of muggers out there, let us say, all disposed to snatch the purse of any victim they can find. But that disposition should not convict any one of them of the theft of any particular victim's bag. Otherwise, anyone generally disposed to a particular variety of crime could be convicted of any particular instance of it. And the law stoutly insists that people should be convicted only for particular behavior and not for a general criminal disposition.

Thus character evidence is a problem. Ruling on it in any given case depends on the balance. The practical implications of this in trials every day are well described by Uviller (p. 218). For example, a jury may have to rule on whether a mother smothered her baby without knowing that she had abused her older child. The jury may have heard of the criminal records of those who testified as witnesses, but the propensity evidence based on the previous actions of the defendant has been kept from them by the prohibition on character evidence. The prohibition seems unreasonable because it restricts the jury's ability to arrive at a commonsense decision. But it also seems reasonable because of the fear that the mother's prior abusive conduct might prejudice it to leap to a hasty conclusion, wrongly finding her guilty of the homicide charge.

One argument for the ban on character evidence in law derives from a view that was once fashionable in the social sciences called situationism. According to this view, behavior is so much influenced by individual circumstances that cross-situational attributes like properties of character are not predictive of future behavior (Sanchirico, 2001, p. 1240). This view is no longer generally accepted by researchers on criminal evidence in the social sciences. According to Sanchirico (2001, p. 1241), "most researchers would now agree that past criminal behavior is quite predictive of future criminal behavior". Redmayne (2002, pp. 687–689) has provided a short survey of the state of psychological research on the uses of character evidence to predict behavior. At an early stage, many social scientists appeared to believe that character cannot be used to predict behavior. Even earlier research had assumed a trait theory that held that people had relatively stable personality traits that could be used to predict their behavior, and there had been a reaction against this theory. In the 1960s there was a devastating critique of trait theory that led to an emphasis upon an opposed approach called situationism. Out of this conflict of opinions on the predictive value of character evidence arose a compromise that still holds (Redmayne, 2002, p. 688). This compromise is to the effect that human behavior can be analyzed in terms of broad dispositional tendencies, but that such evidence is highly variable and dependent upon the significance of situations.

Another more common argument stems from the recognition of the possibility of what is called cognitive error in the social sciences, or fallacious reasoning in logic. The argument is essentially that people generally have an inflated belief in the value of character evidence, and hence juries tend to overvalue it (Sanchirico, 2001, p. 1244). This argument can be countered by the claim that although people do often tend to be more strongly influenced than they should be by character evidence in everyday argumentation, they can also be taught to recognize this error, and to correct for it. To these arguments the third argument can be added that using argumentation based on character seems unavoidable in law anyhow. For example, it is hard to imagine witness testimony working very well as a source of reliable evidence in trials if the honesty of the witness could not be questioned. What has happened in evidence law is therefore a compromise. Character evidence is considered as relevant in some instances, but only in special circumstances, like the cross-examination of a witness. Generally it is banned, if used to try to prove conduct.

If the jury is supposed to be able to engage in the kind of critical thinking needed to assess the arguments on both sides, why should the danger of its being prejudiced need to be guarded against? As Tillers (1998, p. 6) pointed out, there are good reasons to be suspicious of the claim that practically all people are incapable of judging the true value of character evidence. It can be argued that ordinary people are often quite good at judging character evidence. A judge or jury, as Tillers (p. 7) noted, has time for reflection in a trial, and is capable of self-correction when warned of the force of character evidence. But perhaps there is a reasonable explanation for this kind of worry. Character arguments can mislead. Use of a person's character and reputation, for example, can be extremely powerful as arguments in some cases, even when the evidence supporting the argument is very slim. The reasons for this impact are hard to understand. Perhaps one reason is that people find character very interesting; they take a lively interest in it, even when other evidence in a case may not be all that interesting. Another reason is the principle, "Where there's smoke there's fire", meaning that people will often take a suspicion, particularly when it is based on innuendo attacking a person's character, and make it a basis for having reservations about that person. This principle is what underlies the power of slander, innuendo, gossip, and character assassination. It may take years to build up a good reputation, but one attack can easily destroy it, even if the attack is based on very little evidence, or even on no evidence at all.

1.4 Innuendo and Attacks on Character

Many powerful attacks on character are based on rumors and innuendo that impugn a person's reputation. As noted already, such attacks can be extremely powerful, even if based on very little evidence. An attack on a person's character can raise suspicions that have a way of sticking, and may be extremely hard to rebut, or defend oneself against. The dangers posed by the use of innuendo in character assassination, and the difficulties of trying to rebut character attack, can be well illustrated by the Francis Bacon case.[7]

When character is judged, either positively or negatively, it is generally on the basis of an account of the person's deeds or words, related by a second party. In law, this second party is a witness, who gives testimony. In history or in biography, sources are cited. Very often these sources are witnesses, or accounts based on what a witness wrote or said. But there are various problems about using evidence based on what a witness said. One is that the account may simply be false. The witness may be lying or mistaken. Another is that the account may be misleading. It may be based on an element of truth, but many aspects of it may be distorted and exaggerated, so the wrong conclusion about character is drawn from it. Another problem is that evidence may be scarce, and it may be hard to determine whether the

---

[7]For details of this case, see Section 5 below, in this chapter.

account is true or false. The allegations may be based on rumor or innuendo, and it may not even be known who the original source was. Or the original source may be dead, or for other reasons may not be available to be questioned further. The problem here is that attacks on a person's character, even if based on a rumor that is hard to document or verify, can still have an extremely powerful effect in ruining a person's reputation. Such allegations have a powerful staining effect, even if based on weak evidence, or an unreliable source. And, once reported by the media, for example, they may stay around for years, even though the accused party has taken strenuous efforts to deny and disprove that. The advent of tabloid journalism has escalated the scale of this problem. But gossip has always had the same effect. A story is magnified and distorted as it is passed from mouth to mouth. Sometimes what is said at a later stage is the exact opposite of what was reported at an earlier stage. It is very difficult, perhaps even impossible, to protect yourself against this kind of indirect attack on your character. Politicians, for example, have become expert at "leaking" a rumor, by getting a third party to pass on an allegation to the press. The media may then attribute the story to "sources close to the governor", or something of that sort.

In a character attack, the focus of the argument is the bad character of the person attacked. For example, the second party may be said to be a liar, or a hypocrite, or to have some other bad quality of character. How does this kind of argument work? It works by attacking the credibility of the party who is said to have a morally bad character. In many cases, the plausibility of a person's argument will depend on the perceived character of that person. If a person's character is thought to be morally good — for example, if the person is thought to be a man of honesty and integrity — his argument will be found more plausible. But if a person's character is thought to be morally bad — for example, if he is thought to be a liar or hypocrite — his argument will be found less plausible. This aspect of argumentation has long been known to rhetoricians, like Aristotle, who cited argument from character (*ethos*) as an important device of rhetorical persuasion.

The first to clearly articulate the connection between character and political persuasion was Isocrates in his work, *Antidosis* (278–279). The section quoted below is from the English translation in the Loeb Classical Library edition (1966, p. 339).

> The man who wishes to persuade people will not be negligent as to the matter of character; no, on the contrary, he will apply himself above all to establish a most honorable name among his fellow citizens; for who does not know that words carry greater conviction when spoken by men of good repute than when spoken by men who live under a cloud, and that the argument which is made by a man's life is of more weight than that which is furnished by words. Therefore, the stronger a man's desire to persuade his hearers, the more zealously will he strive to be honorable and to have the esteem of his fellow citizens.

Isocrates added (p. 280) that an honorable reputation for excellent character not only adds persuasiveness to the words of the man who possesses it, but even enhances his actions. So reputation for good character supports not only single points in an argument, but the persuasiveness of the argument as a whole.

Isocrates explained why character is extremely important to the persuasiveness of arguments in public discourse — and, in particular, in political discourse. But his explanation has two sides. Reputation for good character is vitally important for a political speaker who wants to persuade his audience. To preserve this reputation, the politician will zealously strive to be honorable, and to have the esteem of his fellow citizens, as Isocrates says. But the opposition political forces will also grasp the importance of such a person's reputation, and try to attack it.

Character judgments put forward as arguments in law and in politics do seem to carry weight as an important form of evidence in some cases. They have a subjective or emotive aspect. They are in fact often used as powerful arguments to prejudice an audience or jury. But they also seem to have a kind of factual basis. If someone claims you are a liar, for example, she may have factual evidence that supports the claim. You, in turn, may have evidence that goes against the claim. In judgments made about the character of a famous personage in a history book, evidence of a factual sort is often presented at much length. On the other hand, there can be disagreements, and such disputes can be notoriously difficult to resolve. Biographers, for example, can flatly disagree. One biography can make a person out to be an altruistic humanitarian, while another portrays the same person as an egotistical villain.

1.5 Character Assassination and Panegyric Discourse

An interesting case of historical judgment of character is that of Francis Bacon. Bacon (1561–1626) made notable contributions to science, philosophy, history and literature, and much has been written about him as a founder of modern ways of thinking. In addition to being a philosopher and scientist, Bacon was also very active in law and politics. He was a member of the House of Commons in England, solicitor general, attorney general, lord keeper of the great seal, and finally, lord chancellor at the age of fifty-seven (Cranston, 1967, p. 236). Inevitably drawn into the political maneuvering that was then common in the circle around the monarch, Bacon was accused of bribery and corrupt dealings in chancery suits in 1621. He was tried on these charges, and admitted his guilt. He was fined, and never sat in parliament again. This incident cast suspicion on his reputation, brought out masterfully in a famous essay "Lord Bacon" by Thomas Babington Macaulay (1856). This essay used innuendo not only to try to minimize the importance of Bacon's intellectual contributions, but to blacken his character by portraying him as corrupt and dishonest. This negative view of Bacon's character seemed to stick, and over and over again it was described in highly negative terms in many textbooks and standard historical sources. Bacon was portrayed as a dishonest and manipulative person who lacked integrity and was corrupt.

There had long been questions about Bacon's character, and doubts about whether the negative view of it was really justified by the facts. The editor of Bacon's works, James Spedding, had shown that many of the attacks on Bacon's character were not really supported by the known facts. But the negative view had gained such a momentum that it persisted, until recently. The question of Bacon's integrity has now been re-assessed. Especially noteworthy is the very thoroughly researched work by Mathews (1996), which clears Bacon of the charges of corruption and fraud in office, cites irregularities in his trial in the House of Lords, and generally rehabilitates his character. What Mathews shows most impressively and interestingly is how easy it is to blacken someone's reputation, and how hard it is to reverse this, once the character attack has circulated. The allegations seem to be passed on from one source to another, without any real attempt at critical examination of their truth.

The problem set by Mathews (1996, p. 431) is to determine why, after Bacon's character was vindicated by Spedding over a hundred years ago, the untruths he refuted continue to flourish. Mathews notes (p. 432) that many writers still go back to all the false charges made by Macaulay, and base their accounts on the latter's colorful but demonstrably false story. Many subsequent commentators bypass Spedding's accurate account, and instead draw from the more colorful but dubious accounts of Bacon's numerous detractors. The pattern seems to be that as time goes on, there is a layering of secondary sources upon secondary sources. Those who wrote about Bacon took their material from previous secondary sources. But once some of these had painted Bacon as a villain, the charges simply kept getting passed on through each new generation of writers, even after these sources had been thoroughly refuted. Although the professional Bacon scholars may have known that the vilification of Bacon's character was only a popular opinion or "myth", they were powerless to keep the myth from being retold in encyclopedias and other popular writings.

This historical pattern of passing on charges not founded on what can be determined about the facts is comparable to the more simple kind of everyday case where false charges, once made, leave a stain of innuendo that can never be erased. Once a charge has been made, even if it can be shown to be false, it always leaves a rumor in place which seems to stick in the public consciousness. In many cases, all people can recall is that they seem to remember something bad about this person. And even the vague feeling that something bad has been said about a person can lead them to have a negative impression about him. The popular expression is, "Where there's smoke there's fire". The assumption is that if a charge was made against the person, maybe there's something in it. What seems to be lodged in place in such cases is a presumption of guilt. The mere rumor seems to have a life of its own, even after it has been refuted and been shown to be false.

Character assassination is one extreme in the portrayal of a person's character; its opposite extreme is panegyric. Panegyric is a form of biographical presentation designed to artfully praise the character of a person by exploiting the admiration of the audience. Notable examples can be found in Isocrates, in the *Life of Sir Thomas More* by Nicholas Harpsfield, and in the *Life of John Donne* by Sir Izaak Walton (Rewa, 1983, p. xi). According to Rewa (p. xi), these works celebrate the virtues and achievements of the persons eulogized : "They appeal to an audience's capacity for admiration rather than its appetite for information". The panegyric mode of biography was long considered a respectable form of discourse in its own right, but since the seventeenth century it has been criticized on the ground that it is not true to the historical data. In modern times, the very term "panegyric", to the extent that it is recognized, is seen in a negative light.

For the Greeks, panegyric was seen as having an ethical function. It was used to portray the person in a biography as having ethical virtues of the kind written about by the Greek ethical philosophers. Among the different kinds of rhetoric that Aristotle classified in the *Rhetoric* is a demonstrative type, including panegyric discourse, that has the goal of creating admiration in the audience, rather than persuading it to do something. According to Aristotle, demonstrative rhetoric produces emotions in listeners who are already inclined to agree with the viewpoint discussed. It is thus different from persuasion dialogue, where the aim is to get the audience to accept a proposition that they do not presently accept.

The traditional genre of panegyric fits into Aristotle's demonstrative category of rhetoric, because its aim is to excite admiration for the virtues of the person whose life and actions are described. The panegyric biography was seen as performing a hortatory function of extolling the virtues, and showing their value and importance to young people, or to anyone who reads the biography. Until the seventeenth century, this kind of biography was seen as a legitimate genre. But times have changed. At the end of the twentieth century, we are extremely suspicious about an ethical enterprise of this kind. We tend to suspect it as "propaganda" used to stir up an audience emotionally for some cause, ideology or special interest. We also see it as departing from the empirical facts in a way we find dubious, and therefore categorize it as "biased". We are generally very cynical about any so-called "ethical" purpose of such discourse, seeing that as just a mask for some ideology or political agenda.

However, it could be argued that panegyric discourse still exists. For example, in times of war, the actions and character of soldiers who have been decorated are described in language designed to excite admiration and stir the imagination of readers. In television programs relating struggles over civil rights, leaders like Martin Luther King are portrayed as persons with virtues of character of the kind needed to persevere in a worthy cause. But such panegyric discourse is not confined exclusively to times of war, civil conflict or national emergency. It also appears, in a more subdued form, in peaceful times. An example is the use of "role models" in many popular media stories to show how happy the working woman is, and how important and self-fulfilling her work is. These biographical portrayals feature what are taken to be the virtues of the person whose actions are described, with the aim of appealing to the imagination and admiration of the audience. Their authors might not like the classification of their stories as panegyric. They might claim that they are only describing the facts and letting the facts speak for themselves. But it is not hard to see that there is a definite panegyric element in such discourse. The intent is to evoke admiration for what are taken to be the excellent qualities of the person portrayed in the discourse. What is perhaps the key difference between ancient and modern panegyric discourse is that there has been a shift from what was taken to be a single set of ethical virtues to fragmented sets of different virtues for different groups.

The existence of panegyric discourse and character assassination suggests that character judgment is often set in a framework of rhetorical argumentation. In such cases, the emotive aspect of the argumentation is prominent. But the evidence used to support the advocated viewpoint is selective. These phenomena may suggest that character judgment is not based on objective evidence, and is subject to rhetorical persuasion. On the other hand, they may also suggest the value of coming to understand the process of logical reasoning that lies behind such argumentation. If we could grasp the structure of that reasoning, we would have a means of using critical thinking when confronted by panegyric and character assassination. This rhetorical use of argumentation could be judged more critically. The weak links in the reasoning could be made evident. We would be less vulnerable to the kinds of fallacies and deceptions that can occur in this kind of emotive rhetoric.

1.6 Reputation and Character

Character attack can be very powerful in influencing a public audience, even if the allegations put forward are not proved. For once the allegation is stated, the effect is to lodge a presumption in the minds of the audience that it could possibly be true. The problem is that evidence of character can have a strong presumptive effect even where it should only carry a small amount of probative weight. Hence there is a tendency, in assessing questions of character, to jump to conclusions, based only on suspicions. Character slurs can be based on false allegations, or unsubstantiated rumors. But even when based on some evidence, they can be blown out of proportion, and used to create suspicion about a person's character. In the character attack argument, such suspicions throw a dark cloud over a person's credibility.

In some cases where a victim is attacked by false allegations, his main line of defense is his good reputation. The following account (Editorial, 2002) illustrates how important a reputation is in research, and at the same time how fragile it is. Dr. Josef Penninger, a leading research scientist in the field of immunology, was attacked by negative allegations about conduct in his lab made by a colleague at the University of Toronto. After colleagues began to question him at scientific meetings about the rumors that began circulating, and repeated pleas for help at the University of Toronto led to no action, Penninger approached an executive of an American biotechnology firm. He set up a human resources inquiry to enable an expert panel to probe the allegations. The review concluded that the remarks made by the colleague who had attacked Penninger were "inappropriate" and that the behavior of the colleague was "unacceptable" (p. A13). Despite this vindication, Penninger was upset that his own university did not intervene to help him. He made some remarks that are worth quoting (p. A1):

> It must be understood that the reputation of researchers is the most important thing they have, something I and the people associated with me have worked our whole lives to achieve. That such a reputation is attacked based on false accusations is simply not acceptable.

These remarks bring out the importance of reputation in research, and show how the work of a lifetime can so easily be destroyed by the unfounded innuendo and rumor emanating from a false allegation. As a result of a mediated agreement, letters were sent to funding agencies advising them that the allegations were unfounded and expressing confidence in the integrity of Penninger's lab (p. A13). Still, he was very upset that his own university did not defend him, and he felt that the students in his lab had been harmed. So he accepted a generous offer from the Vienna Academy of Sciences and moved the lab to Austria.

One problem is that reputation rests on the view generally held of a person by those who know him in a community. This community can be expected to be comprised of enemies as well as friends, or by people who, for whatever reason, pass along rumors and gossip. Upholding a good reputation may not be easy, if other people find it in their interest to try to destroy it. Once an allegation is made, it tends to stick in the community's memory, even after it has been proven false.

The activity of casting aspersions on an opponent's character is, of course, engaged in on a large scale currently in politics. The second half of the twentieth century is the age of the political character attack. But character attack, as noted in this chapter, has always been one of the most important kinds of legal argumentation. In a court case, there are reasons of self-interest why both parties will try to attack the character of the other. The problem in these cases is that allegations of bad character can be made by simply passing on rumors, without taking on any burden of proof, or even investigating the claim made in the rumor.

At any rate, the reputation sense of the term "character" is subject to many abuses associated with character attack arguments. Any ethical analysis of the concept of character should take these aspects into account, when determining how allegations about a person's character should be proved or disproved. Unfortunately perhaps, the whole area of rumor, gossip and innuendo comes into consideration in such cases. Stone (1991, p. 254) takes the legal example of the allegation that a certain person is a "drunkard". This allegation might be proved by calling in another party who gives an opinion based on his own personal observations. But suppose that this other party has something to gain by casting the subject's character in a negative light. Close questioning of the testimonial basis of his opinion, supposedly based on his acquaintance with the subject, might reveal a lot of inconsistencies, exaggerations, and unsubstantiated allegations that are not very plausible. How should we judge such a case? One thing that should be said is that such reports and condemnations should not be taken at face value, and need to be looked at in a spirit of fairness to the person against whom the allegations have been made. It is just this kind of fairness that the principles of burden of proof in law are designed to support. And the same should be true of ethical reasoning about such cases. In historical writing, for example, positive or negative ethical judgments may be made by a writer about some famous historical figure. But the critical and fair-minded historian should take such claims with a grain of salt, and look at where they are coming from. Questions should be raised about the critic, and whether he was friend or foe of the party about whom the judgments were made.

In short, in ethics as in law, attributions of character have an important place, but they should be seen as somewhat accusatorial kinds of judgments, not to be taken at face value without being critically questioned. They represent conclusions of inferences in a chain of reasoning that has a certain dialogical logic. We need to look at what the critic is saying, and then relate that to the testimonial evidence of the first-person acquaintance that has been presented. It is important to look at the evidence on both sides of a case, and judge the strength of the conclusion alleged by weighing the evidence on both sides. The whole body of relevant evidence needs to be summed up and weighed together, looking at all the small but relevant arguments and testimonies on both sides. In this respect, the kinds of reasoning used to support allegations of good or bad character are common to law and ethics. In the past, it did not seem possible to evaluate character evidence in any precise scientific way that might provide a logical analysis of reasoning based on character judgments. The notion of reputation, for the reasons cited above, always seemed too subjective and personal in nature. Now, however, technology is grappling with the problem of how to automate this kind of reasoning.

One of the latest developments in computing is the construction of software systems to engage in electronic commerce and carry out other sorts of communications with human users or other software systems on the internet. Although they are programmed to achieve specific goals, like collecting information or engaging in profitable negotiations, such systems need to be relatively autonomous. One system may have to make a decision about whether another can be taken to be a reliable source of information, or can generally be trusted in some electronic transaction that is being considered. Computing has now been confronted with the problem of how to automate such decisions in a way that will allow for web commerce and other internet transactions of a kind that occur every day. Concepts like honesty, cheating, moral character and reputation, that were formerly studied mainly by philosophers in the field of ethics, have now become important to computer science (Conte and Paolucci, 2002, p. 1). Reputation systems are increasingly being seen as solutions to transactions that take place at a distance between unfamiliar partners where problems of trust can arise (Conte and Paolucci, 2002, p. 31).[8] Of course, such software systems are based on relatively simple and abstract notions of character and reputation that do not fully represent the way we deploy such notions in ethics or law. But they do require a logical model of reasoning based on reputation or perceived character of a kind that is precise enough to be programmed. Thus these new software reputation systems are extremely interesting from the viewpoint of studying logical inferences, based on data, to a conclusion about

[8]As Bons *et al.*, (2001, p. 30) have pointed out, currently most electronic commercial transactions are done by credit card. But high value business transactions (over fifty thousand U.S. dollars) are carried out using purchase orders, invoices and bank transfers. Hence trustworthy trade procedures will have to be developed for these kinds of electronic transactions.

character, or conversely, from a premise about an agent's character or reputation to a conclusion about the likely or possible actions of that agent.

These developments reveal interesting connections between four areas of research that have not previously been combined. The first is the study of virtue ethics, or ethical qualities of character. The second is the study of inferences based on character in evidence law. The third is the development of automated systems of reputation management in distributed computing. The fourth is the study of forms of inference called argumentation schemes in argumentation theory and informal logic, and especially certain forms of argument like *ad hominem* (personal attack) arguments, often associated in the past with fallacies or deceptive argumentation tactics used to unfairly get the better of a speech partner. The investigation of character evidence brings all four areas of research together into an interesting and fruitful junction in which each can benefit from the others.

1.7 Character Attacks and *Ad Hominem* Arguments

Personal attacks on character of the *ad hominem* variety, where the attack on a person's character is used to attack his argument, have become a special subject of concern in media reporting of political discourse in modern democracies. Such personal attack arguments have often proved to be so effective, for example in election campaigns, that, even while condemning them, politicians have not been able to stop using them. They tend to be kept in reserve, as heavy artillery to be used if a candidate begins to feel that she is so far behind in the polls that this is all she has left offering a chance of last-minute victory. Although the dramatic increase in the use of character attack arguments in recent political campaigns is remarkable, use of this type of argumentation in politics is not new. In the 1860s Northern newspapers attacked Lincoln's policies by attacking his character, using the terms "drunk", "baboon", "too slow", "foolish", and "dishonest". Steadily on the increase in political argumentation since then, the character attack has been carefully refined as an instrument of "oppo tactics" and "going negative" by the public relations experts who now craft political campaigns at the national level. It has been so prominently used in the major political campaigns, debates and ads of the past few years that there has been a reaction against it — a feeling that we have gone too far in this direction and that some kind of restraint is needed.

As noted above, negative campaign tactics are not new in political rhetoric. Abraham Lincoln was a frequent target of them. After Lincoln's nomination in 1860, he was called many names, including "ape", "baboon" and "low-bred obscene clown" (Wecter, 1947, p. 87). In 1861 Southern newspapers described him as a "cross between a sand-hill crane and an Andalusian jackass" (p. 88). During the Civil War, hostile clergymen called him a "usurper, traitor and tyrant", and an "old monster" who was "thirsting for more blood" (p. 87). Even after his death, he was described as a "gawky, coarse, not overly clean, whisky drinking and whisky smelling Blackguard" (p. 47). Under such a constant barrage of *ad hominem* argumentation, one would have expected Lincoln to attack his attackers. Indeed, by recent standards of political rhetoric, a failure to do so might be taken as a failure to show strength. Lincoln's reaction to this stream of personal attack revealed something about his character. He didn't use *ad hominem* arguments to attack his critics. Indeed, he didn't seem to resent these attacks, or to feel he should respond in kind.

> Under abuse and vilification Lincoln showed an absence of bitterness which no other American hero — neither Washington nor Jefferson, Theodore Roosevelt nor Woodrow Wilson — has ever quite matched. The man seemed to have no personal resentment. "If the end brings me out all right, what is said against me won't amount to anything," he once told Nicolay. "If the end brings me out wrong, ten angels swearing I was right would make no difference." He understood the unimportance of malice (Wecter, 1947, p. 88).

By present standards of political discourse, Lincoln's attitude and actions are remarkable. He showed, by personal example, a higher standard. This conduct revealed a certain selfless quality in his character. To him, the *ad hominem* attacks seemed to appear in a different perspective. He didn't seem to feel that he needed to respond by attacking his attackers. It is normal to have hatred and bitterness towards one's enemies. When anyone shows a higher standard in personal conduct, a kind of spirituality of character is indicated. This higher standard shows a supererogatory quality, one that is above the call of duty, or above the standard that is normally considered ethical conduct.

Of course, there could be many possible explanations for Lincoln's failure to reply to these *ad hominem* attacks with countering ones. But his own words are part of the evidence that explains his conduct. He felt that what he did would be evaluated on how it worked out, and that, in the end, the *ad hominem* attacks of his enemies would not matter much in comparison to that. This attitude was consistent with much of what we know of Lincoln's life. He was known to be very kind and tolerant, even remarkable for his absence of malice. Unfortunately, times appear to have changed, and recent political events have shown that presidents and presidential candidates have fallen well below Lincoln's high standards of spirituality. Character attack arguments have not only become commonplace at the highest levels of democratic politics, but at all levels.

A revealing case study of an election campaign in which the *ad hominem* was the decisive instrument of victory for an "underdog" candidate has been provided by Cragan and Cutbirth (1984). But since that time, the character attack has been used even more effectively and commonly by politicians, raising much concern about "negative campaigning" and "attack ads". Although character attack arguments have been around for a long time, now more than ever, the problem of how to deal with them in a critically balanced way, is a matter of concern for public discourse in a democracy. What is needed is a method or normative framework that a consumer of political rhetoric can use to critically evaluate these arguments.

In the case described and analyzed by Cragan and Cutbirth, Adlai E. Stevenson, the son of the presidential candidate Adlai E. Stevenson, was criticized in an election campaign for the governorship of Illinois, on the ground that he belonged to an all-male Chicago club. Stevenson overreacted to the criticism by complaining that he had been treated as "some kind of a wimp". Once this comment appeared in print, his opponent, who at that point was behind in the race, made much use of the so-called "wimp factor", portraying Stevenson as a kind of fussy patrician type who had claimed that he only belonged to this club because he couldn't find any other decent place to eat lunch. Stevenson lost, and, according to Cragan and Cutbirth, the perception was that the "wimp factor" argument was the instrument of his defeat.

An extension of the character attack argument is the *ad hominem* argument, in which one party in a dialogue attacks the character of the other, and then uses this character attack to try to devaluate some argument of that other party. But not all character attack arguments are *ad hominem* arguments. To be an *ad hominem* argument, the character attack must be used to devaluate some specific argument that the one party in the dialogue has put forward. For example, in the Stevenson case, the argument used against him would only be an *ad hominem*, strictly speaking, if it was used to detract from some specific argument he had put forward.

The *ad hominem* argument can be a reasonable way of questioning an arguer's credibility by throwing doubt on his character (for veracity, in particular), and using that allegation to throw doubt on whether his argument has much weight in supporting its conclusion. But this type of argument can be used wrongly if the claim is that the arguer's conclusion is absolutely wrong (or indefensible), as opposed to the weaker claim that the argument for the conclusion is open to critical questioning. In other words, the *ad hominem* argument is a relative one, and runs into difficulty as soon as it becomes an absolute claim that the proposition advocated by the arguer is false. The critical thinker must watch out, in evaluating cases, for words like "certainly" and "must" that rule a claim out absolutely. In keeping with character arguments generally, the *ad hominem* has a two-sided nature. It can provide evidence to support a conclusion in some cases, while in other cases it can be a highly prejudicial, even fallacious form of argumentation. Because the *ad hominem* argument has long been classified as a fallacy in logic textbooks, the study of it as a special species of character argumentation falls into the field of logic.

1.8 A Problem of Reasoning and Evidence

As indicated above, the research enterprise of this book can be seen as one of logic or epistemology. But in historical perspective, it could be seen rather as a treatise in applied casuistry, roughly in the sense outlined in Jonsen and Toulmin (1988). The problem is one of taking a set of facts or observations in an individual case, and judging, from the account of actions given in the case, whether qualities of the agent like courage or integrity or cowardice or hypocrisy can be ascribed or not. The project has been acknowledged above to be one of ethics, but it is also one concerning the kind of evidence used to support a hypothesis. This evidential aspect is concerned with the justification of the reasoning used in arriving at such moral judgements. What needs to be explained is what kinds of reasons can be given to support or question these kinds of moral judgments, and how they are themselves supported or evaluated in some kind of systematic way. The word "systematic" is important, because what is needed is to understand the framework of reasoning underlying the way such conclusions should be drawn from the right sort of evidence in evaluating a case ethically. Unless there is such a sequence of reproducible steps drawn by logical inference from some body of evidence in a case, even the most convincing and well supported hypothesis about a person's character is only an individual, emotional response to the facts of the case. What usually happens is that the dispute proceeds along ideological lines, and it goes on and on without any precise logical basis for the passionate arguments put forward by both sides.

The issue of whether character evidence should be admissible in trials seems to coincide with the opposition between left and right political views. This was shown dramatically in a reported debate on a criminal justice bill in the British House of Commons on the issue of whether character evidence should be allowed in trials (Morgan and Mason, 2003). The historical position of the courts in England and Wales is that the defendant's character should generally not be introduced as evidence before the courts, subject to exceptions. The left (Liberal Democrat) and right (Conservative) parties took opposed views on the issue. The Liberal Democrats strongly supported the traditional view. They argued that a fair trial should not depend on evidence concerning a defendant's previous life, including previous convictions and matters of the defendant's character. On this basis, they argued that evidence of bad character should not be admissible in trials. They argued that it would be dangerous to go down the road of allowing more character evidence since this would mean that people would be judged on the basis of their past history, rather than on the specific allegations before the court. They argued that admitting evidence of previous character would provide the police with an incentive to take the approach of "rounding up the usual suspects". They contended that regular offenders would more likely be at risk, and would not get a fair trial. The Conservatives argued that evidence of bad character should be admitted in more cases, citing two recent ones to show the need for reform. In one case, the jury was not told about the previous convictions of a man accused of murdering a woman by stabbing her 81 times. In these previous instances, he had in some cases used a knife and had beaten his victims in others. In the other case, a woman who alleged she had been raped by her physician was not allowed to tell her story, as it would have revealed the physician's previous convictions for sexually assaulting nine patients. The Conservatives argued that putting too many restrictions on bad character evidence leads to injustices because the jury does not learn all the relevant facts of the case.

Such disputes may show that arguments about the relevance of character evidence in law may just reflect the individual biases or opinions of the observers and commentators (as so frequently happens in conversations about a person's character). Hence there is some basis for the worries about subjectivism, emotivism and relativism that quite rightly are central preoccupations about the objectivity of ethical judgments. The worry is that ethical judgments may be seen as mere matters of subjective opinion, lacking any basis of reasoned evidence that could be used to rationally resolve conflicts. Ethics has problems being taken seriously as a discipline precisely because of the apparent lack of a structure of reasoning behind ethical justification of conclusions about values and character. This perceived absence seems to make ethical conclusions individualistic. The aim of the analysis advanced in this book is to get beyond this apparently individualistic approach by providing a framework in which the evidential backing needed to support one judgment of character as opposed to another, is shown to have a logical structure.

At present there is no known logical method of criticizing the extremes of panegyric and character assassination, when trying to evaluate ethical conclusions that have been arrived at about a person's character. Neither panegyric nor character assassination can really be refuted or criticized on any basis that has a clear epistemological structure. As noted above, this problem affects many fields, including law and history. But it certainly is a central problem in ethics, raising many doubts about ethics as an objective field of inquiry. The basic problem is that we judge character on the basis of some past actions of a person in a given case. But once that case is in the past, it can never be re-lived in exactly the same details. We can judge only on the basis of hindsight, which is always imperfect. Thus one agent can try to put herself in the mind of another, at the time the other acted in certain ways, but the situation will have changed. The judging agent will not have all the same information about the facts of a case that the original agent had. Inevitably, when one agent tries to judge the character of another, the process involves guesswork and estimation, in a situation of incomplete knowledge. It is easy to simply shrug, and say, "Well, one person's opinion is as good as another's". In consequence, it is easy to get away with distorting someone's character, either in a positive or a negative way. In character assassination, the bad qualities are emphasized, and blown out of proportion. In panegyric, a flattering portrait of a person's character is painted, in which good qualities are puffed up, and bad qualities are ignored or suppressed. How can such abuses be contained or criticized unless there is some kind of structure of reasoning underlying the arguments used to puff up or deflate a person's supposed character?

1.9 Character Properties in Law and Ethics

There are all kinds of character properties, or so-called traits of character, that might be chosen and studied. In ethics, the so-called cardinal virtues are at the center of much of the discussion of character as an ethical notion. The concerns of common law have centered on broad propensities of a kind that carry over from one alleged action to another action of the same person. The motivation in legal rules of evidence has been to exclude character judgments of a kind that might tend to prejudice a jury. For example, suppose a man is accused of armed robbery, and there is evidence that he was previously convicted of committing an armed robbery, thus showing a propensity to commit this kind of crime. Would this be evidence in a trial about the new accusation? The answer, according to current rules of evidence, is that "a defendant cannot be shown to have the propensity to commit a crime by the use of evidence that merely shows that the defendant committed another crime that has the same statutory description" (Park, 1998, p. 719). Following this line of thinking, evidence law prohibits arguing that evidence that a person committed a crime can be based on a supposed propensity to commit this type of crime. Among the character properties of this sort cited by Park (1998, p. 718) are being "a liar, violent, trustworthy, intemperate, a thief, cruel, kind, lazy, conscientious, careless". It is not hard to appreciate how these traits of character are easily fitted into evidential inferences of a kind that are very significant cases at trial. What is worrisome, from a point of view of rules of evidence used in trials, is that a jury might easily attach far too much importance to an argument like "He is a violent man, therefore he committed the armed robbery at issue in this case". Even though such an argument has some probative weight in everyday reasoning, the worry is that, in the hands of an aggressive prosecuting attorney, it might be used fallaciously to persuade a jury to find an accused person guilty. The problem is that even though it might be true that the accused person is a violent man, or at least that there is evidence linking his past actions to such a character property, nevertheless he might not be the one who committed the armed robbery in this case. The problem is one of possible wrongful conviction. If the defendant looks guilty, if he looks "weird", unpredictable, or possibly dangerous or violent, a jury may be sufficiently impressed to leap to the conclusion that he must be guilty. Accordingly, the rules of evidence have classified arguments of this form as irrelevant. Their slight probative weight is counterbalanced by their tendency to prejudice a jury. Hence the character ban in legal rules of evidence.

For these reasons, the literature on ethics has centered on different properties of character than the legal literature in evidence law. The concern of evidence law has been with excluding arguing from general character propensities to allegations about whether a specific action was carried out by a particular person. The concern of virtue ethics is with the way general character properties, like honesty or integrity, can have ethical import in judging actions as good or bad, and with the kinds of evidence that should be used to support or criticize claims about such general properties in a person. Evidence law is very much centered on inference drawn from a person's alleged character traits to specific actions that person is alleged to have carried out. Thus the problem is seen in a logical way. The central questions are how such an argument can be evidence in a court of law, and when it should be considered relevant. In ethics, the problem is more one of the status the virtues have as general properties of character bestowing positive or negative value on a given action. The concern in ethical theory is to see how virtues, or ethically positive or negative qualities of character, provide a basis for evaluating actions as right or wrong, as an alternative to utilitarian theories that judge actions ethically on the basis of their probable consequences. The central problem for virtue ethics has been to define the virtues in some clear and precise way, so that they can be linked inferentially to specific actions that we want to evaluate ethically.

These differences stated, there are common concerns and elements. Both fields are centrally concerned with the property of honesty, for example, and how that property relates to instances of lying. In law, one of the leading exceptions to the character evidence ban is that the character of a witness for honesty (veracity, or truthfulness) can be attacked during cross-examination of the witness. One might think that this kind of inference is fairly simple, and could be the best place to start investigating the common elements of character evidence in law and ethics. Honesty, one might think, can very simply be defined as a propensity to tell the truth, and dishonesty as a propensity to lie, or not to tell the truth. Thus the following kinds of inferences seem straightforward.

Inference from Lying to Dishonest Character
He lied.
Therefore he is dishonest.

Inference from Dishonest Character to Lying
He is dishonest.
Therefore he is lying now.

But casuistic problems that arise in ethics, as well as the problems cited above arising from developments in evidence law, have shown that such inferences are a lot more problematic than they initially seem. First, it is not easy to define what lying is. Telling a lie is not just saying something false. This can happen through ignorance, or being misinformed. Telling a lie needs to be defined along the lines of intentionally saying something false, or that one thinks is false, with the intention to deceive (Bok, 1978). Another complicating factor is that some lies, like "white lies", may not be evidence of having done something that is ethically wrong. Telling this kind of lie is not evidence that a person is dishonest. For example, there is a famous incident of a knight, Adrien de la Riviere, who had been captured in earlier clashes before the Turkish assault on Malta (Bradford, 1972, p. 153). Under torture, he told the enemy falsely that the fort of Castile was a weak point in the defenses. When the Turks attacked the fort, they took heavy casualties, losing hundreds of their best troops, because the knight had been lying. Once they realized that de la Riviere had been lying, they beat him to death. It can be argued that although the knight lied, what he did should not be taken as evidence that he was a dishonest person. Quite to the contrary, what he did was altruistic, and could be considered highly courageous. Yet another complicating factor is that there are famous borderline cases in ethics where intentionally saying something vague or ambiguous can be misleading, but is on the borderline of being a lie. President Clinton's famous statement "I did not have sexual relations with that woman" is a case in point. Arguably, he did not say something false, or commit perjury by telling a lie, because of the vagueness or ambiguity of the expression "sexual relations". Cases of this sort are famous in casuistry.

Considering some of these traditional ethical problems about lying shows that trying to analyze the form of reasoning connecting what appear to be simple statements, like those connecting honesty with instances of the act of lying, is not as easy as it looks. Because a person has lied, it does not necessarily follow that he is dishonest. Or if a person is honest, it does not necessarily follow that he is telling the truth in a given instance. Definitions of key terms defining a character trait or a type of act can also be highly problematic. Defining what honesty is, or what lying is, runs into problems that are far from trivial from a logical point of view. Nevertheless, it does seem that there are common concerns in the two fields, and that both are centrally preoccupied with the same kinds of inferences connecting general character properties with specific actions a person is alleged to have carried out in a particular case. The common concern is to elucidate the structure such inferences have, and to show how they can be modeled in a way seen to represent reasoning of some clear and precise sort.

The implications of these difficulties are far-reaching. Once they undermine some of our preconceptions about reasoning based on character evidence, the proportions of the problem faced can be appreciated. It is easy to assume that the two inferences cited above are inductive. In the inference from lying to dishonest character, it is easy to assume that one only needs to count up the instances of a person's lying, and then reason inductively from that evidence that the person is a liar with a greater or lesser degree of probability. In the inference from dishonest character to lying, it is easy to assume that one is reasoning inductively from a probabilistic propensity to lie to make a prediction about the likelihood that the person in question will lie in the future. But each of these ways of viewing the reasoning can be shown to be erroneous. To take the former one first: just because a person has lied before, one can't conclude that he is dishonest. It depends on the purpose of the lie, and the circumstances. Just because the knight de la Riviere lied to deceive the enemy in war, it does not follow that he was a dishonest person. On the contrary, we conclude he was a very brave person with strong principles, and that under normal circumstances, he could be relied on to be very honest and upright. And with regard to the latter inference: is the person's supposedly dishonest character a mere summing up of all the cases in which he is known to have lied in the past, perhaps as compared with all the cases in which he is known to have told the truth? It does not seem so. For example, if he lied inconsequentially in some instance in order to avoid being cruel, and hurting someone vulnerable, this act would not count very strongly for the conclusion that he is generally a dishonest person. But if he lied in a business deal, using deception to try to profit unfairly from the deal, that act would count very strongly for such a conclusion. In other words, a simple counting of actions to make a probability argument to or from a character property is not the kind of reasoning that is involved.[9] The circumstances, and how we describe them, seem to count as factors in judging the strength or weakness of the inference.

---

[9]McKinnon (1999, p. 67) argued for the same thesis when she concluded that character cannot be simply the sum of one's innate dispositions.

It is these sorts of problems that gave rise to the complaint of Anscombe (1958) about the poverty of our moral descriptions and evaluations in ethics. As McKinnon (1999, p. 103) expressed the problem, "we seem to be almost completely in the dark when we are asked to describe carefully the motivations and characters of bad persons". The same could be said about the motivations and character of good persons. So-called ethical virtues, like courage, honesty and integrity, although important in common inferences we draw in ethics and law, as well as in everyday practical reasoning, are very little understood. They are more than just propensities, or summations of positive or negative instances of behavior. Virtuous qualities of character are chosen and acquired, and they serve as motivating reasons rather than compelling reasons to act (McKinnon, 1999, p. 66). They depend on circumstances and interpretation, and they relate to single instances in a rather complex way that makes inferences based on them subject to exceptions and to defeat in special cases.

1.10 Character Evidence in Law and Artificial Intelligence

Character evidence is clearly very dangerous in legal argumentation. The general ban on character evidence makes this perceived danger clear. Attacking the defendant's ethical character, or attacking the character of a witness for honesty, is such a powerful form of argument in law that the rules of evidence have been specifically designed to contain it. But character evidence is also fundamentally important in law, as shown by the exceptions to the ban. To cite just one exception once again, the character of a witness may be the crucial evidence that decides many a case. Anglo-American law has developed rules for judging character evidence, based on centuries of experience of having to deal with it in trials. But the subject of this book is how we should arrive at judgments about character by some process of logical reasoning and how such judgments, once made, should be supported or criticized by evidence. It is about the kind of evidence or reasoning used to justify character judgments. As shown below in this section, the logical aspect of character evidence ties in with recent developments in computing. There has arisen recently a strong need to standardize communication between humans and software entities, and between these software entities themselves. In electronic commerce, for example, parties need to reason together in an organized way that follows organized standards for logical reasoning. In some cases the character of a person, like whether that person is trustworthy or has a good credit rating, can be relevant to communication. These developments offer many clues on how reasoning about character evidence should be formalized as a clear procedure.

Character evidence is a powerful force that cannot easily be swept aside or dismissed, as the history of law shows. As indicated in section 3 above, in Roman law a trial was all about the character of the defendant. If the defendant was shown to have a good reputation, that was taken to be a good reason for concluding that he was not guilty of the crime with which he was charged. If he was shown to have a bad reputation, that was taken to be a good reason for thinking that he was guilty. Although now banned by the rules of evidence law, such arguments to some conclusion about what a person did, or might do, are extremely common in everyday argumentation. Business deals, for example, are often based on the perceived honesty and trustworthiness of another person. Perhaps one of the most important skills in business is the ability to make this kind of judgment. Around the beginning of the nineteenth century, however, a general ban on the use of character evidence began to be an important part of Anglo-American law. Since then, the so-called "character evidence rule" has become firmly established in law. There seems to be a fundamental conflict here. Character evidence is one of the most important elements in everyday life argumentation and in business, and does seem to be predictive. Yet, as we have seen, the rules of evidence ban character evidence if used to prove conduct in a specific instance. Even so, the law itself seems conflicted, because of exceptions to that rule.

In many a trial, the issue of whether character evidence should be deemed relevant has been highly contested. In the televised criminal trial of O. J. Simpson, for example, the two sides argued with the judge about the admissibility of evidence that Simpson has beaten and stalked Nicole Brown Simpson even before the trial started (Park, 1996, p. 748). The defense contended that it was character evidence, and therefore should be excluded. The prosecution argued that it was relevant because it showed motive. Judge Ito excluded some of this evidence but admitted most of it, on the ground of a California ruling in favor of admitting evidence of prior assaults in homicide cases. But in general, character evidence is quite strictly hemmed in by Anglo-American rules of evidence. The rules allowing or forbidding use of character evidence are complicated, and many a trial is taken up with argumentation in which the attorney for one side tries to get character evidence admitted while the attorney for the other side tries to keep it out. Why all this concern about character evidence in law? The answer suggested above is that it is such a powerful form of argument that it could be used to deceive or prejudice a jury by fallacious argumentation. Even though it is assumed in our system of law that a jury is capable of judging argumentation, it is also assumed that there are limits to this capability that need to be taken into account in order to have a fair trial.

The character evidence rule has been subjected to "withering criticism in recent years", and has been subject to erosion, but still has many defenders (Tillers, 1998). The policy of excluding character evidence in criminal trials has been challenged in English law. Redmayne (2002, p. 684) reported that a proposal was made to weaken the presumption of inadmissibility of character evidence in 2002. One English judge had even suggested in 2001 that revealing a defendant's previous convictions at the beginning of every trial should be considered. As Anglo-American law has evolved to its present state, the issue of character evidence has become complex and controversial. The issue raises many basic questions about why character evidence should be banned. But it also raises even more basic questions about what character is, and how conclusions can be drawn on the basis of a person's character. Character is an internal property of a person. It is not visible to a judge or jury in a trial. And yet triers do often draw significant conclusions from what they take to be a person's character, based on reports about how that person acted. How could such inferences be verified or falsified, based on what should properly be called legal evidence?

The subject of this book is how we should arrive at judgments about character by some process of logical reasoning and, once such a judgment has been made, how it should be supported or criticized by evidence. It is about the kind of evidence or reasoning used to justify character judgments. This logical aspect of character evidence will be shown to tie in with recent developments in computer science, in a new field of distributed computing called multi-agent systems. In agent communication, two software entities called agents need to communicate with each other. For this purpose, it is vital that one agent be able to make judgments about whether the other agents may be assumed to be cooperative and honest, or to have other qualities of character or disposition. These recent developments in computer science, especially in AI (artificial intelligence), and linguistics (especially in pragmatics) have cast new light on the structure of reasoning used when one person draws a conclusion based on what she assumes is the thinking of another person. Indeed, the field of multi-agent systems has grown up around the basic idea of intelligent agents being able to act and plan together. An intelligent agent is an entity, either a human or a software or hardware entity, that can not only act, but can also sense its environment and have goals. Having a useful multi-agent system requires agents not only to carry out reasoning in an organized practical manner, but also to reason with other agents. To have agent teamwork, one agent not only has to have some grasp of how another agent is thinking when both of them are trying to carry out a task together, but also must be able to communicate, to ask questions, and process the answers. It is necessary for agents to deliberate with each other on how to proceed with carrying out planned actions. But to do this in an intelligent and informed way, the agents also need to grasp incoming information and to use it in their deliberations. Through this research in computing several new tools have been developed that are extremely useful in giving a precise structure to interpersonal reasoning.

The special approach taken in the abductive theory of character evidence developed in this book follows recent developments in the new field of computing called computational dialectics. This term was coined when Ron Loui and Tom Gordon organized an AAAI workshop with Johanna Moore and Katya Sycara under the name Computational Dialectics in Seattle in 1994 (Lodder, 2000, p. 255). The workshop (Loui and Gordon, 1994) described the field as the study of structured dialogues used in multi-agent communication systems in which agents reach agreement to achieve common goals through rational interaction in a fair and effective way. The field comprises intelligent computer support of discussion, negotiation and collective decision-making processes. Such interactions include asking questions to get information from other agents, assessing the worth of that information as a basis for arriving at an intelligent decision, and reasoning together to solve a problem or resolve a disagreement.

The theory of planning, and especially the notion of plan recognition, are centrally important for the study of character evidence. The idea behind this notion is that a second agent can recognize the plans and goals of a primary agent, by observing what the other agent is doing. Another idea important in plan recognition is that the two agents can engage in a dialogue. Thus if the second agent comes up with a hypothesis about what it thinks the other agent is thinking, it can get evidence to confirm or refute the hypothesis by asking the other agent a question. Other fields besides computer science have also developed resources that are useful tools for studying reasoning based on empathy. The notion of simulative reasoning has been studied in psychology and philosophy of mind. And the field of pragmatics in linguistics has examined the way participants in a conversation can draw defeasible inferences from each other's utterances or speech acts that are part of the conversational flow. The Gricean notion of conversational implicature posits that human communication in everyday life depends on inferences that one contributor draws by supposition from what the other says. For example, if one person asks another where he can get gas, and the second person says, "There is a gas station around the corner", the first person would act on the supposition that the gas station is open, as far as the second person knows. Such implicatures are typically unstated, and are taken for granted in everyday conversational exchanges, but knowing about them is vitally important for understanding reasoning based on reenactment as a logical process. Putting all these pieces of the puzzle from computer science, psychology, philosophy and linguistics together, it can be shown that character judgments are not just subjective, but are reasoned conclusions of a kind that can be verified and falsified by reproducible evidence. These tools from various fields will be used to show that there is a process of reasoning behind character judgments.

The clue that offers a way forward is that in everyday reasoning, character evidence is often used to predict a person's future conduct based on the known facts about her past conduct. This kind of reasoning is essentially inductive in nature. It goes from past to future. Social scientists can then collect data, for example data on repeat offenders and so forth, to debate whether the inference from past conduct to future conduct through character propensity is a strong or weak form of argumentation. However, in a typical case at trial, character evidence is not used in this way. In a trial, character evidence is just one piece of fallible evidence that is weak and conjectural by itself. But it can swing a balance of consideration to one side or the other in a trial, where there is a conflict of opinions, and where the situation is one of uncertainty and lack of complete knowledge. The knowledge is incomplete because the issue is about an event that happened in the past. This key difference between predictive reasoning and the typical kind of reasoning used in a legal case at trial is well brought out by a kind of case cited by Park (1998, p. 723): "While it may be true that only one in a thousand men who physically abuse their wives goes on to kill her, if a wife is found murdered and the husband is suspect, the evidence of abuse is certainly worth considering". Predictively, the argument from the premise of known abuse to the conclusion of murder may be weak. But as one bit of evidence in a case where the wife has been found murdered and the husband is suspect, the same argument retroductively (going from the known facts as premises back to a conclusion about something that supposedly happened in the past) is definitely relevant and important.

The problem is that such evidence may be fallible and potentially misleading by itself. Put in the context of a larger mass of evidence, however, it can be highly significant in the legal context of a trial. But what kind of reasoning is this? How can it be judged strong or weak? And how can it be judged, in particular cases, to be relevant or not? Answering these questions will take us on a long road. The first step is to philosophically define what character is, in a clear and precise enough way that it can be distinguished from allied notions like habit, motive, propensity and bias. Only then will we be in a position to study how character evidence should properly be used in argumentation, and to determine when it is used in a fallacious way.

Chapter 2

DEFINING AND JUDGING CHARACTER

What is character? The problem is that in the past we have swung between two extremes in trying to define it. Character has traditionally been taken to be an internal property of a person. It is the "inner citadel" of ethics. But because it is internal, and hence subjective, it is said to be impossible to define it legally in any helpful way.[1] The question is how, if it is subjective and personal, it can be based on objective evidence. How can one person judge the character of another person? Character judgment is a form of inference that is based on observations of actions and data that are external to the person who is the source of the actions. But of course, given the problem of other minds, such an inference is always indirect and conjectural. There is always a logical leap from the data to the conclusion drawn from that data. So how can we be sure that any character judgment is right if it is based on a guess or leap of inference to something unobservable that is hard to grasp, define, or even imagine? These difficulties have led to a second view. On this view, character is a habit, propensity or disposition to carry out a certain type of action. This way of defining character is based on probability. Its logic is based on inductive generalization. For example, "x has the character trait of being honest" means "x generally tends to tell the truth". As will be shown in this chapter, this way of defining the notion of character doesn't work very well either. The problem is that neither extreme really works. Hence we are driven to try to find some new approach.

A new way of defining the notion of character is presented in this chapter. According to this, character is more than just a general tendency or propensity. It is an ethical notion tied to an interpersonal judgment in which one agent makes a value judgment about another, based on how the one

[1]Allen, Kuhns and Swift (1997, p. 677).

agent sees and interprets the actions of the other. Solutions to these problems are shown in this chapter to be found by redefining the concept of an agent, in line with new research on how agents reason and carry out programmed tasks in artificial intelligence. An agent is an entity that carries out actions, but also has an internal structure. It has goals and commitments. These may be long term and even abstract in nature. The agent carries out the actions based on its goals. An agent also has the capability of perceiving its external environment, to some limited extent. In particular, it can see its own actions as they are carried out, and can see at least some of the immediate consequences of those actions. An agent is an autonomous entity that moves along on its own, constantly perceiving, acting, and judging its own actions in relation to its goals and what it sees happening. In this chapter, character will be defined as a property of an agent.

2.1 Bias and Character

The distinction between character evidence and bias is very important in legal argumentation. As noted in chapter 1, character used to prove a specific act is not admissible by Federal Rule of Evidence 404. In a criminal trial, for example, the prosecution cannot use the argument, "He has a bad character in some respect, therefore he must be guilty of committing this crime as alleged". In contrast, the argument that a witness is not credible because he is biased is generally regarded as relevant in law. The reason is that witness testimony is an important form of evidence in law. And if a witness is biased, it is important for the jury to know this, in order to properly evaluate this evidence. So the same argument can be irrelevant as character evidence, yet be relevant as evidence of bias. This point was illustrated in the part of the criminal trial of O.J. Simpson that was outlined in chapter 1. The defense argued that Detective Fuhrman's recorded racist declarations were relevant because they showed a racial bias against black persons. Aware that "evidence of specific instances of conduct is not admissible to attack the character of witness for honesty or dishonesty", the defense argued that the evidence of Fuhrman's racist statements "was relevant to more than character for dishonesty because it also showed bias and hostility towards the defendant" (Park, 1996, p. 757). The distinction between character evidence and evidence of bias was significant here.

However, in practice, if you look at argumentation in a trial, it may not be easy to draw a clear distinction between character evidence and bias evidence. Some questions are raised by some problematic borderline cases cited by Allen, Kuhns and Swift (1997, p. 677). Suppose a witness tries to bribe another witness. Is this evidence of bad character, or is it evidence of bias? Or could it be both? What about evidence of gang membership? Is that character evidence or evidence of bias? Or could it be both? According to Allen, Kuhns and Swift, these issues are "difficult to resolve in part because the term character is not defined and is probably not definable in any helpful sense". The lack of a clear definition is a problem for evidence law that leaves open avenues of exploitation by a clever lawyer. Character evidence may not be admissible. But if the very same character argument can be smuggled into court under the heading of bias, it will have the same powerful impact on the jury. Lawyers know this, and, being advocates, they will exploit it. The problem is such a difficult one that Allen, Kuhns and Swift even consider whether it might be desirable to abandon the distinction between character and bias.

In principle, however, it should be possible to make a clear distinction between the two. Character should be defined as a long-term disposition, generally of an ethical nature, that an agent has. It is an internal characteristic that can be assessed externally by examining what that agent has said and done over a long period. Bias, on the other hand, is a matter of an agent's attitude as judged by his performance in argumentation. In many kinds of argumentation, it is vitally important for an arguer to be open to fairly taking into account the argumentation of the other side. For example, in a critical discussion, a participant must not distort or discount the other party's arguments automatically. It is also important for a participant to be open to defeat, should he recognize that the other party has a convincing argument. This quality in argumentation is often called open-mindedness. An arguer must look at and fairly consider both sides of an argument. An arguer who fails to exhibit this quality may be said to be biased. In other words, bias in this sense is a kind of one-sidedness in argumentation. The biased arguer always advocates only his own side, and automatically discounts the arguments of the other, even if they are rationally convincing and strong.

How can bias be judged in a given case? The evidence is to be found in an agent's argumentation. If he always sticks to one side and never admits any arguments put forward by the other side, even when they seem reasonable, that is evidence of bias. If he has an interest at stake, and always promotes this interest, even against the evidence, that is evidence of bias. If he uses slanted language and one-sided persuasive definitions, that is evidence of bias. Such evidence is found in the recorded dialogue showing the agent's performance in argumentation. Thus bias is contextual. Whether it is normal, or whether it interferes with the proper progress of a dialogue depends on the context of dialogue. In some contexts, bias is normal, and is not a fault of argumentation. If we are negotiating, and I always press for my interests, then that is a bias, but not a bad bias. But if we are supposed to be engaged in a critical discussion, and I keep pressing for my interest in one-sided advocacy, then that is bad bias. It is a matter of how argumentation is put forward in a context of dialogue. If the dialogue is supposed to be a critical discussion, the type of argumentation that should be used is two-sided. A participant needs to be open to the arguments of the other side, and to take them into account. Sometimes he should even be persuaded by them, and change his commitments because he is so persuaded. Failure to be two-sided in the way required for this type of dialogue is evidence of a negative kind of bias. A finding of this kind of bias can rightly be used to question or attack an arguer's credibility.

The relevance of character evidence in law is also contextual. It depends on the goal of the type of dialogue the parties are supposed to be engaged in. Character evidence tends to be irrelevant (subject to exceptions) in the main argumentation stage of a criminal trial where guilt is to be determined. As noted above, Rule 404 of the Federal Rules of Evidence bans the general use of the argument that the defendant must be guilty because he has a bad character. But the same character attack argument that was deemed irrelevant at the main argumentation stage of a criminal trial can be highly relevant later at the sentencing stage. The difference between how relevance of character evidence is judged in these two types of dialogue has been well brought out by Landon (1997). Essentially, the goal at the main argumentation stage is different from the goal of the dialogue at the sentencing stage. At the main stage of a criminal trial, the goal is to look backward to try to determine what happened on a particular occasion. In contrast, the goal at the sentencing stage is to look forward, and to try to determine what sentence is appropriate for punishment (Landon, 1997, p. 613). Evidence of the character of the offender is relevant in this type of dialogue. For example, evidence of bad acts or convictions in the past could be relevant to judging whether a repeat offender is a habitual criminal (p. 614). Thus judging both bias and character as evidence in legal argumentation is contextual.

Bias is a kind of proclivity, and so is character. But they work in different ways. Identifying the difference between the two in a specific case is contextual. But the basis of the distinction is there. Bias is a kind of one-sidedness, and a failure to be open in considering both sides of an argument. The evidence is to be found in the person's argumentation, and in how he reacts to criticisms and opposed viewpoints. Character is a general disposition a person has to act in certain ways. Evidence of character is found in the person's actions and words, as known or reported. But character can also be revealed by the way a person acts in argumentation. For example, the way he replies to critical questions about his actions may be very important in revealing a person's character. Thus there is overlap in the kinds of evidence for character versus bias. Evidence of an attempt to bribe a juror, or evidence of gang membership could fall into either category, depending on how it was used in a given case, and what it was supposed to prove.

As noted in chapter 1, character evidence can be used in a trial to prove motive intent or plan. If it can be shown to come under this heading, character evidence that would normally be considered inadmissible could become admissible. Thus it is very important in legal argument to draw a distinction between character and motive. The importance of this distinction was illustrated in part of the O.J. Simpson criminal trial described in chapter 1. The defense cited the rule against the admissibility of character evidence to argue that the evidence of Simpson's spouse abuse was not relevant. The prosecution argued that this evidence was relevant because it showed that Simpson had a motive of controlling and dominating his wife. The distinction between character and motive was thus crucial here to determining relevance of evidence. In principle, this distinction is very important in evidence law.

In practice however, as shown above in connection with bias and character evidence, it can be problematic to decide whether evidence falls under the one category or the other. Suppose a person can be shown to have bad motive, like a motive to cheat or kill another person. Very likely that finding would also tend to suggest that he has a bad ethical character. To approach this problem, it is useful to begin by looking at some legal argumentation about character evidence as used and supported in trials. It is useful to try to see how character judgments are in fact supported by evidence or by supporting arguments.

2.2 Habit, Propensity and Motive

Character is not fully defined in evidence law, but certain key attributes of the notion are clearly stated or implied by the way the rules concerning character evidence are formulated. The way character is understood in law, it is a general tendency or propensity. In Federal Rule of Evidence 404 (a), it is defined as "a generalized description of one's disposition, or of one's disposition in respect to a general trait, such as honesty, temperance, or peacefulness". But not any habit, or propensity to carry out a certain kind of action, is the same as character. According to the way the legal notion is understood, character may also be taken to have an ethical requirement. Park *et al.* (1998, p. 132) have articulated this point very clearly.

> To constitute a character trait, one would think (though this is not settled) that the tendency must arise in some reasonable degree from the person's *moral* being — from traits over which the person has a substantial element of choice, and which cause observers to regard the person more favorably or less favorably upon learning of the individual's behavior.

Park, Leonard and Goldberg (p. 132) also offered some nice examples of general tendencies or propensities that would not be considered character traits. For example, a stroke victim's propensity to forget would not be seen as a trait of character, but as a medical condition. And despite the Advisory Committee's reference to "temperance" as a character trait, one could argue that the intemperate use of alcohol is a medical condition rather than a character trait — though admittedly this view has not achieved general acceptance. Thus while there is room for argument on some borderline cases, in general, character is not just any disposition or propensity, but one arising from an agent's choice, leading observers to make ethical judgments concerning the associated actions, positive or negative.

The rule of evidence banning the use of character evidence in trials is complex and subtle, because there are several important exceptions to it, and judging whether something is an exception often requires careful consideration. What is not allowed is to argue from character to alleged action. More specifically, the rule says that character evidence is barred when it is used to argue that a particular action was in conformity with a person's character. For example, consider the common kind of case in which a person's prior bad act is cited to show he has a bad character, and this conclusion is then used as evidence to argue that he committed a specific crime. This kind of argument is not allowed, because it is based on character or disposition. However, suppose evidence of a prior bad act is used to establish motive or opportunity to commit a crime. Then the argument would be admitted, as long as the evidence of the prior bad act was not offered to show disposition. Thus, as indicated by a comment of Park *et al.* (1998, p. 134), there is a rather fine line to be drawn in such cases.

> There is a varying and hard-to-define line between general character-based disposition, which embraces such traits as honesty, peacefulness, and the like, and specific disposition, which embraces evidence of "habit", evidence of modus operandi, and evidence of other relatively narrow tendencies of a person.

Among the exceptions to the character prohibition rule cited by Park, Leonard and Goldberg are the following. When character is the ultimate issue, as in a defamation of character case, the ban against character evidence does not operate (p. 134). A defendant may offer witnesses to attest to his or her own good character (p. 139). This move, however, may then open the floodgates for an attack on character, which is now relevant, by the other side (p. 141). Arguments concerning the character of the victim may be allowed as evidence in some criminal cases. For example (p. 144), in a homicide case, the defendant may claim the victim was the first aggressor. It is allowed to attack the character of a witness for honesty by citing prior convictions or by offering testimony about the bad character of the witness for truthfulness (p. 151). Evidence of reputation can sometimes be used to prove certain kinds of claims. For example, a person's reputation in the community or workplace can sometimes be used as relevant character evidence, provided the witness has personal knowledge of the person's reputation (p. 152). Evidence of past crimes can be used to show a pattern or *modus operandi*, provided it is not based on the character of the defendant (p. 157). The distinction is a rather subtle one. You can't argue that the defendant is the type of person who commits bank robberies, for example, and that it is therefore more likely that he committed this crime of bank robbery. But you can argue that since he used a distinctive method of bank robbery in other cases, it is more likely that he carried out the bank robbery in the case at issue, which used the same method. Another exception is that past conduct or propensity could be used to prove motive (p. 163). Here, a careful distinction needs to be drawn between motive and character. Past conduct can also be used in criminal cases to prove opportunity to commit a crime (p. 168), guilty knowledge (p. 169), or preparation to commit a crime (p. 175).

The need for such careful distinctions has arisen from the prohibitions on character evidence. Park *et al.* (1998) have identified two contrasting general patterns of inference of this sort. The first one (p. 158) is a character inference based on past actions.

Inference from Character to Alleged Criminal Act

Factual Premise: The defendant committed one armed robbery.
General Premise: The defendant is the type of person who commits armed robberies.
Conclusion: It is more likely that the defendant is guilty of the present crime than would otherwise be the case.

The second type of inference can look superficially quite similar to the first in a given case. But the general premise is subtly different. It is not based on a generalization about character, but on one about using a repeated pattern of action, a *modus operandi*, literally a way of operating or doing something methodically. The precise form of this contrasting type of inference has been set out by Park, Leonard and Goldberg (1998, p. 159).

Inference from *Modus Operandi* to Alleged Criminal Act

Factual Premise: Defendant robbed other banks using exactly the same method.
General Premise: Defendant is a bank robber who uses that distinctive method to commit the crime.
Conclusion: Defendant is the person who committed the crime at issue.

Note that the inference from *modus operandi* to an alleged criminal act is based on the habit or propensity of an agent to carry out a certain kind of action in a certain pattern or according to a certain method of doing things. What is the difference, then, between the two inferences, if character is also to be defined as a propensity or disposition?

The difference has to reside in the notion that character is a narrower notion than a pattern or method of acting, or a general propensity to act in a certain way. Thus the general premise in the inference from character to alleged criminal act is not just a claim about an agent's disposition, or usual way of doing things. This kind of inference is based on character in some fuller sense of the term. But what is this fuller sense? One clue, of course, is that it is an ethical notion of some sort, tied up with values and judgments of praise and blame. But that may hinder more than help, as it also suggests a problem. How can the inference from character to an alleged criminal act be used to show evidence of having committed a crime (a bad or punishable type of action), if it depends itself on the judgmental notion of an action being good or bad? Thus puzzles remain about this form of inference, and how it is to be evaluated in specific cases where it plays an important role as evidence.

2.3 Agents, Practical Reasoning and Character

The key to seeing how judgments about a person's character can be verified or falsified by evidence lies in the concept of an agent. An agent is an abstract model of what a person should be like if that person were thinking and acting rationally, according to a certain standard. That standard is one of practical reasoning. In law, the expression "the rational man" is often used to evoke a certain kind of standard to judge in a given case how a person would likely have acted if he had been rational or reasonable, and had therefore done what was (presumably) the reasonable thing to do at the time. This device of the rational man is used to draw conclusions in the form of hypotheses about what probably (or plausibly) happened in a given case. The concept of an agent needs to be used in the same way in making hypotheses about a person's character, and in verifying or refuting these hypotheses.

An agent is an entity that has goals, and has the capability of carrying out actions in a particular situation. An agent also has information on the situation. This may be incomplete, and may even be mistaken, but an agent has the capability of bringing in new information, and of correcting or revising the old information, as the situation changes. There are two other important characteristics of an agent. In particular, it has the capability of perceiving the consequences of its actions, once it has acted. And it has the capability of changing its actions, once it perceives these consequences. These last two capabilities are called "feedback". For example, if an agent is a machine that has the goal of hitting a target, and its previous actions are falling short of the target, it can see that, and correct its aim accordingly.

Agent technology is widely used in computer science, especially in robotics and artificial intelligence, as shown below. In this perspective, an agent can be a machine, or a software package. But we can also look at human actions as if they were carried out by an agent. To look at a human action this way, of course, is to adopt a particular point of view. An agent is predictable, while in many cases human actions would not be so easily predictable. An agent always does the rational thing, whatever that is. Of course, what the rational thing to do in any given case may be very hard to judge, because the particulars of the case may be highly complex, and in certain key respects, not known. Nevertheless, an assessment may be made of what the agent would do, and this assessment can be compared, in any actual case of a human action, to judge what the rational thing would be for the person to do. This information, in turn, can be used, like the legal rational man model, to make hypotheses about what the person likely did, assuming he was "rational". This finding, in turn, can be used to assist in formulating hypotheses about the person's character.

What kind of reasoning, then, do agents use when they carry out goal-directed actions? The answer is that they use practical reasoning. This kind of reasoning is already somewhat familiar to philosophers, and is increasingly so in computer science. In fact, it was known to Aristotle as *phronesis* or practical wisdom (Drefcinski, 1996). Nowadays it is generally referred to as practical reasoning (Audi, 1989). The basic unit in the structure of practical reasoning is the type of inference traditionally called the practical syllogism, which can be explained as an inference of the following general form (first person pronouns like "I" and "my" refer to the agent),

My aim is to realize a certain goal.
This action is the means to realize that goal.
Therefore, I should carry out this action.

This form of inference is called a type of syllogism because the major premise states a goal or aim that can be general, and the minor premise states a specific action, or course of action, that fits into the goal, thus generating the conclusion. Unlike a proper syllogism however, this form of inference is (at least typically) not deductively valid. It can be deductively valid in cases where the database of the case is assumed to be complete. But in typical cases of practical reasoning, of the kind used in ethical reasoning for example, the inference is made in conditions of uncertainty. The database cannot be assumed to be closed. The kind of reasoning typical of such cases is what

Wellman described as conductive. It represents a different type of reasoning from the traditional deductive and inductive kinds that have been dominant in logic. It is tentative and subject to revision if new information comes in. It is judged on a balance of considerations in a case where the issue may be controversial. While the agent needs to take action in an uncertain situation, it should not be dogmatic, and should be aware of the fallible nature of its reasoning. An agent needs to be flexible and prudent.

If an agent has a goal, and it sees that in a given case, the means of achieving that goal is a specific action, then it will carry out the action. But agent reasoning needs to take many factors into account. If the agent sees that more than one action is available as a means, it will have to consider which action is better from its point of view. Or if it carries out the action that is the obvious means, but then sees that there is a better means, once it sees the consequences of its previous action, it will correct by feedback. It will "change its mind" and switch to the new action. In general, though, what the agent does is mechanical and predictable, compared to what a human agent might do in the same situation. Human beings are often irrational, at least judged from the agent point of view. A human being may see that an action is the best means to carry out his goal, but then through weakness of will, or for whatever reason, simply fail to carry out that action. The agent point of view is only an abstract model of what the practically reasonable thing to do is in a given situation. It does not necessarily correspond to what any actual human would really do in that situation.

A goal is very similar to a motive. Both of these notions are also close to the notion of an intention. Here the problem of distinguishing between motive and character thus arises again. Determining what an agent's goals or motives are is surely an important part of the evidence used to support or refute claims about that agent's character. And yet a goal, even though it may be general and lasting, is different from a quality of character. So even when we bring in the agent model, the problem of how to distinguish between an agent's goal (motive, intention) and an agent's character remains to be solved. It seems to be a limitation of the agent model that it does not, at least immediately, offer a clear basis for drawing this distinction.

Despite this limitation, the agent model is quite useful in broad outline for showing how both character hypotheses and hypotheses about goals can be based on observations about the actions carried out by an agent. The agent model is useful for deriving plausible conclusions abductively in the form of hypotheses about not only human motives, but human character as well. One of the most recent advances in computer technology is the advent of multi-agent systems. In a multi-agent system, a group of agents needs to act together in order to carry out a task. In order to act together in a co-ordinated and useful way, its members need to communicate with each other about the task at hand. In order to do that, one agent must act on presumptions about the character of another agent. For example, in order to communicate and co-ordinate the carrying out of a task, one agent may need to act on the presumption that the other agent is honest, meaning that when it says something, it is saying something that it thinks is true. In other words, it may be important for the one agent to be able to act on the assumption that the other agent is not lying. But is such an assumption in fact justified in a given case? If there is evidence that it is not justified, the first agent needs to take that information into account in deciding what steps to take in order to reach the goal. Curiously enough then, hypotheses about character play an important part in agent technology.

2.4 Character as the Property of an Agent

The term "agent" is used in computer science to refer to an artificial kind of structure called an agent architecture (Huhns and Singh, 1998, p. 5). An agent architecture allows a man-made entity to perform tasks that it is programmed to carry out. With the expansion of the internet, software entities that performed tasks in an open information environment on behalf of a user came to be called agents. These help a human user to deal with a complex internet environment in which there is a lot of information available and certain tasks that the human user wants to perform. The widespread use of this technology has changed the way we look at agents. In the past, behaviorism or positivism was the dominant view. On such a view, all that can be observed are the external actions, or so-called "behaviors" of an agent, and so nothing at all can be said objectively about an agent's "inside". With the advent of agent technology, it became necessary to program software agents that could perform useful tasks. The new approach meant overcoming behaviorism, and exploring the "black box" inside the agent. Deductive reasoning could not capture the kind of thinking necessary for an agent to be programmed to carry out the needed practical tasks. The agent came to be seen as an entity that acted on the basis of goal-directed practical reasoning. This model has now come to be what the artificial intelligence community mainly has in mind when it uses the term "reasoning". Many current theories of agent reasoning use the term "commitments" (Huhns and Singh, 1998, p. 14) to refer to the internal beliefs and intentions of an agent. Another important notion is that of an agent having social commitments, or of one agent having commitments to another (p. 15). And especially important are problems relating to understanding coordination as a property of groups of agents performing in a shared environment (p. 15).

These developments suggest a new way of defining "agent" as a concept in ethics. Presumably the agent is that in which the supposed virtue of courage resides. But what is an agent? The development of software agents in computer science has reached the point where this question has not only been asked, but some answers to it have been proposed. Franklin and Graesser (1996) have surveyed a number of proposed definitions offered by computer scientists doing so-called agent research. Among the characteristics cited in these definitions are the abilities of an agent to perform actions autonomously (p. 22), to "perform domain oriented reasoning" (p. 22), to "perceive its environment through sensors" (p. 22), to "act on its environment" (p. 22), to "realize a set of goals and tasks" (p. 22), to act autonomously (p. 22), to perceive, affect and interpret dynamic conditions in the environment (p. 22), to "employ knowledge of the user's goals or desires" in carrying out some set of operations (p. 23), to "engage in dialogs and negotiate and coordinate transfers of information" (p. 23), to carry out "autonomous, purposeful action in the real world" (p. 24), to be "goal-oriented, collaborative, flexible, self-starting, and to have character, adaptiveness, mobility and communicative skill" (p. 24). The items on this list are multiple and varied, but the central concept of the agent has been expressed by Wooldridge and Jennings in a comprehensive summary of all an agent's characteristics. These authors distinguish between two meanings of the term "agent" in the computer science literature (Wooldridge and Jennings, 1995, pp. 116–117): a stronger and a weaker use of the term. According to the weaker use, an agent is a computer system that has the following four properties (p. 116).

1. *Autonomy*, meaning that it has control over its actions and internal states.
2. *Social Ability*, meaning that it can interact linguistically with other agents.
3. *Reactivity*, meaning that it perceives its environment and reacts to changes in it.
4. *Pro-activeness*, meaning that it can take the initiative in its goal-directed actions, so that it is not just responding to these changes in its environment.

According to the stronger use, an agent is an entity that possesses not only the above four properties, but also the following (p. 117).

5. *Mobility*, meaning that it can move around an electronic network.
6. *Veracity*, meaning that it will not knowingly communicate false information.

7. *Benevolence*, meaning that it will do what is asked, and not have conflicting goals.
8. *Rationality*, meaning that it will act in order to achieve its goals, and not prevent its goals from being achieved (in line with its beliefs about these matters).

According to Wooldridge and Jennings (1995), the weaker usage of the term "agent" is well established and is relatively uncontentious in computer science, whereas the stronger one is "potentially more contentious", and less widely accepted.

What should we say about this list? Some of the items on it are questionable, and not very clear as defining characteristics of the notion of an agent that would be useful in ethics. But still, the list suggests a certain direction that could be valuable. The weaker notion of agent ties in well with the framework of practical reasoning used in (Walton, 1986), where an agent is seen as interacting with its environment, and overcoming obstacles and dangers in realizing its goals in that environment. But some items in the stronger usage, particularly items 6 and 7, suggest qualities of character of a more long-lasting sort that may be difficult to analyze. In particular, the property of rationality makes it problematic to distinguish between the character and the bias that an agent might be thought to have.

Another aspect of the concept of an agent suggested by the list is that its characteristics naturally fall into two subclasses. The first comprises the characteristics of the reasoning agent as it interacts with its natural environment by acting on its meaning. The environment is seen as passive. This subclass comprises the reasoning used by the agent as it perceives its external circumstances, and its ability to take into account its knowledge of these circumstances as it carries out goal-directed actions (and perceives their effects on the changing external circumstances). The second group of characteristics has to do with communication with other agents. The same kind of reasoning is used, but instead of acting on passive circumstances the agent is acting on other agents, who may respond by acting in turn on the original agent. A key difference between these two kinds of cases is that in the second kind, there is the possibility of communication between the two agents. What becomes important is not only physical actions but also speech acts. A whole new dimension is introduced by considering cases of multi-agent reasoning.

Multi-agent reasoning poses a number of philosophical questions, and also suggests a number of directions in which the field of ethics can and should be extended. But even within computer science, there are fundamental problems about how to proceed in this area. According to Jennings and Wooldridge (1995, p. 364), a major problem with multi-agent systems is that "the overall system is unpredictable and nondeterministic: which agents will interact with others in which ways to achieve what cannot be determined in advance". What is needed, according to their account, is "a sophisticated means of dealing with incomplete and conflicting viewpoints", so that agents can help with decision support tasks (p. 365). What is needed is some kind of systematic framework in which it can be understood how agents communicate with each other in various ways, and what one is to conclude about such attempts at communicative action. A vehicle that is being found more and more useful for this purpose is argumentation theory. Two (or more) agents are seen as putting forward their individual views on a matter under discussion in the form of arguments. A second party is seen as reacting to the argument a first has put forward by asking critical questions, or making other kinds of appropriate moves. The idea (Grice, 1975) is that both parties are contributing to a collaborative goal-directed conversation. According to the Conversational Principle (CP) of Grice, each needs to make the moves that are appropriate at any particular stage of the dialogue to keep it moving forward towards its goal. Thus there will be rules or maxims that will govern the conduct of a polite and productive conversation. Using this kind of dialogue framework, computer scientists have begun to get a better insight into how agents can collaborate on teamwork tasks that require not only co-ordinated actions, but also communication among the agents, in which priorities and decisions can be sorted out as a basis for intelligent action.

2.5 Evaluating Witness Testimony

A witness is someone who is in a position to know about something that he directly observed, or otherwise has access to the facts. A witness makes a statement that, presumably, represents an accurate account of the facts as he saw them or as he understands them. But how can we, as users of witness testimony, have any grounds for drawing an inference that the witness's statement is true? We are warranted in drawing such an inference if the best explanation of what the witness said is that the account he gave is a true account of what really happened. Thus appeal to witness testimony can be seen as a form of argumentation. The following argumentation scheme represents its form. It is expressed as a defeasible kind of argument in which the major premise has the form of a warrant. A warrant (Toulmin, 1958) is a general rule that is subject to exceptions but can support an argument by combining with other premises. The variable *A* in what follows stands for a statement.

Appeal to Witness Testimony
Position to Know Premise: Witness *W* is in a position to know whether *A* is true or not.

Truth Telling Premise: Witness *W* is telling the truth (as *W* knows it).
Statement Premise: Witness *W* states that *A* is true (false).
Warrant: If witness *W* is in a position to know whether *A* is true or not, and *W* is telling the truth (as *W* knows it), and *W* states that *A* is true (false), then *A* is true (false).
Conclusion: Therefore (defeasibly) *A* is true (false).

The argumentation scheme for appeal to witness testimony presents a kind of tool that can be used in evaluating witness testimony as evidence in a given case. One can ask whether the three premises above are supported or not by the given facts in the case. One can also judge how strongly these premises are supported by the facts. If there is good evidence supporting each of the premises, or at least, if there is no good evidence that undermines any of the premises, the argument can be accepted as supporting the conclusion. Of course, such an argument is rarely if ever conclusive. But it could have a certain weight or probative value as evidence that could provide a rational basis for arriving at a decision, despite the lack of access to the facts. Under conditions of uncertainty and lack of knowledge, such an argument can still provide good reasons for tentatively accepting a conclusion, if one keeps an open mind. But there are hard cases and easy cases. In a hard case, there is a conflict of opinions, and arguments that provide good reasons on both sides. In hard cases, there tends to be a different "story", or account of what happened, on the two sides, and one story may directly conflict with the other.

A witness will often, for example, when testifying in court make not just a single statement, but will present an account which Hastie, Penrod and Pennington (1983, pp. 22–23) call a "story". In a plausible story, a whole set of connected statements will hang together. Pennington and Hastie (1991, p. 526) presented an analysis of what makes such an account plausible by citing three key factors: goals, physical conditions and psychological conditions. Pennington and Hastie (1993, p. 197) outlined what they called an abstract episode schema. In this schema, psychological states like motives or goals initiate actions, which result in consequences. The abstract episode schema explains how goal-directed practical reasoning can explain the sequence of events and actions in a story. For example, a person may have a goal, and we can understand her account of what she did on some occasion because we understand that she was trying to achieve this goal. But physical conditions might block a person's working towards her goal, making her angry. The anger may then function as a psychological condition that she needs to overcome. In logical terms, the account makes sense to a person to whom the story is told because both parties can grasp the sequence of practical reasoning. Both parties are familiar with goals, and with the kind of means-end reasoning used in trying to achieve them. Pennington and Hastie

(1991) applied this theory to legal argumentation, and especially to witness testimony. If a witness presents testimony that hangs together, in which the actions and goals all fit into a coherent story of the kind that makes sense to the jury, the jury will tend to find the story plausible. If the story appears bizarre or unfamiliar in relation to the expectations of the jury about the way things normally go in their experience, the latter will find the story implausible. It will tend to question it, or even to reject it as evidence. Hastie *et al.* (1983) carried out empirical studies showing that the order in which the elements of a story are presented to a jury will affect whether it evaluates testimony as plausible or implausible. Pennington and Hastie (1991, p. 522) found by studying cases of witness testimony that one story will be picked out by the jury from the competing accounts given by witnesses. The jury will then draw a conclusion to accept this particular account as the best explanation of what happened in the case.

The most important kind of evidence in both history and law is based on witness testimony. But witness testimony is a fallible form of evidence. As the many recent cases of unjust conviction, as shown by DNA evidence, have indicated, witness testimony is often wrong. Eyewitness testimony is very often wrong, because of the fallibility of human memory (Loftus, 1979). And witnesses often lie. It is often in their best interests to lie. Sometimes, too, they are biased, and the problem may be a combination of lying and distorting the facts to suit their own interests or preferences. If witness testimony is so fallible then, how can it be tested or evaluated? After all, a witness is in a special position to know. A jury has no direct access to the facts. What criteria can be used? As Pennington and Hastie showed, one test is how well the story hangs together internally. But there is also another method of evaluation. A story can be tested against other evidence, like physical evidence, for example, that is independent of the account given in witness testimony. This process of checking a story in relation to independent evidence is called "anchoring" by Wagenaar *et al.* (1993, p. 39). A story presented by a witness, according to their analysis, can be made more plausible if it is supported by what they call "safe anchors". They cite the case of a defendant in a criminal case who has an alibi. He claims that he was elsewhere at the time the crime was committed. This claim may not be very plausible without further support. But suppose that two police officers give sworn testimony that they saw him exactly where he claimed to be when he claimed to be there. The police officers' testimony then provides an anchor to the defendant's story. The anchor makes the story more plausible than it was without this supporting evidence.

The anchoring of a story, or the lack of it, is thus an important factor in evaluating any appeal to witness testimony. But just as such appeal is a defeasible form of argument, so anchoring is itself a defeasible process of argumentation. According to Wagenaar *et al.* (1993, p. 39), anchoring involves a kind of evidence based on general rules subject to exceptions. For example, as a general rule, it may be assumed that police officers are reliable witnesses, whose testimony would strongly support a claim made in court. But of course, there are cases where police officers are known to have lied in court, to have given testimony that turned out to be wrong. The anchor itself can be undermined as evidence, or even refuted by further argumentation.

When evaluating an appeal to witness testimony, direct verification, by first-hand observation of the facts, is not possible. Witness testimony, unlike scientific evidence based on observation and experiment, is not reproducible. It can be tested against the facts. But in a typical case in law or history, especially in controversial or hard cases, what the facts are, and how they should be described, may be subject to interpretation and disputation. The testing of an account presented as witness testimony is based on a different kind of argumentation. Consistency of the account is the focus of the evaluation. But consistency refers to how well the account hangs together as a story, and how well the story is anchored. Testing the consistency of an account given by a witness can be carried out by the process of asking the right critical questions. The following are five critical questions that can be so used.

CQ1: Is what the witness said internally consistent?

CQ2: Is what the witness said consistent with the known facts of the case (based on evidence other than what the witness testified to)?

CQ3: Is what the witness said consistent with what other witnesses have (independently) testified to?

CQ4: Can some kind of bias be attributed to the account given by the witness?

CQ5: How plausible is the statement *A* asserted by the witness?

If the account given by the witness is biased, finding it so detracts from the probative weight of the appeal to witness testimony as evidence.[2] The fifth critical question concerns the plausibility of the claim. If a statement made by a witness is highly implausible, that will adversely affect the plausibility of the whole account that he or she has offered. However, the third critical question can also play a role here. If two independent witnesses have made the same implausible claim, that could suggest in some cases that their observations are careful and accurate.

[2] There are many indicators of bias when questioning the account of a witness. One is a finding that the witness has something to gain by testifying.

The initial argument, in the form of an appeal to witness testimony, carries a probative weight if the requirements for supporting the premises are met. The argument then works by shifting the probative weight from the premises to the conclusion. This process, when it works, makes the conclusion appear to be plausible. But as noted above, such an argument is defeasible. It is not a conclusive form of argumentation, even though it can function as evidence under the right conditions. In such a case, the argument is judged to be plausible. But that plausibility can be removed, or undermined, by asking the right critical questions. If the critical question that has been asked is answered appropriately, the appeal to witness testimony is once again plausible. But if the critical question is not answered appropriately, the argument is defeated.

2.6 The Structure of Abductive Reasoning

Abduction is a process of hypothesis formation that is used at the discovery stage of scientific investigation. The hypothesis is formulated as an explanation of an observed event, or set of data. It is just a guess, but it can be supported or refuted by devising an experiment to test the hypothesis, or by collecting empirical evidence that is relevant to it. But abduction is very common in ordinary reasoning as well. Suppose my car won't start. There might be various explanations. It might be out of gas. There might be a short in the wiring. The spark plugs could be blocked with carbon. Each of these possible explanations is a hypothesis. Which is the right one? To answer this question, empirical evidence can be collected. I check the gas tank. There is gas in it. I check the wiring. It looks all right. I take out one spark plug. I observe that the base of the plug contains a black substance filling the spark gap. I can then draw an inductive inference that probably the rest of the plugs are in similar condition. The right hypothesis is that the spark plugs are blocked with carbon. The inference to this hypothesis is no longer just a guess. It is now based on some empirical evidence that supports it.

Abduction sounds mysterious, described in the abstract, but two examples given by Peirce go a long way towards helping to explain it. The first, quoted below, comes apparently from personal experience, and is an illustration of how abduction is used in everyday reasoning (Peirce, 1965, p. 375).

> I once landed at a seaport in a Turkish province; and, as I was walking up to the house which I was to visit, I met a man upon horseback, surrounded by four horsemen holding a canopy over his head. As the governor of the province was the only personage I could think of who would be so greatly honored, I inferred that this was he. This was an hypothesis.

The second example quoted below (p. 375) is an instance of the use of abduction in science.

Fossils are found; say, remains like those of fishes, but far in the interior of the country. To explain the phenomenon, we suppose the sea once washed over this land. This is another hypothesis.

In both cases, the inference is based on a premise citing an observation of a "curious circumstance". The pattern of reasoning is what is now commonly called inference to the best explanation. To explain the initial observation, an assumption is made in the form of a hypothesis. Note that in the fossils example, Peirce actually used the word "explain". The given observation suggests an assumption in the form of a hypothesis that explains the observation, and becomes the conclusion of the inference. The process of explanation is based, according to Peirce's description, on the use of a "general rule". In the four horsemen case, the general rule might be something like the following: only a very important person (like the governor) would be likely to have a canopy supported by four horsemen. In the fossils case, the general rule might be something like the following: anywhere remains like those of fishes are found is likely to be a place where water once was.

The term "abduction" has recently become a very common expression in computer science, especially in artificial intelligence. A comprehensive theory of abduction as a distinctive type of inference has been presented by Josephson and Josephson (1994). According to their account, it is equivalent to inference to the best explanation. Of the many examples cited by them, the following one (p. 6), in the form of a brief dialogue, helps to explain the kind of reasoning they categorize as abductive.

Joe: Why are you pulling into this filling station?

Tidmarsch: Because the gas tank is nearly empty.

Joe: What makes you think so?

Tidmarsch: Because the gas gauge indicates nearly empty. Also, I have no reason to think that the gauge is broken, and it has been a long time since I filled the tank.

It is not difficult to see how the reasoning in this case can be described as inference to the best explanation. Tidmarsch considers two alternative explanations for the indication presented by the gas gauge. One is that the tank is nearly empty. An alternative explanation is that the gauge is broken. But, as Tidmarsch says in the dialogue, there is no evident reason to think that the gauge is broken. Perhaps Tidmarsch does not remember when he last filled the tank. Or perhaps he does remember that he has not filled it for quite a while. Given this evidential situation, the best explanation is that the gas in the tank is nearly empty. The inference begins from an observed fact, namely the observation that the indicator on the gas gauge points to "empty". Other relevant data are taken into account, like Tidmarsch's remembering when he last filled the tank. Then a conclusion is drawn by inference from what has been observed. This is that the gas tank is nearly empty. Based on this conclusion, appropriate action can be taken. Tidmarsch could drive to the nearest gas station.

Peirce (1965, pp. 372–375) offered the following example to illustrate the difference between inductive, deductive and abductive reasoning. Suppose you have a bag full of beans. You draw out a handful at random, and they are all white. You can infer by inductive reasoning that all the beans in the bag are (probably) white. Suppose you reason from the premises that all the beans from the bag are white, and that this bean is from the bag, and conclude that this bean is white. This inference, according to Peirce (p. 374) is an example of deductive reasoning. Abductive reasoning is different from both deductive and inductive reasoning. Suppose you find a red bean in the vicinity of a bag of white beans. You may infer by abductive reasoning that this bean is from the bag. You don't know whether the bean is really from the bag for sure, or, indeed, where it came from. But in the absence of any plausible data to the contrary, you can assume that it is from the bag. Some might think that abductive reasoning is a special kind of inductive reasoning. Peirce (1992, p. 142) did not. He wrote, "There is no probability about it. It is a mere suggestion which we tentatively adopt". Peirce also used the terms "hypothesis" and "best explanation" in describing abductive reasoning, indicating that he regarded it as a special kind of reasoning, inherently different from induction.

Peirce (1965, p. 375) defined abduction as a kind of inference that works by the supposition of a hypothesis to explain some observed data. He described it as a process "where we find some very curious circumstance, which would be explained by the supposition that it was a case of a certain general rule, and thereupon adopt that supposition". This description is especially interesting because it contains the three terms "supposition", "general rule" and "adopt". "Supposition" appears to be another word for "assumption". If so, then abduction involves a kind of assumption-based reasoning that makes it different from deductive and inductive reasoning. You could reply that deductive and inductive inferences are also based on premises that are assumptions. And that is true. But it could be that abduction is especially assumptive in a way that relates it to presumption. Peirce often associated it with what he called "guessing". So perhaps the notion of supposition is an important characteristic of abduction as a tentative form of reasoning. The word "adopt" also suggests the tentative nature of abduction. You can adopt a hypothesis as a provisional commitment even if it is subject to retraction in the future, and even if you are not sure of it. Finally, the expression "general rule" is significant. A general rule may not hold in all cases, or even in most or countably many cases. It may only hold for normal cases, and fall outside this range of cases. At any rate, Peirce's use of the three terms suggests that abductive inference leads to a conclusion that is only a supposition, that can easily fail and have to be given up if it falls outside a range of cases of the "general rule".

Abductive reasoning has often been equated with inference to the best explanation (Harman, 1965). In the bean example, the hypothesis might work as an inference to the best explanation as follows. First there are the given data. I see the bean on the table near the bag. I know that the bag contains white beans. From these data I construct the hypothesis that the bean on the table came from the bag. Such a hypothesis would explain how the bean came to be on the table. It didn't just appear on the table. It came from somewhere. But what could explain where it came from? There is no other information, let's say. The room is bare except for the bag, the table and the one bean. Appearances suggest that the bean may have come from the bag. That would be one explanation of where the bean came from, and no other explanation is suggested by the given data. The explanation posits a hypothesis about the source of the bean.

What is the structure of abductive reasoning? Although it is much written about in current work in computer science, there is still not complete agreement on how to define it or to give a precise account of its structure. Abductive reasoning is often contrasted with deductive and inductive reasoning, and is thought to be weaker and more provisional in nature than these two more familiar (in logic) kinds. An abductive inference is said to draw a conclusion in three steps. First, it begins from a set of premises that report observed findings or facts. Second, it selects out a proposition describing the so-called best explanation of these facts. Third, it draws a conclusion that the selected proposition is true, or at least acceptable as a hypothesis. Abductive inference is defeasible, meaning that the conclusion is only a hypothesis that is subject to defeat if new facts come into a case that show that it no longer holds. Such inference is most useful when a tentative hypothesis is the best conclusion to adopt temporarily in a situation of incomplete and advancing knowledge. Abduction is often associated with the American logician and scientist C.S. Peirce, and a good initial idea of what abduction is can be gotten from examining some of Peirce's insightful remarks on it. But Peirce's remarks, while highly original, are contoversial to interpret, perhaps because he was so far ahead of anyone else in originating ideas that later came to be extremely important in logic and science. Abduction has come to be an extremely important concept for recent work in artificial intelligence. Even here, many questions remain open on how to define or analyze abduction by exact methods appropriate for logic.

The general form of the abductive inference is represented by the following schema, according to Josephson and Josephson (1994, p. 14). In what follows *H* is a hypothesis.

Form of Abductive Inference (Josephson and Josephson)

D is a collection of data.
H explains *D*.
No other hypothesis can explain *D* as well as *H* does.
Therefore *H* is probably true.

The reasoning used in the gas tank example starts from the observed data that the gas gauge indicates nearly empty. Tidmarsch formulates a first hypothesis to explain the data — namely the hypothesis that the tank is nearly empty. He then formulates a second hypothesis that the gas gauge is broken. But the second does not explain the data as well as the first hypothesis. Therefore Tidmarsch draws the conclusion that the first hypothesisis is probably true.

According to Josephson and Josephson (p. 14), the judgment of likelihood associated with an abductive inference should be taken to depend on several factors.

1. how decisively *H* surpasses the alternatives,
2. how good *H* is by itself, independently of considering the alternatives (we should be cautious about accepting a hypothesis, even if it is clearly the best one we have, if it is not sufficiently plausible in itself),
3. judgments of the reliability of the data,
4. how much confidence there is that all plausible explanations have been considered (how thorough was the search for alternative explanations).

Beyond the judgment of likelihood, Josephson and Josephson (p. 14) list two additional considerations on which willingness to accept the conclusion of an abductive inference should depend.

1. pragmatic considerations, including the costs of being wrong, and the benefits of being right,
2. how strong the need is to come to a conclusion at all, especially considering the possibility of seeking further evidence before deciding.

Josephson and Josephson's account of abduction suggests that this form of argument has a comparative aspect. Two or more competing hypotheses that explain the same data are being considered. There is a conflict of opinions about which is the best one. The question is which one explains the data better. Thus the abductive inference structure presented by Josephson and Josephson is not like a deductive or inductive argument where a conclusion is drawn only from a fixed set of premises. Instead, two potential conclusions are possible, and the one conclusion is opposed to, or at least different from the other in some respect. The conclusion to be accepted turns on which is the better explanation at some point in an investigation or collection of data that may continue to move along, so that new data may suggest new alternative explanations that may even be better than the one now accepted. The conclusion does not have to be certain, or beyond doubt. Even if it is a guess or hypothesis, if it is an intelligent guess, based on the body of information presumed to be true and accurate in the given case, it can be justified by the evidence.

2.7 Character as an Interpersonal Notion

It is easy to think of character in ethics as being a psychological notion of disposition. But in ethics, the notion of character plays a different role, more akin to the one it plays in the law of evidence. What is centrally important in ethics is making positive and negative evaluations of actions, and of persons as well in some instances. For example, if a person is said to be courageous, this strongly positive evaluation has all kinds of implications about judging that person, and her actions, from a moral point of view. The framework of evidential reasoning about character ascriptions is parallel, or comparable, in legal argumentation. If a witness is alleged to have a bad character for veracity, as shown in the example in section 2 above, the evaluation of his character could be relevant to the conclusion at issue in a trial, because the weight of the witness's testimony depends on his credibility. The same kind of reasoning is a central aspect of how we think ethically about actions outside law courts, how we judge such actions, and what conclusions we draw from them.

According to Stone (1991, p. 254), the term "character" has at least three distinct meanings in law. The first is "the actual propensities or dispositions of a human being as a psychologist would think of them". In ethical reasoning, this meaning is actually less important to ascriptions of courage, or other qualities of virtue or vice, than the remaining two meanings. The second meaning is "the opinion of a nominate person concerning that human being's propensities as a personal acquaintance would think of them". This meaning is fundamental in the notion of character in ethics, as well as in law. The base line is how one person thinks of another on the basis of personal acquaintance with that other person. It is this element of personal acquaintance that provides the data for drawing conclusions about character. The third meaning (Stone, 1991, p. 254) is that of "the anonymous opinion of the class of men with whom that human being comes into contact — the neighborhood or 'reputation' sense". This third sense is a kind of abstraction derived from the first. Reputation has to do with what the community at large takes to be the character of the given person, as based on evidence derived from the first-level acquaintance evidence.

In modern culture there is yet another level of thought about character, which relates to the perceived public persona or *ethos* (sometimes called the image) of a person who is known to the public, like a famous politician. Such a person is perceived to have a certain character, or certain qualities of character like courage, based on snippets of what the public is told about that person by the media, which may be highly selective. This public image is constantly changing, for example, when a politician is in office. And politicians have public relations experts who are in the business of manipulating this public image of character — putting a certain spin on it, as they say. Their aim may to be put a positive spin on their person's character, and to put a negative spin on the perceived character of a political opponent. Such manipulation of public opinion has become a huge industry in the twentieth century.

But the important thing is that character ascriptions need to be seen, in ethics as in law, as being based on a distinctive kind of reasoning which attributes positive or negative values in drawing conclusions about a person. These positive and negative attributions are vitally important in ethics. You might even say that they are what ethics is all about. So it is essential for us to figure out how they work, what their logic is, and what kind of evidence is needed to support or critically attack them. The same is true in law, and indeed, the kind of reasoning used in ethics and law is, in this instance, very similar. The conclusion drawn is that so-and-so is a good or bad person, in a certain ethical respect. The fundamental data on which such a conclusion is based is the reported say-so of those who have been in intimate social contact with that person over a period of time, or possibly in a crisis. The basis of such reasoning is what Stone (1991, p. 254) calls a "testimonial opinion medium". Those who know the person relate facts that support their ethical valuation of him or her as, say, courageous or cowardly. At a second level, others of us are then free to critically question the evaluation and the reasons given to support it. It is not hard to see that the framework for such evaluation is that of a dialogue or challenge-response. Certain arguments are brought forward, with their supporting reasons, and then those of us not directly involved can question and evaluate the judgments made, perhaps by comparing the conflicting conclusions drawn by different parties who have a first-level acquaintance with the subject whose personal qualities are being discussed. It all sounds a bit like it could degenerate into gossip, and there is a danger of it doing exactly that, in a bad sense. To overcome this danger, conclusions about a person's ethical character need to be based on evidence. In the sequel, more will be shown about how relevant information is used as evidence to justify or challenge hypotheses about a person's perceived character.

The question then remains: what exactly is character? The answer is that character is something that one agent perceives as being "inside" another agent. Character, so conceived, is based on a relationship between two agents. It is not just a set of stable characteristics or dispositions that one agent has, it is something constructed by one agent in order to explain, predict and evaluate the actions of another. The character isn't inside the one agent, as it is seen by some of the views examined in this chapter. It is something constructed by another agent, based on evidence that this other agent can see. This new way of defining character could be called the interpersonal concept of character. An agent is defined as a kind of structure or platform that can be used to define a somewhat artificial, but extremely useful, concept of character. An agent is an entity that engages in goal-directed reasoning. It can be seen as a programmable entity that reasons by continually cycling back and forth between its goals and its actions, as it gathers information from its environment, including information about the perceived effects of its own actions. And that is all it does, and all it is. So an agent is not a real person, with real beliefs or intentions. It is only an abstract model of how a person would think and act if that person were a practical reasoner in a situation with a given database of information and given goals. The new interpersonal way of defining character is therefore artificial. It is a mere model, useful to show how character judgments can be based on evidence drawn from a given database by a process of logical reasoning that can be duplicated and verified. The interpersonal definition provides an answer to the question, "What is character?" But like all definitions, it has a purpose. It is a philosophical definition meant to deal with ethical questions, as well as related legal and historical ones, about character judgments seen as based on some kind of logical reasoning from evidence. Thus the definition has a normative purpose. It is meant to provide a theory that tells us how such reasoning should be done.

To explain the interpersonal concept of character, two agents are needed. The one, the primary agent, carries out certain actions. The other, the secondary agent, is in a position to observe these actions. The secondary agent cannot always see the actions of the primary agent directly. The secondary agent may have access to testimony, perhaps in the form of written records describing the actions and speech of the primary agent in a particular situation. It is this testimony, or record of observed actions and speech, that provides the evidence for character judgments. The secondary agent uses it to arrive at hypotheses about the character of the primary agent based on abductive inferences. But how can the secondary agent accomplish this feat, using a kind of reasoning that can be tested and verified? The answer is that the secondary agent is himself an agent who deliberates and acts in real situations comparable to the kinds the primary agent is perceived to be acting in. Both agents have goals, in many instances similar goals involving common needs like safety. So the one agent can extrapolate from the actions and situations of the other agent. The secondary agent can conclude, "this is what she is doing now, and this is why she is doing it". What makes this possible is that there is problem-solving at two levels. The primary agent is deliberating on how to solve some problem. The secondary agent looks at the given data and grasps the problem, or at least understands how the primary agent is acting to solve some problem. The two agents might be quite different. They may even be from different periods in history. But they will share some common framework. For both are agents, and both use the same kind of practical reasoning to try to solve problems. Often, as well, both agents may have the same, or comparable kinds of problems. So there is a certain common framework of reasoning there. It is because of this that the secondary agent can draw inferences about what he takes to be the character of the primary agent.

2.8 Evidence for Character Judgments

Each of us may think we know our own character. But really we do not. What we know is that we have certain goals, or things we think important, and we have learned ways of achieving these goals. These habits and routines are observed by other persons, and these other persons try to put them into some kind of pattern. They try to make up some kind of hypothesis that will fit what they have observed into a package or pattern. The package or pattern they use is character. Somebody may say that Bob is very patient and calm in difficult and stressful situations, or that Shirley is a brave person who has often risked her own life to do life-saving work in dangerous conditions. These are things we say about other people. We do not say them about ourselves. If we did, it would seem somehow inappropriate. And when we say them about other people, still others can verify or dispute these statements based on what they have seen, or what they know about their actions.

My character is something I create by everything I do. But it is not something I construct, or put into a formula that expresses what it is. That is done by others who observe my actions. They summarize and explain the information thus found by making statements about facets of my character. My character thus is just a device constructed by others by abductive reasoning, in order to compress data into some kind of ethically useful and interesting package. But how are such abductive inferences possible? They are possible because both the drawer of the inference and the person about whose character the inference is drawn, are agents. The common agent framework is based on Kupperman's (1991) notion of normal patterns of thought and action. Let's say that the secondary agent sees the primary agent in a dangerous situation. How does he know that the situation is dangerous? The answer is that he will know what is normal and expected, and can therefore judge if a situation is unusual. If the primary agent is caught in a storm in a small boat far from shore, then we can judge that the situation poses a danger, and we can see why the person in the boat would be afraid, and with reason. So it is this commonality of context and thinking that enables one agent to appreciate the situation of another, and to draw inferences which judge how the other reacted in that situation. The secondary agent can put the situation into a perspective. He may not have all the information; but he may have enough to draw an inference about the presumed character of the primary agent. How should such an inference be drawn? What are the links in the chain of reasoning? Already, the kind of inference used has been shown to be abductive. It leads to a conclusion drawn by a process of selecting out the best explanation from the given facts. Some account is needed of why the person was trying to do what she was doing, and we need to know why doing it, in the given situation, was risky or dangerous for her. We need to be satisfied that what she was trying to do can be judged by us (the critics, or evaluators) as morally good, and that she thought it was good. We also need to know other things about her character, to have a sketch filled in roughly of what this person was like. Such an account should be plausible and consistent. It should also be balanced.

Commitments can be goals or intentions revealed by the actions of the agent. The two factors fit together to fill out the practical reasoning component. The goal fits in with the actions carried out so that we can make a rationale for the sequence of actions carried out by the agent. As Bratman (1987, p. 54) writes: "Given an intentional action we can normally work our way back to an intention which guides the action, and then to the deliberation and habits responsible for that intention". As Bratman pointed out, this way of making an inference from an action to a presumed intention involves a rationality assumption. We reason from the agent's carrying out of the action to his/her intention by assuming that his/her goal or intention guided her action deliberately. Of course, such an assumption might be false in a given case, even though the evidence in the case makes the conclusion a plausible inference to draw.

The third component is our set of assumptions about what is normal, or what should reasonably be expected to take place, in this kind of situation. The rational agent is one who is relatively consistent in trying to carry out goals she is committed to, and who foresees the normally expected consequences of her actions. But in some cases, the assumption of normality will break down. An act described as courageous will not be something that would normally be expected of anyone who would find themselves in that situation. Instead, as noted in the previous section, it stands out as something exceptional and, very often, something beyond the requirements of duty, or what would normally be expected of someone in that kind of situation. As noted above, the inference to the best explanation takes place on two levels. It involves a kind of meta-reasoning in which one person tries to enter into the thinking of another. How is such a leap of inference possible? The answer seems to be that the two parties share a common frame of reference. What is normal, familiar and expected for the one is also normal, familiar and expected for the other. When I am told the facts of a case in which a person acted courageously, I can put myself in his/her situation, by an act of transference. I can't actually go into the actual situation. But I can imagine what it was like, to some extent. How? The answer is that although the situation may not be one I have personally been in, many aspects of it are familiar. I know the expected consequences of rushing into a burning building without any sort of protection. I can easily appreciate how that sort of situation would be dangerous and threatening to me. I may even find it terrifying. Thus I can grasp how the principal agent in the case must have thought and reasoned. This mental leap is possible because we share a common grasp of the way things can normally be expected to go in familiar situations. All of us can predict the normal consequences of certain kinds of actions with some degree of plausibility.

That much holds true for individual actions, and for intentions that can be inferred from them by making assumptions about normality and rationality. But how do we get from there to attributions of character, to judgment that so-and-so is courageous or brave as a person? This is really a tough question, and Nussbaum is right to describe it as taken to be "a complex interweaving of beliefs, motivational desires, and emotional responses". Two obvious factors are (1) that such attributions of character are long-term stable traits that take other actions of the agent into account, and (2) that they delve deeply into the agent's goals and intentions, not just in the given case, but more generally. But that is not all there is to it. Yearley (1990, p. 107) shows that the notion of a human disposition is involved, and also that this notion has to be seen as one factor in a complex framework of other factors, including actions and capacities. Kupperman (1991, p. 103) states that to describe someone as generous or courageous is a complicated matter that involves more than just an account of the person's abilities. Hamblin (1987, p. 206) sketches out the parameters of the problem very well when he observes that the ingredients of Aristotelian practical wisdom fall roughly into four groups (1) a knowledge group, including perception and intuitive reason, (2) an art or skill group, including cleverness, (3) a group concerned with the weighing of ends, including deliberative excellence and judgment, and (4) moral virtue (*arete*). A whole complex of factors of these general kinds has to fit together in the right way, in a given case, to support the conclusion that the person whose actions are described can be called courageous. Kupperman (1991, p. 152) also states that someone cannot be a genuinely virtuous person unless there is an ability to weigh and balance relevant factors of various sorts.

2.9 Drawing Conclusions by Abductive Reasoning from Given Data

As cases like those studied above suggest, practical reasoning is not just an abstract calculation that can be fitted onto a given case, and used to draw or refute the conclusion that the agent in question has a quality like courage. When we do draw such conclusions, often a huge amount of data is involved, and the way it is woven together into a coherent body is extremely complex. For example, a biographer may write a book showing that the subject of the book has integrity. The biographer may relate a whole series of incidents, from stories of the protagonist as a small child to her career and experiences in later life. The whole book could be seen as a long presentation of information that has the theme of integrity woven into it. The person's actions and presumed goals are a major part of the whole picture, but not all of it. The readers have to be brought to sympathize with the protagonist, and the author must be able to deal with certain kinds of reservations that many readers will likely have. If the protagonist is seen often changing her professed views for selfish reasons and thereby causing needless harm to others, these perceptions will be negative or disconfirming evidence. They will go against the conclusion that the protagonist has integrity.

Given a mass of data that record how an agent acted in various situations, a hypothesis may suggest itself. The person may come to be seen as having integrity. But how is such a hypothesis constructed, and what kind of evidence supports it or challenges it? The answer is that the evidence comes from the mass of data describing the actions of the agent. The person who is writing the historical account can interpret those data, using the model of practical reasoning. She sees the agent as taking part in a situation that tests that agent, and she sees how the agent responds. Using these data, the historian (or it could be any reader or commentator) formulates explanations of the actions described. The historian or reader of the set of facts has to grasp how the agent in question acts as an agent. Thus the historian or reader also needs to be seen as an agent — a second-level or secondary agent. To make the process work, the second-level agent has to put herself into the practical reasoning of the first-level (primary) agent by an act of empathy. At a second level, she can then extrapolate from the data describing the actions and events at the first level, and formulate hypotheses that explain how the agent acted and why he did certain things in a certain way. Among these hypotheses are attributions of qualities of character to the agent.

According to the model suggested above, there is a given set of historical data or presumed facts that comprises the knowledge base in a case. Besides describing actions carried out by a primary agent these data may contain many other facts that suggest that the agent has various commitments. The secondary agent can use practical reasoning to set up hypotheses that explain how the primary agent acted, and what his goals (presumably) were. Among these hypotheses will be statements about the qualities of character that may supposedly be attributed to the primary agent. But as indicated above, these are guesses or suppositions, typically open to discussion and critical questioning. In many cases, there can be several competing explanations of the given data and the problem is often to select the most plausible one. There can be many arguments for and against the competing hypotheses. To evaluate the hypotheses against each other, critical discussion seems to be the best method. This contains abductive argumentation, and the premises of the competing arguments come from the set of presumed facts in the case. The evident fact that the argumentation in such cases can often be highly controversial is often taken as evidence for noncognitivism. But it may be that the leap to noncognitivism is hasty. The conclusion that should be drawn is that there are easy cases and hard ones, and the hard cases are going to be controversial. In some cases, the data themselves may even be contradictory.

Judging courage as a quality of character fairly often requires dealing with a mass of apparently contradictory data. For example, Barton (1947, p. 51) remarked on what appeared to be a contradiction in Lincoln's character.

> Lincoln had a remarkable combination of caution and courage. His caution was nothing less than abnormal. His periods of indecision were marked by what seemed an almost hopeless inability to meet the situation. His hesitation when he was about to marry, so manifested in his relations with May Owens, and again with Mary Todd, are not the only instances of his great caution. He displayed that caution in the earlier periods of his anti-slavery convictions. Again and again it disappointed and even disgusted outspoken abolitionists that Abraham Lincoln did not seem to possess the courage of their convictions. On the other hand Lincoln had abundant courage both as to his own person and acts as to public policies and military movements.

In discussing Lincoln's courage as a quality of his character, Barton looked over a mass of historical data on many aspects of Lincoln's life, including his personal actions, his political actions with respect to public policies, and his actions as a leader in war. Many of his actions in politics and war could be called bold. He often showed a kind of selflessness and disregard for his personal safety. But on the other hand, as Barton indicates, many of his actions show an unusual caution, and even what could be considered indecisiveness. From these data about Lincoln's life, it appears that two contradictory hypotheses can be drawn. He was unusually cautious and slow to act in the face of an important decision. And yet, many of his actions suggest that he was courageous. How can these two conclusions be reconciled? For it would seem that courage is opposed to a quality of character that could be called caution or even indecisiveness. But is it? To resolve this question, it is necessary to analyze what courage is — how it should be defined as a virtue. Caution could suggest a kind of carefulness and thoughtful deliberation that would not be opposed to courage, but could actually be taken to support it. It is also necessary to look at the mass of biographical data on Lincoln's life. It could be that although he was cautious, he did act in a thoughtful but wise way when the time was right. Or maybe, he sometimes acted this way, and sometimes didn't. This kind of apparent contradiction is just the kind of problem a thoughtful biography should probe into. The data are the mass of biographical information concerning different incidents. Hypotheses are drawn from the data. The factual evidence is then considered. Does it support the one hypothesis, or does it tend to weigh more heavily in favor of the opposed ones? The biographer can look at the evidence on both sides, and it is up to the reader to decide what conclusion to infer.

The approach needed here is to look at each case individually, and recognize that an abductive evaluation of the hypotheses in each case on its merits is the best approach. Conclusions about character are drawn on the basis of practical reasoning, but the logical inferences used to draw such conclusions are abductive. The secondary agent constructs a hypothesis, or set of hypotheses, about the supposed commitments of the primary agent. Of course, it is hard for one person to tell, or even try to guess, what the commitments of another person really are or were. Such a judgment is perhaps even more difficult when the events written about are in the past, and the data available are therefore limited. It is necessary to attribute values and ethical goals to another person. The basic reason is that courage comes from an inner commitment that is a habit of the person which stems from personal values. But it is closely tied to altruism, to valuing one's community as a whole. Kupperman (1991, p. 152) has emphasized that aspects of a morally good character include concern and commitments. An act is not something that can be judged by some kind of transparent process of calculation in which the goals and underlying values of the agent are clearly or explicitly expressed and acted on. Worthy qualities of character come from a commitment to others, from values that are most clearly expressed naturally and without thinking, and that were probably learned when the person was very young.

As noted above, in any case where a biographical or historical claim is made that a person has a good character, there will be some sort of "story" or account of some incident in his life that is taken to prove or support the claim. The story is usually a connected account of some incident describing how this person triumphed over adversity in difficult or dangerous circumstances. It is presented as evidence supporting the claim that this person has worthy character qualities. It seems, on the surface, that the historical facts, empirically verified or falsified, function as the evidence that supports the conclusion about the person's character. But here the problem of panegyric discourse surfaces again. Many of these stories are based on an ideological strategy of "puffing up" the hero to support some cause or advocate some interest. During a war, wonderful stories of the exploits of fighter pilots are portrayed in heroic rhetoric to raise morale, encourage recruitment and sell war bonds. Even in peacetime, every advocacy group has to have its heroes and role models. But the supposedly worthy character and actions of the hero, as portrayed in this kind of rhetoric, are open to doubts and suspicions. Too often such accounts are highly selective and biased, overlooking inconvenient details that might be problematic.

Consider a biographical and historical database from which judgments of character are being derived. Some abductive conclusions from the given facts might be subject to little dispute, and quite strongly supported by the evidence. Any biography could be used to show how a body of data suggests apparent contradictions in a person's character. But the character of Abraham Lincoln is especially interesting in this regard. Barton (1947, p. 49) wrote "some aspects of the character of Lincoln lie revealed upon its surface." Among the clearly indicated aspects of Lincoln's character that Barton cites (p. 49) are his "transparent sincerity, his rugged honesty, his exalted sense of honor (and) his kindness of heart." But Barton found that in other ways, Lincoln's personal qualities of character seemed inconsistent. He wrote (p. 50), "few men have been so consistently inconsistent as Abraham Lincoln." Lincoln showed humility by often acknowledging his limitations, "sometimes with sorrow" (p. 50). On the other hand, he often showed that he was conscious of his own power and strength. He was also very ambitious. Sometimes he would defer to others, and be pliable and tolerant, while at other times he would be stubborn and act with finality. He also showed extreme caution in many instances, while in other instances there is no question that he showed courage. He was often visibly unmethodical and disorderly, yet crisp and clear in his thinking and judgments (p. 55). These apparent contradictions can perhaps be explained by what Barton calls Lincoln's "practical sagacity" (p. 55). But they stand as puzzles for the biographer of Lincoln. The body of biographical data affords evidence that can support opposed hypotheses in a character judgment. Resolving the apparent contradiction poses a problem that can only be dealt with by probing into the data, and studying what inferences can be drawn from the known facts. It is this sort of contradiction that is especially interesting to a biographer, it would seem, because it is a test of what inferences can be drawn from the facts by comparing various explanations. In the case of

Lincoln, a study of these apparent contradictions can reveal a subtlety and cleverness in judgment underlying the character of a man who was, in some ways, simple and homely. Lincoln was loved and respected because he constantly showed a kind of simple honesty. He was in some ways unpolished, and did not have what was thought of at the time as the manners of a gentleman. But his ability to hold a group of people together, and get results by navigating through a sea of political interests and strong personalities, is revealing. These abilities, as well as many other personal incidents in his life, show that he did have highly sophisticated social skills.

In legal argumentation in a trial, as shown in chapter 1, character is often an issue. Someone who is supposed to know the person whose character is in question may testify by offering character evidence. For example, someone may testify about the honesty of another person, or may testify that the second person does not have a character for truthfulness. Here, as in the case of a biography or a historical study, the evidence is based on witness testimony. In court, it is assumed that a witness is telling the truth and giving a factual account, but how can that assumption be tested? What kind of evidence is appropriate to support or refute such assumptions? As noted in this chapter, section 7, the testimony of a witness often takes the form of a "story" or connected account of something. The plausibility of the story can be tested through the process of examining the witness in court. Weak points can be questioned. Apparent contradictions can be pointed out and possibly resolved. The story can be tested against the accounts of other witnesses, and against other evidence, like DNA evidence. What we find is that there is a set of presumed facts or data. But the account that is taken to represent the facts is based on witness testimony and other forms of argumentation that are partly conjectural and not conclusive. We presume that the witness is in a position to know. But, as finders of fact, we are not ourselves in a position to know. Still, we can test the account given by the witness by asking the right questions. One agent cannot see directly into the mind of another. But one agent can take the account or testimony of another and judge how plausible it is by probing into it. An account is plausible if it fits together in a natural way that represents a sequence of events and actions normal and familiar to an agent. If it contains an inconsistency, then the account is not plausible unless the inconsistency can be removed or at least explained — perhaps by abductive reasoning.

Agents carry out practical tasks. In this, they need to exercise prudent judgment. To do this they need to reason carefully, in situations of incomplete knowledge. This means using abductive reasoning. They also need to collect information, and to engage in dialogues with other agents who might provide such information. And they need to be non-dogmatic. They need to be ready to revise a hypothesis or retract a previous conclusion should new information come in that alters the facts of a case. But in order to do all these tasks well, agents need to be even more clever. They need to judge the character qualities of other agents that they will interact with and rely on for collective tasks. They have to formulate special kinds of hypotheses about the presumed character qualities of other agents, even though the evidence for and against such judgments can only be inferred indirectly. It is a matter of one agent having to use abductive reasoning in order to judge the abductive reasoning presumably carried out by another, observed to have acted in particular ways in a given case. In other words, as evaluators of cases, we need to examine given cases at a higher or meta level. How is it possible to evaluate the kinds of reasoning involved, using some kind of evidence that leaves reproducible or verifiable tracks?

The answer turns on the definition of character as a kind of stamp that leaves a lasting impression on a case. The evidence of the character of an agent is to be found in the actions and commitments of the agent, as expressed not only in his or her reasoning in the case, but in the context of dialogue as well. As an agent, you can't look directly into another agent's mind to see character qualities there. You have to infer these indirectly. Even so, there can be plenty of good evidence that is relevant to a character judgment. This evidence is fallible, and depends on inference to the best explanation of the known or presumed facts of a case. These presumed facts can turn out to be wrong. Abduction is a kind of guessing that can turn out to be wrong. Correct perceptions of the fallibility of character judgments have caused generations of thinkers to discard them as subjective. But we make character judgments anyway, in politics, law, and everyday personal and business transactions. We need to. We can only carry out organized tasks based on effective teamwork by practical reasoning based on prudent judgments of this sort. But only if we learn the rational structure of the reasoning used in them can we overcome leaping to wrong conclusions based on incorrectly evaluated evidence and poor judgmental skills.

According to the dialectical model of abductive argument, a conclusion about a quality of character of a person is first of all based on a presumed set of facts, called a case in traditional casuistry. The first potential error is in getting the facts wrong. Also, the facts can change as new information is added to a given case. An abductive argument to a conclusion expressing a hypothesis about an agent's character thus needs to be seen as bounded, or relative to the circumscribed facts of a case. It is based on what is called bounded rationality. The next point to be considered is that any abductive argument is an inference to the best explanation — meaning "best for the moment", relative to what is known presently about the facts of a case. Third, evidence for character judgment should always be seen as weighed on a balance of considerations in the given case. Was Napoleon a scoundrel or a hero? Was he courageous or simply an egotistical despot who didn't mind taking tremendous risks and wasting many lives for his own personal glory? Apparently quite plausible historical arguments can be made for both conclusions. Historical explanation and argumentation can only draw on what are presumed to be the facts. Much of the evidence is in the form of witness testimony of one kind or another describing what Napoleon did and said in certain situations as we know them from the accounts of historians. But still, there is historical evidence there. We rightly call it evidence, even though much of it is questionable, and subject to surmise and inference.

Abduction starts with a set of given facts, and then moves to an explanation of them. In some cases, the database is quite small. In other cases, it is quite large. In some cases, one explanation stands out as obvious, and there may not be any other real contenders. Also, the base of information could be quite large, even complete, or close to complete. In such cases, an abductive inference could be quite strong. In others, it could be small and incomplete, and the number of plausible hypotheses could be quite large. An abductive inference could then be quite weak. Judging character can depend on a large or a small body of evidence. If you have been married to someone for thirty years, you have a large body of evidence on how your spouse behaves in different kinds of situations. But in many cases, we make judgments about another person's character based on very limited evidence. We may have just met a person, and know very little about him. But if we see him act in a certain way, we may immediately draw conclusions about his character. In politics, we may never have met a person, but we may have fairly firm ideas about what we think of his character, based on media reports, and how he looks on television. But this evidence may be very selective. Another type of case concerns historical judgments. We may have fairly firm notions about the character of a historical person. But while writings about this person may be considerable, they may be based mainly on a few primary sources. Moreover, many of the writings may reflect the interests and prejudices of the writers. What is claimed in some of these writings may even sharply contradict what is claimed in others. In such cases, the firm base of primary evidence may be fairly small.

It is no fault of character judgment by abductive reasoning that it is sometimes faced with the problem of puzzling contradictions. Of course, noncognivists might cite this fact as evidence that such judgments are merely subjective. Such skeptics might say that there can too often be an opposed hypothesis to an abductive character judgment. They might conclude that abductive judgment is a subjective process that goes on and on, resulting in different opinions, but never leading to conclusive proof of a claim. The problem with this objection is that it is based on a kind of positivistic view that sets its sights for successful justification too high. It sees justification as successful only if it offers a deductive proof that establishes a conclusion beyond all doubt. In the remaining chapters, a method of judging character will be built up that progressively rebuts this objection by showing that contradictions in a database are not necessarily bad. A contradiction should not be taken as a sign to give up, as it is in deductive logic, but rather as something to be explored and evaluated, thus often producing evidence that can support or refute an abductive hypothesis about an agent's character.

2.10 Differentiating Character, Motive and Bias

Given the analysis of character presented in this chapter, the problems now to be addressed are how to differentiate between character and motive, on the one hand, and character and bias, on the other. One level of differentiation is that of definitions. Aristotle's definition of excellence of character as a settled state concerned with choice, situated in a mean relative to us, is a good place to begin. Character, so defined, is a matter of the practical reasoning of an agent who acts on his goals but balances many complexities of a real situation based on good judgment. Practical reasoning is a goal-directed kind of reasoning that concludes in a decision for prudent action, based on the circumstances of a case known to the agent. An agent's goal represents his motive for acting. An agent can be biased, or he can look at all the evidence of a case in an open and balanced way that fairly examines the argument on both sides of a dispute. Bias has to do with argumentation in which there are two sides, and with whether an agent is open to the two sides or not.[3] Character is a long-term ethical tendency to act in certain ways that falls into a certain pattern over a lifetime, and is a matter of habit and disposition. A motive is a goal or intention that is the basis, in practical reasoning, for an agent's action. Theoretically, these three concepts are distinct, even though all of them relate to an agent's practical reasoning.

How can one tell, in a specific case, whether something is character, motive or bias? In a trial, for example, how can one tell whether an attack on a witness is an attack on his character, rather than an argument that he is biased or that he acted out of some motive, like motive for gain? What one has to examine is both the target of the attack and the evidence used to support it. To allege motive is to argue that an agent's action can be explained by showing it to be based on some presumed goal that he was acting in accord with at the time he carried out the action. The focus is on a specific action, and on the practical reasoning or means-end reasoning that presumably led the agent to carry out this specific act. To make this kind of argument is to create a conjectural explanation of the agent's mental state at the time he

[3]Hence the importance of seeing legal argumentation as a dialogue process. Recent work in artificial intelligence that takes the dialogue approach to the analysis of legal argumentation includes that of Prakken and Sartor (1996), Prakken (1997), Feteris (1999), and Lodder (1999).

carried out the action. The reasoning goes abductively from the presumed facts describing the action, backwards to a conclusion about the mental state of the agent, by a process of practical reasoning. The kind of reasoning used in a character judgment is very similar. It also goes backwards from the given factual data to a best explanation of the data in the form of a hypothesis about the agent's mental state. But character is a stable mental state that has to do with ethical qualities and judgment skills over the whole lifetime of a person. Although character is stable, it can evolve and change. It can adapt to different circumstances in different ways. But it is not about a single action.

Differentiating between bias and character is a different problem. Bias can relate to character, because being closed-minded or dogmatic and rigid in one's judgments can be a quality of character. But evidence of bias and evidence of character are collected and assessed in different ways. Bias is primarily a property of argumentation in a context of dialogue. Bias is a problem if the dialogue is supposed to be two-sided, like a critical discussion, but the argumentation is one-sided. Thus bias is judged by looking at a person's argumentation in a context of dialogue. Does it show evidence of fairly examining the arguments on both sides of the issue? Does it give weight and proper consideration to an argument that is in opposition to the arguer's viewpoint or interests? These are the questions relevant to judging bias. Evidence for character assessment is different both in how it is used, and in the conclusion to be drawn from it. Character evidence aims at the agent or person as an entity that is stable, or shows a pattern of responses, over many incidents, decisions and actions. It is put forward as an interpersonal judgment in which two agents are involved. In the legal case studied in section 2 above, the witness presenting character evidence could testify to the other person's character because he knew that other person well. Character evidence needs to be evaluated on a basis of the one party's being in a position to know about the other. In a legal examination, laying a foundation for character evidence is done by establishing prior facts. As indicated in section 2, four prior questions need to be asked. How long has the one person known the other? How often has the one person been in close proximity with the other? How closely have the two persons interacted in intimate social environments? How often has a specific character quality, like honesty or courage, been tested out in the actions the one person has seen the other perform? These questions set out the requirements for character evidence, and show how character judgments should be tested, and supported or refuted by evidence.

Evidence for bias is quite different in this regard. How well the one person knows the other is not especially important here. What is important is how the person who is alleged to be biased performs in the kind of argumentation that is supposed to be appropriate for two-sided dialogue. But of course, there can be overlap. In the case of the alleged racial bias of detective Mark Fuhrman in the Simpson criminal trial, the evidence of bias is also evidence of Fuhrman's character. Persistent racial bias showing unfairness in treatment of others is evidence of bad character. Hence the subtlety of legal argumentation when it comes to the problem of admitting evidence or judging it to be irrelevant in a trial. Evidence of bias, in a specific case, can also be evidence of character. Thus a jury could draw all kinds of implications about a person's character from evidence that he is biased. The same facts could partly be used to prove the one or the other.

The evidence required to support a character judgment in legal argumentation has its special characteristics. Typically there is an interpersonal judgment involving two parties, the person making the character judgment and the person whose character is at issue. Let's call the former the witness and the latter the subject. The first requirement is that the witness be in a position to know about the character of the subject. To be in such a position, the witness must have known the subject under conditions in which he could have observed how he acted in different situations. The length of time the two parties knew each other can therefore be an important factor. So can the kinds of situations the witness saw the subject acting in. In a trial, a lawyer who is interviewing a witness to get character evidence will use a technique of argumentation called "laying a foundation". Several prior questions will be asked before the main question, in order to make the answer to the main question more persuasive. Observing how this technique works in cases of character evidence brings out some of these characteristics.

Moody and Coacher (1998, p. 165) have presented a useful example of how the technique of laying a foundation can be employed in examining a witness who is supposed to provide character evidence. In the example, the witness's character for truthfulness (veracity) is cast into doubt.

Q: Mr. Jones, how long have you known the witness, Mr. Henderson?

A: I have known Mr. Henderson for four years.

Q: How do you know him?

A: He is my next door neighbor.

Q: How often do you see him?

A: I see him almost every day.

Q: Under what circumstances?

A: Well, for the last year, we have worked in the same office in the post office and I deal with him every day there. In addition we see each other as we do yard work or things like that. We have seen each other socially on several occasions and our sons are members of the same scout troop.

Q: In his dealings with you does he ever have an opportunity to make representations of fact to you concerning work or other matters?

A: Yes, he does.

Q: Based upon your knowledge of Mr. Henderson do you have an opinion as to his character for honesty and truthfulness?

A: Yes, I do.

Q: What is that opinion?

A: My opinion is that he is not truthful.

The strategy of the questioner is to attack Mr. Henderson's character for truthfulness in order to raise doubts about his credibility as witness. As shown in this chapter, section 7, appeal to witness testimony is a form of argument that depends on a premise that the witness is telling the truth. If this premise can be cast into doubt, the credibility of the witness will also be cast into doubt. If the credibility of the witness is impugned, the appeal to testimony will be weakened as an argument, or even put in question as evidence. Suppose that Mr. Henderson's character for honesty is attacked, as in the sequence of dialogue above. What impact will it have on a jury? The jury will have good reason to draw the conclusion that he may not be telling the truth in his testimony in this particular case.

How does the questioner lay a foundation for the allegation made via the opinion put forward by the witness? It is done by getting the witness to answer several preliminary questions that establish several facts.

1. The witness has known the subject for a significant length of time.
2. The subject is in close proximity with the witness every day.
3. He interacts with the witness in intimate social environments, like work.
4. The subject has often made factual statements to the witness.

These four factors, once established, lay the foundation for the final question put to the witness. What is his character for honesty? When the answer comes, it is convincing because the prior assertions by the witness have provided evidence of the sort required to back up the ultimate statement that the subject is a dishonest person.

These observations about how character judgments are typically supported by evidence in legal argumentation offer some clues on how to go about differentiating between character, on the one hand, and motive and bias on the other. In character argumentation, there is a special dialogical interpersonal relationship between the person providing the evidence and the person whose character is being evaluated. The former needs to be in a position to know about the character of the latter. The four factors listed above specify the requirement of being in a position to know. But couldn't these factors also be applicable in making judgments about a person's bias or motive? It seems that in many cases they could be relevant considerations. Hence the problem of differentiating character from these closely related aspects of legal and ethical argumentation has not been solved. To solve it, a deeper philosophical analysis of the concept of character is required.

In this chapter the analysis of character, along with the tangential remarks about motive and bias, give a philosophical basis for making a distinction between what one is aiming at in presenting evidence to prove a claim about character, rather than about motive or bias. Character is hard to define, and hard to separate from other notions vitally important in legal argumentation and evidence. But it is not impossible, in principle, to define it, or to separate it off from these allied notions. The same facts can sometimes be used to support or refute a claim about character and a claim about motive or bias. And the same kind of process of abductive reasoning is used to lead from the evidential facts to the conclusion. The goal, however, — the conclusion that the reasoning is aimed at — is different. Moreover, the evidence itself is of a different kind, even if it is sometimes overlapping. Character evidence is based on a special kind of interpersonal relationship between agents.

Chapter 3

INTEGRITY AND HYPOCRISY

Not all virtues or ethical qualities of character are judged in the same way. A virtue that appears to be different from others like courage, generosity, honesty, or patience, is the ethical quality of integrity. When a primary agent judges that a secondary agent has, or does not have integrity, the primary agent concludes that the secondary agent has shown that she has certain ethical values. He concludes that she shows a pattern of sticking to these values even at the cost of some sacrifice of her own narrower self-interests. Integrity is quite a broad quality of character, as contrasted, for example, with courage, that typically tends to involve a more narrow kind of judgment. Integrity comprises many other qualities of character, because it represents a kind of wholeness in which a character hangs together as a unity. A person who has integrity is a reliable person who has a certain kind of consistency, so that he or she can be depended on to do what is expected of an ethical person with principles and standards. On the other hand, a person who is attacked because his conduct is not consistent with his professed principles is said to be a hypocrite. Hypocrisy is the opposite of integrity. If someone's integrity is questioned, that is a telling form of criticism that undermines the person's whole reputation for good character. If someone is said to have integrity, that is a high form of ethical praise, suggesting that he is not only of good character ethically, but is also a thoughtful kind of person who has depth of character. To allege that someone showed evidence of hypocrisy is a character attack.

Integrity and hypocrisy can be defined as qualities of character, but there are many open questions about the sort of evidence that should be used to support or refute a claim that a person either has or lacks integrity. This chapter begins by defining integrity as a quality of a person's character, and then raises a number of questions about how one can judge whether a person has this quality or not. Integrity is judged by the relationship between an agent's actions and professed ethical commitments. This chapter will also examine a case of alleged hypocrisy. The basis for arguing that a person is a hypocrite is that there is an inconsistency between his actions and his professed ethical commitments. Judgments of integrity and hypocrisy raise many of the same problems as judgments of courage and cowardice. Both kinds of judgments require a framework in which one agent judges the character of another agent. The two kinds of judgments use similar tools of reasoning. What makes judgments of integrity and hypocrisy different is that they are based not only on straightforward abductive inferences from action to commitment, but also on a juxtaposition of an agent's observed or reported actions with his or her supposed commitment to some ethical value or goal. What is under examination is consistency or inconsistency between words and deeds.

3.1 The Three Central Characteristics of Integrity

Integrity is one of the most important qualities of character. As a quality, it has three centrally defining characteristics. First, it is a property of persons, as shown in the last chapter. More particularly, it is a property of a person's character. Second, it is based on the person's having an ethical position. Third, it requires the person's sticking to that ethical position with some degree of consistency, even in cases where it would be expedient to deviate from it. Halfon (1989, p. 13) asks who would qualify as a person of moral integrity, and replies by proposing Socrates, Mahatma Gandhi and Martin Luther King. Asking what these persons had in common, Halfon (p. 14) answers, "One trait they share is that each made a commitment to pursue some objective and maintained that commitment steadfastly". It would appear, then, that Halfon is in agreement with the three-part analysis proposed above. To develop this analysis further, the three components — person, commitment and consistency (in the sense of "steadfast" ness) — need to be clarified, and fitted into some method or structure that can be used to evaluate cases where a person is said to have integrity (or not).

One problem with evaluating integrity in specific cases is that this consistency is not rigid. It needs to have a certain flexibility, in order to deal with problematic cases in ethics — like those where there are conflicts of principles and exceptions to rules. To have integrity, a person must be "steadfast" in carrying out commitments. But too unbending a steadfastness might be more the sign of a fanatic or zealot than of a person with moral integrity. Integrity is often associated with honesty, but as McFall (1992, p. 80) notes, "the apparent centrality of honesty may reflect a general but defeasible commitment to what is taken to be a sound moral principle, allowing for cases of deception where this is morally condoned or required . . .”. McFall cites the following case to show that integrity can, in some cases, be consistent with deception, if not with outright lying: “If you are living in Germany in World War II and a Jew is hiding in your basement, no one except Kant would claim that you suffer a loss of moral integrity if you tell the Nazi at the door that you are the only one home”. The conclusion suggested by such cases is that the kind of consistency required to define integrity is not rigid. It involves implementing general rules or principles, like the rule to be honest or tell the truth, that are subject to exceptions in particular cases. They are defeasible, meaning that they are subject to defeat in particular cases, even though they hold generally. The problem is how to define consistency in the appropriate sense, referring to a kind of steadfast sticking to a general ethical principle or position that is nevertheless somewhat flexible in the light of circumstances.

Another problem is that the commitment to which the person must be steadfast has to be one we accept as morally justified, and even laudable. Stalin or Hitler stuck to their commitments right to the end, but that does not mean we are entitled to say they had moral integrity. They did display a sort of consistency by sticking to their goals, and pursuing them relentlessly even under dangerous adverse conditions. And that could amount to a sort of “integrity”. But we stop short of saying that either of these men was a person of moral integrity, in the sense sought after here. The reason, presumably, is that they had commitments that we do not see as representing morally good values of the kind we want to advocate. Halfon (1989, pp. 134–136) raised the question of whether a dedicated Nazi might be said to have integrity. The answer is that he could only be so judged by a person who was also a Nazi, or who at least thought that Nazism was a morally acceptable position. Most of us think that Nazism is not an ethically acceptable position, and that it ought to be strongly condemned. Judging the question on this basis, a dedicated Nazi is not, and could not be, a person of integrity. In contrast, Claus von Stauffenberg was a person of the highest integrity even though, as a German officer, he had taken an oath to follow Hitler. Instead, he tried persistently, even though unsuccessfully, to kill Hitler. Such evidence could be taken to show a certain lack of consistency. Nevertheless the right judgment is that von Stauffenberg was a man of integrity while Hitler was not. Hitler showed a rigorous consistency in sticking to his goals against all kinds of opposition and adversity, but it would be quite wrong to say that he was a person of integrity.

Socrates, Gandhi and King, in contrast, were all, in Halfon’s terms, “committed to what they believed were admirable goals in the face of adversity” (Halfon, 1989, p. 14). Not only that, we — the evaluators of whether these men had integrity or not — agree that their goals were admirable. Socrates was committed to philosophical dialogue giving birth to new insightful ideas. Gandhi was committed to nonviolent resistance to injustices in India. King was committed to nonviolent action against bigotry and segregation. These represent moral positions that all of us can presumably accept as morally worthy. Not that there can't be controversy about these commitments, or about how each man lived up to them. But generally speaking, all three goals are arguably worthy as moral commitments.

Integrity refers to a certain kind of wholeness that makes a person's character hang together as an ethical unity. The term "integrity" is derived from the Latin word *integritas*, meaning "as a whole". Wholeness requires there to be a certain connectedness, making the parts of a person's character hang together as an ethical unity. But what is this whole, and what are its parts? That is the problem of defining integrity as a quality of a person's character. The answer given here is that the unity is the person's whole ethical position — the person's set of commitments on ethical matters that she judges to be important in the conduct of her life. Integrity has to do with how that unity is adhered to and followed out.

3.2 Judging a Person's Integrity

The problem posed here is to judge a person's integrity on the basis of some relevant evidence. To do this properly, several assumptions need to be made. When judging the integrity of a particular person, it is assumed that you have some information about two things. It is assumed, first, that you have some information about the person's professed or presumed moral principles; and, second, information about their actions that has ethical implications in relation to the principles cited in the first assumption.

In a typical case, information about the person's actions comes from some account of his life, or what he did in a certain instance. This may take the form of a biography, which could be quite long, or an account of some incident that the person allegedly participated in. But where does the other sort of information, that about the person's professed or presumed moral principles, come from? It could come from many sources. It could come from a speech that the person made, or some other discourse in which he professed certain moral values. Or it could just come from ethical presumptions that we normally make about people when we engage in everyday personal transactions with them. For example, if there is no evidence to the contrary, we assume that a person is polite, honest, reasonably fair, and so forth. These are just the normal moral expectations we have of people we deal with. We hold them to certain standards, and if they fall below these standards in a given case, we judge their conduct accordingly, and we may also be more guarded in dealing with them in future. We assume that people have certain moral standards of personal conduct. If evidence from their actions indicates otherwise, that finding is of interest in indicating how one should treat that person in personal dealings with him or her. It is from this sort of information that evidence about a person's ethical position comes. Of course, in some instances, we can interpret this evidence quite wrongly, or draw the wrong conclusions from it.

Suppose that a woman tells her son that smoking is bad for one's health, and that he should not smoke. It would be appropriate to judge, from this lecture, that the mother has a commitment to the proposition that smoking is a bad practice. However, suppose her son points out that she herself smokes. What should we conclude from this statement? The son may conclude that his mother does not practice what she preaches — in other words, that his mother's commitments are inconsistent. He may further conclude that her argument about smoking is worthless, and that he can disregard it. This kind of case raises a lot of questions about the conclusions that can be draw from a person's commitments for an account of his or her actions.

One thing to note about this case is that it may be too hasty to infer that because the mother smokes, and even admits it, therefore she is committed to smoking as a policy. When confronted by her son's criticism, she may reply that she has tried to quit smoking, but that smoking is addictive, and she has not been successful so far. She may even add that because smoking is addictive, and because it is so hard to stop once it becomes a habit, that is another good reason why the son should not take up smoking. What does such a reply tell us? It tells us that we need to be very careful about drawing conclusions about a person's committments, on the basis of what has been observed about her actions. Actions often speak louder than words, but not always. There may be qualifications and exceptions about what seems to be implied by an action in a given case.

In this case, if the son argues that his mother is a hypocrite who says one thing and does another, the basis of his argument — namely that her actions appear to be inconsistent with her words — may be quite accurate. Yet the son would commit a fallacy if he rushes to the hasty conclusion that his mother's whole argument about smoking is worthless. The mother may have presented good evidence to show that smoking is unhealthy. Casting her argument aside as worthless would be a mistake. To some extent, the son has a good argument. But if he takes it too far, it becomes a bad one. Unfortunately, it is very easy to take this kind of argument too far, and draw the wrong conclusion from it.

The general lesson is that a person's actions do generally express her commitments, or may be presumed to do so in the absence of evidence to the contrary, but what is generally true may be false in a given case. A person's actions may appear to express her commitments to a certain policy or proposition. That may be a reasonable presumption, from what we know.

But once the person has explained her position more fully, it may become clear that she is not really committed to that policy or proposition at all. To assume that she has to be committed to it could be a kind of prejudice. When a primary agent judges that a secondary agent has or lacks integrity, words can be as important as deeds. The primary agent may observe the actions of the secondary agent, and try to explain them, drawing abductive inferences from this data. But if the primary agent herself offers explanations, and tries to express her commitments verbally, this speech data cannot be ignored. Often an apparent inconsistency can be "explained away" once the primary agent has had a chance to make her position clear.

3.3 Commitment and Integrity

Some would define integrity as sticking to principles believed to be morally right. Such an account would define it in terms of beliefs. But beliefs are psychological entities. To judge what a person actually believes or does not believe, in a given case, is a question of psychology. Psychology is an important subject, highly relevant to the study of integrity, but having to judge a person's integrity by determining what his or her beliefs actually are makes the subject more difficult than it needs to be. To make ethical judgments about a person's character and integrity, this may not be necessary. It may be enough to get evidence about the principles or ethical propositions that the person professes to believe, and to evaluate these in relation to what he actually does, or has done. What is important is not what the person actually believes, but what he advocates as his ethical position. What is important is the principles he argues that everyone, including himself, should follow. In short, a distinction should be made between acceptance and belief. Judging integrity in line with what a person accepts, or may be taken to accept on the basis of what is known about what he has said and done, is the approach taken here.

According to this, an agent's actions and words in a given case provide a body of evidence that is a basis for another agent's judging what that primary agent's commitments are. The primary agent's commitments are the propositions he may be presumed to have accepted on the basis of this evidence. An agent's commitments are inferred from his actions. But actions include speech acts. For example, suppose that a particular person, Bill, makes a promise to pay you some money by a certain date. Then Bill has made a commitment to the proposition that he will pay you that amount of money by that date. How do we know he has made such a commitment? What is the evidence for it? It is that Bill has gone through a ritualized performance called making a promise. This speech act typically includes the uttering of certain words like "I promise to pay you this money by such-and-such date".

Once Bill has made this kind of statement, in the right circumstances, he has made a commitment.

There is a difference between commitment to a proposition and commitment to an action. If you go on record as claiming that a particular proposition is true, then it may be truly said that you are committed to this proposition. Active commitment to a proposition of this kind carries with it a burden of proof. If challenged to prove that the proposition is true, you are obliged to either give some evidence to support it, or retract your commitment to it. In the cases of commitment to action, you are committed to carrying out that action, or at least to living up to it. What counts as living up to a commitment is discussed below. The problem here is that you may not be able to carry out the action, even though you remain committed to carrying it out. In this respect, commitments to propositions are somewhat easier to deal with.

In some cases, it is quite clear that a person is committed to a specific proposition. But in others, judgment is more problematic. For example, a person may be committed to a general policy, abstractly stated, but it may be hard to judge what proposition or course of action that commits him to in a specific case. A person may profess commitment to safety, say, but sometimes ride his bicycle to work, knowing that this action is somewhat risky. Should we conclude that he is not really committed to safety? Not necessarily. The person may claim that risks to his personal safety thus posed are relatively minimal, or risks he can live with. And he may argue that he also has a commitment to health, and that riding his bike to work is healthy for him. Also, he may argue that his health is related to his safety since, if he gets exercise like cycling, he is less likely to have a heart attack. What, then, should we say about this person's commitments? In general, he is committed to safety, but in this particular instance, it appears he is not committed to his personal safety. But once he explains his position, we can see that the initial appearances were misleading. His commitment to safety can be reconciled with his personal actions of riding his bike to work.

What can be seen in this kind of case is that it is one thing to have a general commitment to some policy or goal in the abstract, but another to judge exactly what that policy commits a person to in a specific case. The particular commitment is not precisely determined by the general commitment, and vice versa: there is a slippage or indeterminacy between the general policy and the specific case. This observation is extremely important when it comes to judging a person's integrity. Integrity requires a certain kind of consistency. But typically what is involved is not just logical consistency. It is the kind of consistency that relates a general policy to actions in a specific case. The indeterminacy between general and specific leaves room for raising questions about such judgments. Although a lack of integrity may be suggested by a conflict between actions and professed policies or general commitments, further specifics of the case may resolve the apparent inconsistency.

In any given case, there can be many probing questions that need to be asked, and it may be quite difficult to pin down in some proposition that can be stated precisely exactly what the person in the case is supposedly committed to. For example, Socrates was cited above as an individual who would be considered a leading example of a person having integrity. After all, Socrates persisted with his activity of raising philosophical questions right up to the point where he took the hemlock, even though he could have avoided this outcome if he had given up the activity. Exhibiting this kind of commitment would appear to make Socrates a person of outstanding integrity.

The problem is that while the historical Socrates probably did fit these requirements, our judgment of his integrity will be drawn mainly from the account of his actions given in the dialogue written by Plato. These dialogues are literary works, and Socrates is often portrayed as a "poster boy" for Plato's own philosophical and ethical views. The views that Socrates himself was allegedly committed to are often negative and circumspect. For example, he did not claim to know, but only claimed to have the wisdom to know that he didn't know. So, if it is somewhat hard to pin down his exact views or commitments, it may be hard to give the exact kind of evidence required to prove that he was a person of integrity.

According to Kateb (1998, p. 78) the "strangeness of Socrates" is owing to his negativity. As evidence of this, Kateb notes that Socrates wrote nothing, and claimed to know nothing (p. 78). He questioned the doctrines and theories of others but did not claim to have produced one of his own (p. 14). Despite this negativity, Kateb thought that it might be useful to see Socrates as a person of integrity on two grounds (p. 79) (1) that he shows intellectual integrity in his relentless pursuit of wisdom, and (2) that he shows moral integrity in his strict avoidance of injustice. But both claims are subject to questions and doubts. Kateb used the text of the Platonic dialogues *Crito* and the *Apology* as evidence to support various hypotheses about how Socrates showed integrity of both sorts in his reported words and deeds. The evidence shows that, on balance, it is not difficult to make out a case for considering Socrates a person of integrity, but there are many questions about exactly what his integrity supposedly consisted in, and how it was shown by his actions and words conveyed in the Platonic dialogues. For all this evidence, it remains that the Socrates portrayed in the dialogues is, partly at least, a fictional construct designed for philosophical and literary purposes. The dialogues are a kind of blending of the historical Socrates with the device of Socrates as the philosopher interlocutor in the dialogues written by Plato, his student. The best we can do is to judge integrity from the database given. But of course, other questions can be asked about the truth of the database. Historical evidence may indicate that Socrates was like, or unlike the philosophical hero in the dialogues, in various ways.

3.4 A Case Where a Person's Integrity is in Doubt

Studying actual cases of judgments of integrity, or lack of it, can be quite revealing. In one interesting case (Kranhold, 1999), a man who co-founded one of the first environmental public-interest law firms, John Bryson, was hailed as a "green" utility executive when he became head of the electric utility Edison International. Bryson announced plans to reduce emissions, convert to electric vehicles, and introduce tough smog-control policies. He claimed to be "among the handful of leaders among electric utilities in the country in terms of environmental commitments" (Kranhold, 1999, p. 1). However, many of Bryson's fellow environmentalists described him as a "turncoat" or "chameleon", saying that he and his utility were helping to pollute the Grand Canyon, killing marine life off the California coast, and blocking the development of alternative power sources. One of these critics, James Caldwell, questioned Bryson's integrity by saying, "Here John Bryson sets himself up as being a steward of the environment. He is investing in coal plants, they are building coal-fired plants. Where does he get off calling himself green?" (p. 1). Caldwell alleged that Bryson was "as green as AstroTurf".

In this case, Bryson's critics are contrasting his professing a green position with his actions or track record as head of Edison International. In their opinion, these don't live up to the green position on environmental issues that he had so long and so strenuously expressed a commitment to. In other words, the critics allege that his real commitment, or what we may take to be his real commitment from the evidence of his actions, is to his company, not to the environmental cause. On the other hand, since Bryson still professes commitment to the green position in his speeches, there is a certain lack of consistency between what he says and what he does. The allegation is that he does not practice what he preaches. The allegation is not just one of a failure of logical consistency; it has an ethical thrust. The criticism is essentially that Bryson lacks integrity.

Notice that the judgment of character in this case, while it conveys an extremely powerful criticism of the ethics of the person whose integrity is doubted, is not final. Presumably, Bryson would be able to reply to this attack in various ways. He might argue that the company, under his leadership, has actually done much better on environmental issues than the critics allege. Or he might argue that he has led the company in an environmental direction as well as anyone could, but that there are limits to how a large organization can be steered, one way or another. This is typical of many such cases in that there is relevant evidence on both sides. The criticism of Bryson's integrity is telling, but it is just one side of the story. The whole case takes the form of an ethical issue with two sides. Bryson should have a right to reply to criticism, of course, and it is quite possible that his reply would throw a different light on the question of his integrity.

This case is typical of the way an argument may be used to cast doubt on a person's integrity. The argument used is that the facts of the case show an inconsistency. First, facts about Bryson's background and views he has advocated, backed up by evidence from quotations from his speeches, show his commitment to the green or environmentalist position. But then other facts are cited about things the utility did when Bryson was head of it. These are taken to suggest that, when it comes down to the real actions Bryson took, it appears that he is not really committed to environmentalism. In other words, the argument cites a pragmatic inconsistency between what Bryson professes and his actual deeds. What is this contradiction taken to show? That Bryson is a hypocrite.

There is much to be said on how to evaluate this argument. It does present relevant evidence, and makes a strong point unless it can be rebutted. But what is weakest in the argument is the inference that because the utility did various things under Bryson's leadership, these actions accurately indicate the latter's real commitments. As head of an organization, a leader may not have total control over everything that is done. Far from it, in many cases. So to evaluate the argument, one should question this inference. On the other hand, there is a legitimate connection there. If Bryson was aware that the utility was taking actions that were against his principles, perhaps he should have resigned, or otherwise protested in some way.

The basic thrust of the argument is an attack on Bryson's integrity. The bottom line is that Bryson lacks integrity because he has professed commitments that he does not live up to. Bryson is alleged to be a hypocrite — a person who propounds principles that should apply to everyone, but then reveals by his actions that he does not follow these principles himself. To charge someone with hypocrisy is to imply that this person is a morally bad person. The argument, as in this case, mounts an attack on the credibility of the person attacked. That is one reason why this form of argument is so powerful. For if a person's credibility is destroyed, then he or she will not be taken seriously in any future arguments.

3.5 Living Up to a Commitment

Integrity is not always following one's commitments exactly, because it may be hard to say which specific action that one might carry out counts as following one's commitments. For example, suppose I have a commitment to peace. What action I might take would count as following this commitment? Some would say that disbanding the armed forces is the action required by a commitment to peace. Others would say that it is maintaining them. But no matter which action I take, what I need to do, in order to be a person of integrity, is to connect up my action with my commitment to peace. In making such a connection, means-end reasoning (practical reasoning) will be involved. What will also be involved however, is the notion of living up to a commitment.

According to Hamblin (1987), living up to a commitment is not necessarily the same thing as performing any single action dictated by that commitment. Living up to a commitment, according to his analysis, requires making strategic decisions and estimates of circumstances that are partial strategies for acting in accord with the commitment. A simple example to illustrate this has been presented in (Walton and Krabbe, 1995, pp. 18–20). Let's say that John has made a commitment to take out the garbage. Let's say, for example, that he has promised Mary to take out the garbage before 7:00 a.m., putting it in the place where the garbage is usually collected. If John sleeps in until eight o'clock, then he has failed to live up to his commitment. But what if John's son Bill unexpectedly takes out the garbage at 6:30 a.m.? Has John lived up to his commitment? Well, he has not lived up to his commitment to take out the garbage himself. But if he woke up and saw Bill take it out, and realized that it was no longer necessary for him to do it personally, then it would seem reasonable to say that he has lived up to his commitment. It would certainly be inappropriate to say that he defaulted on his commitment. Many other puzzling questions can be posed by extending the example. Suppose John got up on time, and thought he was taking out the garbage, but what he really took out was a bag of sweaters that someone had left, in a bag that looked the same as the garbage? Did John live up to his commitment to take out the garbage? It would seem that the answer is yes, provided that John thought he was taking out the garbage, and there was no visible evidence that he was not, when he put out the bag.

Hamblin (1987) built a theory of imperatives around this notion of living up to a commitment. Walton and Krabbe (1995, Appendix) showed how Hamblin's theory fits into the theory of commitment in dialogue. Norman and Reed (2000) showed how Hamblin's theory fits into multi-agent systems in computing. This theory is very useful for reconstructing cases in which there is assumed to be a connection, or a chain of reasoning, between an action or omission by an agent and some prior commitment the agent supposedly has. Hamblin's theory sees the world as a chain of states, or so-called possible worlds, connected by what he calls deeds and happenings. An imperative, like "Take out the garbage!" can be satisfied extensionally by those worlds in which the garbage is out. The mere fact of the garbage being in the right place by the right time, in other words, extensionally satisfies the imperative. But extensional satisfaction is a weak notion, not very useful for giving some adequate account of what it is to live up to a commitment. Hamblin's notion of wholehearted satisfaction is much better for this purpose. As Norman and Reed (2001, p. 136) explain this notion, it is based on what Hamblin calls a partial strategy, a set of incompletely specified strategies for fulfilling an imperative. The wholehearted satisfaction of an imperative by an agent is defined as being the agent's adoption of a partial strategy and by the execution of a deed based on that strategy. In the case of the garbage example, John could have wholeheartedly satisfied Mary's imperative, "Take out the garbage!" by adopting various partial strategies. For example, realizing that he might not be able to take out the garbage himself, he might have paid Bill to do it, knowing that Bill was normally an early riser, and was reliable in carrying out household tasks when paid to do so.

3.6 Integrity and Living Up to a Commitment

Suppose you are committed to an action, but for reasons beyond your control, you don't actually carry it out. For example, suppose Bob tells Rita in the morning that he will meet her at Harris Hall at four o'clock that afternoon, but on the way to Harris Hall at 3:45 there is a vehicle accident that delays him. Let's say that Bob has to stay at the scene of the accident in order to help the accident victims until the ambulance arrives. As a result he does not meet Rita at Harris Hall at four o'clock. Has Bob lived up to his commitment? Bob has not fulfilled his commitment to meet Rita at four o'clock at Harris Hall. But suppose he arrives late, finds Rita waiting for him, and explains to her about the accident. It would be appropriate to say that Bob lived up to his commitment to meet her at the appointed time. He did his best, under the circumstances, but something else intervened that delayed him. He could have just ignored the situation of the accident, and arrived at Harris Hall by four o'clock. But that would not have been the right thing to do. So Bob had a good reason, a valid excuse, for failing to be at Harris Hall at four o'clock. There is thus a sense in which we could say that Bob lived up to his commitment to be there at four o'clock, even though he didn't actually get there at that time.

On the other hand, suppose that at noon, Bob took the train to O'Hare Airport, and then at two o'clock, got on the flight to Amsterdam. We could then truly say at 2:15 that Bob has not lived up to his commitment to meet Rita at Harris Hall at four. Why? Because he has taken a course of action that moves him further and further away from meeting Rita at four o'clock at Harris Hall. Presumably at some point, it becomes impossible for him to fulfill that commitment. Of course, Bob might have some very good reason for going to Amsterdam. And that could alter the question of whether he was living up to his commitment to meet Rita. But as things stand, the evidence strongly indicates that Bob has not lived up to his commitment.

Living up to a commitment is different from actually fulfilling that commitment by carrying out specified actions needed. It seems more like moving towards fulfilling the commitment, unless you are diverted from this by some other commitment that rightly takes precedence. The problem is that when we judge integrity, and when we consider evidence for a person's commitment to some plan, policy, action, or value, we assess how well he has lived up to that commitment. We do not necessarily conclude that because a person failed to carry out some action, he was not really committed to carrying out that action.

A person's commitment may be said to be of an active or a passive sort. An active commitment is one that a person has gone on record as explicitly making, and in many cases, even defending and justifying as important and worthy. A passive commitment is one that has been taken on indirectly, or that has been simply conceded. For example, if I make passionate political speeches that every woman should have the right to an abortion, it would be justifiable to conclude that I am committed to the proposition that every woman should have the right to an abortion. Or if I have gone on record as claiming that there are aliens on other planets who are trying to communicate with us, then I have an active commitment to the proposition that there are aliens on other planets who are trying to communicate with us. If someone doubts this assertion, and asks me to prove it, then I am called on to give evidence in support of my commitment. Passive commitments are less firmly fixed in place. For example, during a discussion on the abortion issue, I may concede for the sake of argument that the fetus is a person in the third trimester. I may not actually believe this myself, but I may be willing to concede it, because you believe it, and I have no need or wish to strenuously dispute it. Once I have conceded it, I am committed to that proposition, but only passively. If challenged, I may quite justifiably reply that I am not obliged to prove it, because my argument does not rest on it, and that I only accepted it for the sake of moving the argument along.

It is often possible to alter, or even retract one's commitments, in everyday moral deliberations. For example, if Bob phones Rita and says that it is a problem for him to make it at four o'clock, the two of them may agree to meet at five o'clock instead. But you can't always retract a commitment without an acceptable explanation or justification of why you have changed your mind. Indeed, people who appear to constantly retract their commitments for no apparent reason, for no better reason than something like convenience or self-interest, are judged to lack integrity. At the other extreme, sticking to commitments rigidly, when there may be reasons for changing your mind, is also a fault that could suggest you are not a person of integrity.

For example, suppose you have committed yourself to a planned merger with another company. Many of the details of the proposed agreement have been drawn up by the lawyers for both sides. The merger looks like it would be good for both companies. But then you find that the other company has concealed some facts about its debts, and about some illegal business arrangements it has gotten into in the past. This new information suggests to you that the merger would be highly problematic, and might get your company into a lot of trouble, once these matters come to light. At this point, you decide to retract your commitment to the planned merger. Revealing the new information to the board of your company, you try to persuade the other board members not to sign the merger agreement. In this kind of situation, you may have a firm commitment, but when new information comes in, you may only be doing the right or prudent thing if you retract it.

In general, a person of integrity will stick to her commitments, once made. But in a specific case, she may retract a commitment, and yet still be judged to be a person of integrity. In some cases, retracting a commitment would even be the appropriate thing for her to do. This may be obligatory to retain her integrity. But such required retraction can even go beyond what should be done in a specific case. It may be possible for a person to change his whole position, and adopting one quite incompatible with the old one. When this kind of change of position occurs, it is generally suspicious, from the standpoint of judging integrity. But it is possible nevertheless. For example, suppose that a politician who has long been a member of the liberal party "crosses the floor", joins the conservative side, and for the rest of his life is a staunch conservative, vociferously opposing policies that he earlier supported. It may seem that he is radically contradicting himself, and perhaps he is. He might often be attacked by his opponents on these grounds. Yet it could be that he has had a genuine conversion, or change of political convictions. If so, his retraction of his previous commitments could be judged to be reasonable, or at least explainable.

A person may easily profess a commitment, but his or her actions may raise doubts about how deep that commitment is, and about how serious he or she is about it. As noted above, actions, especially under certain conditions, are often taken as a more reliable indicator of a person's real commitments than what the person says. Three types of conditions provide tests of commitment that are especially indicative. One is action carried out against a person's interests. A second is action carried out under adversity. A third is action that resists some kind of temptation.

A person may profess some noble goal or lofty ethical principle, but one may wonder how deep their commitment is to it? Actually carrying out an action that is meant to realize this goal in a situation where it costs something personally, would be a very good indicator of real commitment. Often the situation has something to do with altruism. For example, a person may profess to hold the nurturing of children as an important value for everyone. But suppose that when her own children need her care, she decides to stay at work, because she wants to further her career. She may give speeches about children's rights and the value of "quality time" with children, but her personal actions may reveal her real commitments more accurately.

The second test has to do with adversity. If a person persists in carrying out a commitment to some principle even in difficult conditions that would deter other people, then it shows how deeply he is committed to that principle. Another special test is that of danger. If a person carries out some value, like helping others, even in conditions that pose a danger to her, then her action clearly reveals her commitment. Courageous actions fall into this category. Suppose that under conditions of extreme stress in battle, where everyone is justifiably afraid, a medical orderly calmly and carefully binds up the wounds of others, even though seriously wounded himself. One World War II veteran remembered a situation like this, and tears always came to his eyes when he described it. This kind of situation, bad as it is, is a wonderful test of commitment that says a lot about the qualities of character of the medical orderly. The deepest test of commitment is adverse circumstances, such as those occurring in floods, earthquakes, wars, and so forth. The worst brings out the best.

The third test has to do with temptation. A person may sincerely profess commitment to some principle or value, like marital faithfulness. But can or will he or she stick to it in a situation where behavior to the contrary looks very attractive and pleasurable, and where there seems little chance of getting caught? If so, then that person has shown that he really does have a serious commitment to the value or goal he professed. Relevant to this kind of test also is weakness of will, or what philosophers call *akrasia*. Suppose a person is on a diet, and is strongly committed to losing weight, but is presented with a box of chocolates. He may love these particular chocolates, even though they are very fattening, and he may have a whole box of them where nobody can see him eating them. He may really be committed to losing weight, and be strongly convinced that losing weight is necessary for his health. He may place a very high value on health. But in a weak moment, he may eat all the chocolates anyway. This kind of situation poses a philosophical problem, because many would insist that his commitment to all these values is real, even though, in a moment of weakness, he acted contrary to them. The truth of the matter is that his eating the chocolates is evidence that goes against the seriousness and depth of his commitment to the value of health and to the policy of losing weight as a means to his health. At any rate, if he resists temptation, and gets rid of the chocolates somehow, instead of eating them, he will have given a very good indication that he really is committed to the value in question. The situation provides a good test of his real commitment to this value, and how sincere he is about it.

The whole body of evidence in a given case sets up a network of reasoning that is all part of the justification for any claim that the principal agent in the case may be said to have some ethical quality of character, like courage. The supposition that the agent has such an internal quality appears to be arrived at by a process of abductive reasoning. The supposition that he is courageous seems to be the best or most plausible explanation of the total body of facts in the case. But it would also seem that such a supposition is defeasible. It can be defeated if new facts enter into the case, especially relevant facts that show the agent being severely tested in a difficult situation. The inference is made to a supposition that attributes a certain commitment to the agent. But, as we saw, commitment can be retracted. Evaluators of the case attribute a certain commitment to the principal agent as a best explanation of facts known at that point. But if continuation of the investigation brings in new relevant facts, a better and more convincing explanation may suggest itself. The deeper the case, and the more testing of character it reveals, the more convincing the explanation will be.

For example, suppose a candidate for high political office was a prisoner of war for many years under extremely difficult and degrading conditions. And suppose that under these conditions, his actions were closely observed, and for a long time, by his fellow captives. Someone who survived this situation without losing his moral values, and who showed extraordinary commitment to these values, would have survived a test that few of us will ever have to pass. In such a case, the evidence for an attribution of courage as the best explanation is very strong. Of course, such a person can change, or react differently under different circumstances. But performing well in such a tough situation, shows that the commitment to ethical values goes very deep. In such a case, the evidence is especially strong. In ethics as in legal reasoning, there are easy cases and hard cases.

3.7 Character Attack Based on Alleged Hypocrisy

Many of the judgments of character studied so far in this book have concerned praiseworthy aspects of it — virtues like courage and integrity. But there are cases concerned with alleged negative qualities of character. In the case of Francis Bacon, studied in chapter 1, section 4, a person's character was attacked and his reputation blackened for hundreds of years by the allegations that he was dishonest, ambitious and corrupt. In the case of John Bryson, studied above, a utility executive's integrity was brought in question by saying that he was "as green as Astroturf". The basis of the attack in this case was that Bryson's actions ran counter to his words. He was attacked as being a hypocrite, a person who showed a lack of consistency between what he passionately advocated and what his real commitments were, as expressed in his personal actions. It was argued that he not only failed to live up to his commitments, but actually went against them.

Hypocrisy is the opposite of integrity. Integrity refers to a wholeness of character shown in a consistency between words and actions as commitments. Hypocrisy refers to an inconsistency between words and actions. A hypocrite is a person who advocates a policy or position as generally good, or good for everyone, but then acts in his own case in a way that is contrary to this policy or position. To show that someone is a hypocrite is a powerful form of character attack. For it suggests that the person is not sincere in what he advocates. It reveals a kind of dishonesty or double-dealing — a kind of insincerity that is an ethical defect of character. Moreover, such a defect, once revealed, throws doubt on an advocate's credibility. For if he doesn't adhere to his principles in his own personal conduct, there must surely be serious doubts about whether he really believes them or is personally committed to them. So the charge of hypocrisy is an extremely powerful form of attack on a person's character, particularly in the political arena, where the persuasiveness of a speaker's argument is based both on his principles and his perceived character. Let's study a case of an attack on a politician's character on the ground that he is a hypocrite.

This case comes from *Time* magazine's *Election Notebook* of November 18, 1996 (p. 16), a page on which *Time* gives out "Campaign '96 Awards" to "recognize outstanding achievements by politicians, their relatives and their hecklers". Remarks about two of the awards are directly quoted below.

> THE SLIGHT-INCONSISTENCY MEDAL: To Al Gore, who left not a dry eye in the house at the Democratic Convention as he described his sister's death from smoking-induced lung cancer. Gore failed to mention that for some years following her death, his family continued to grow tobacco and that he continued to accept campaign money from tobacco interests.
>
> THE MOST NAUSEATING SPIN: Gore explained the above by saying, "I felt the numbness that prevented me from integrating into all aspects of my life the implications of what that tragedy really meant."

No author of the *Election Notebook* page was given. It simply appears as an editorial column, with accompanying pictures (including one of Gore, in a speech-making pose).

To classify the type of dialogue to which the argument of this case belongs, one would have to say that it was found on an editorial page of a sort, rather than in a news story. The intent of the entries on the page could be described as ironic and satirical, but each definitely has a political content, in the sense that it is an argument expressing a particular viewpoint. Each is an editorial comment expressing a particular "spin" or opinion. So the function of the discourse can be classified as one of political commentary, which is partisan in nature, as opposed to information-seeking or news-reporting. The case cited above, for example, presents a point of view, expressed in an argument for one side of an issue. In a newspaper report on politics, by contrast, there would be an expectation that both sides would be presented.

The argument in this case is an attack on Gore's character, based on what is claimed to be a practical inconsistency between his words and actions. This apparent inconsistency makes Gore appear to be a hypocrite. The argument against him runs as follows. First, Gore's speech about the death of his sister from lung cancer is cited as showing that he holds that smoking is a very bad thing — something he is strongly against. But the argument then goes on to say that Gore "failed to mention" two key facts. One is that his family continued to grow tobacco, after the death of his sister. The other is that he himself continued to accept money from tobacco interests. The actions cited in these two statements clash with what Gore is reported to have said in his speech. This clash takes the form of a pragmatic inconsistency, from which the reader draws the conclusion, by implicature, that Gore could not have sincerely meant what he (so tearfully) said. The conclusion suggested is that he must be a hypocrite.

Could there be an explanation for this pragmatic inconsistency? The editorial actually gives one, but it makes Gore sound even more insincere. The reader is led to draw the conclusion that Gore must be a bad person — a hypocrite who recommends values and policies in his speeches that are the direct opposite of his personal policies, as revealed by his own actions. In many cases, this kind of inconsistency can be explained. But in this case, the argument seems to be airtight. To seal it up even further, Gore's (presumed) reply offers further evidence of his insincerity. The suggestion is that his tearful speech was a mere rhetorical flourish, and that you can't really trust or accept anything such an insincere man says in politics.

To analyze the argument in this case, the first step is to confirm the allegation of inconsistency — the allegation that Gore's actions and arguments are pragmatically inconsistent, one being the opposite of the other. The further implication suggested by Gricean implicature, as noted above, is that Gore's arguments against the use of tobacco products are not sincerely meant. The idea is that he says one thing but does another, so "actions speak louder than words". The personal attack element of the argument is the suggestion that Gore is a hypocrite — the suggestion that his argument is only political posturing, and is not expressing a conclusion he really accepts personally. But exactly how is the personal attack drawn by Gricean implicature from the circumstantial contradiction that is posed by the argument? The alleged practical inconsistency arises from the clash between the following two propositions.

1. Gore, in a speech, tearfully described his sister's death from smoking-induced lung cancer.
2. For some years following his sister's death, Gore's family continued to grow tobacco and he continued to accept money from tobacco interests.

From proposition 1, the implication is drawn that Gore is strongly against smoking. The fact that his tearful description of his sister's death was part of a political speech implies that this description was relevant politically. In other words, presumably Gore included it in such a public speech because he was advocating the message to the American public that smoking is a bad habit, that he is against smoking, and that the public generally ought to be against smoking. But then proposition two says that Gore, after the time he gave the speech (and the element of the timing is very important to the argument), personally accepted money from tobacco interests and his family profited from growing tobacco. But how exactly does this connection imply a contradiction that reveals hypocrisy?

There is a well-known connection, of course, between the growing of tobacco and the habit of smoking. Growing tobacco is a necessary means for smoking. We all know that cigarettes are produced from tobacco, and that the normal way of manufacturing cigarettes has the growing of tobacco as one of its most important parts. So if anyone is sincerely against smoking, it would be highly questionable for that same person not to be against the growing of tobacco. The close connection between smoking and tobacco makes the advocacy of both propositions 1 and 2 by the same person highly questionable. It cries out for an explanation. And in the absence of one, the conclusion implied (by implicature) is that this person is the worst sort of hypocrite, who will even exploit the death of his sister to move an audience for political gain. The implications of the inconsistency make Gore out to be not only the worst sort of scoundrel, but ridiculous as well.

The photograph presented of Gore, where he appears in a rhetorical pose with a caring and passionate look on his face, adds to the ridicule expressed by the argument. The idea of a speaker looking this sincere and acting in such a hypocritical way is ironic and funny in just the way that the ironies ridiculed by Voltaire and Moliere were funny. The idea of a rogue who can sell things to gullible and unsuspecting buyers of his products or ideas by saying all sorts of ridiculous things that he does not believe at all, in the most sincere way, seems very ironic and funny to people. Perhaps the comedic aspect of it is that the rogue speaks with what appears to be the greatest sincerity, and the buyer pays rapt attention to this absurd performance.

3.8 Evaluation of the Alleged Hypocrisy Case

Next we need to proceed to analyze the character attack argument used in the Gore case to see why and how it was based on evidence that made it at least somewhat persuasive. The important thing is to pinpoint the gaps in the evidence, to show how such arguments can be challenged. The weakest part of the argument relates to one aspect of proposition 2, a conjunction of two propositions. One of them is the allegation that Gore's family continued to grow tobacco for some years following his sister's death. What has to be questioned here is why Gore is being held responsible for things done by his family. For example, it could be possible that he didn't like other people in his family growing tobacco, or that he protested about it, or even that he didn't know about it, and so forth. Personal control over what one's family members do may be minimal, or even non-existent. Who were these family members, and how were they related to Gore? What economic stake did Gore have in the family tobacco-growing enterprise? Until these questions are asked and answered, we don't know what sort of connection Gore had with tobacco growing, and whether the connection can in any way be taken to indicate that he somehow supported or advocated tobacco growing.

So this particular subpart of the character attack argument is very weak, at best, and, as it stands, could be misleading and fallacious. Allied to the other part of the conjunction in proposition 2, that Gore accepted campaign contributions from tobacco interests, this allegation about Gore's family does give the attack an additional push, because it does cite another connection between Gore and tobacco. But on closer examination, it seems rather a weak part of the argument — one that should be scrutinized and critically questioned carefully.

What about the other part of the conjunction? Here the connection is firmer, because these days we expect politicians to at least make reasonable efforts to know whether their campaign funds are coming from special interests. The big question is whether Gore knew that these funds came from tobacco interests. If he did, then it does seem questionable that he accepted them, without any further comment on their source, especially in light of his passionate speech (earlier) on the evils of smoking. The presumption posed by this apparent conflict is that Gore did not really mean what he said in his speech. And the implicature (Grice, 1975) suggested by this presumption is that Gore is a "phony" or hypocrite, who exploited this family tragedy to add pathos to a political speech, no doubt with great effect. So the argument alleging inconsistency is the vehicle used, by implication, to pose a character attack argument to the effect that Gore is not a sincere person who can be trusted to tell us what he truly believes in his political speeches. As is characteristically the case with this form of character attack, the allegation of pragmatic inconsistency leads to the implication that the arguer attacked is a person of bad character.

A general question that needs to be raised in this case is whether the argument is an *ad hominem*, or only an ethical attack on Gore's character. It is a requirement of an argument being an *ad hominem* argument, that it be a personal attack used to undermine the argument of the other party (Walton, 1998). Attacking someone's integrity, or even calling that person a liar or a hypocrite, for example, is not necessarily an *ad hominem* argument. An *ad hominem* is not just any slur on someone's character. It must be a slur aimed at that person's argument (by attacking the credibility of the arguer for that purpose). What matters is not the actual intention of the attacker, but how the argument is used in a given case. In this case then, we need to ask what argument of Gore's the attack on his character (by way of the alleged circumstantial conflict) was aimed at refuting. Presumably, it was his passionate speech which, if relevant to politics at all, was a message to people against smoking. Was the *Time* segment (as quoted above) then meant to attack the argument against smoking? Was it a kind of pro-smoking message? Presumably not. And that raises the question whether the editorial really contains an *ad hominem* argument at all. This question is a subtle one, and requires an analysis of the form of inference (argumentation scheme) that defines the *ad hominem* argument. Such matters will be addressed in chapter 6.

This case looks like a pretty typical example of the character attack argument as used in political discourse. And in certain respects, it is. The allegation of bad ethical character is there, and it is used to mount a personal attack on the integrity of a politician. But some factors of the argument's context of dialogue need to be observed. This is not just the more typical kind of case of one politician attacking the policy or argument of another in a political debate — for example with a "negative ad" in an election campaign, of the kind studied by Pfau and Burgoon (1989). Instead, the argument in this case is an ironic commentary on an editorial page of a major national news magazine by an anonymous author. The purpose is somewhat unclear. It may be more of an attempt to stir up controversy, or to amuse readers who are cynical about politicians, than an attempt to attack Gore's political position, or some specific argument he has advanced. But character attack is very definitely a strong component.

The tricky, and therefore especially interesting tactic exhibited by this case is the conjunction of the two propositions used as a dual basis for supporting the one side of the alleged pragmatic inconsistency. The conjunction is composed of the following two propositions.

(P1): For some years following his sister's death, Gore's family continued to grow tobacco.

(P2): Gore continued to accept money from tobacco interests.

As shown above, the allegation made in (P1) is quite a weak and a questionable basis for an allegation of inconsistency. We don't blame people for things that members of their families (like their parents) do. So unless there is some further link, (P1) is not much of a basis for establishing inconsistency of a sort that shows Gore to be a hypocrite. The real basis of the attack on his character is (P2). While a lot of other politicians probably also accepted money from tobacco interests at the time, still Gore's having done this does clash with his speech about his sister in a way that somewhat supports the allegation of inconsistency against him.

So the trick in this case is to combine a weak but persuasive basis for a character attack argument with a stronger one. The stronger basis, by itself, does not seem all that impressive (probably because all politicians were engaging in pretty much the same practice at the time). But when combined with the weaker one (that somehow looks more impressive, especially when combined with the stronger one), the effect is considerable. The argument, as a whole, succeeds in making Gore look quite ridiculous. Even though the argument is revealed, once analyzed, as weak from a critical point of view, it is highly persuasive when you first encounter it. At least, it certainly would be persuasive to any who are cynical about politicians to begin with, or to those who already suspect that Gore is selling a kind of superficial rhetoric to support his own interests and those of his allies. To the extent that a reader has these cynical attitudes, he is likely to find the character attack argument used in this case easy to accept.

An especially interesting aspect of this particular case is its compactness. Very little is said in the given text of discourse, but a lot is implied. Repeated use of Gricean implicature to suggest propositions is a clever aspect of the argument, showing how easy it can be to mount a character attack argument on the basis of very little evidence, but with a terrific smearing effect. The Gricean implicatures work because the audience as well as the two main agents involved are all familiar with scripts about the way things are normally done. The audience can recognize the connections in the plan and the actions attributed to the agent being attacked. It can put two and two together, so to speak, without the attacker having to fill in all the steps in the sequence of argumentation. The plan recognition capability of the audience fills in the missing steps. The beauty of it is that the attacker, if pressed too hard by a challenge to prove his allegations, can deny that he ever really meant to attack the other agent at all. Thus it is extremely difficult to defend oneself against this type of argument. If the victim attacks it too vigorously, he appears guilty. But if no reply at all is made, or only a weak one, the damage can be just as bad or worse. The usual strategy of challenging the support of the premise seems to be of limited use in such a case. Once the imputation is made, even if the evidence for it is later questioned or refuted, the damage may be done.

This powerful smearing effect, based on Gricean implicature, is the reason why the character attack argument is so powerful as a device of persuasion. Such an argument can backfire, and make its proponent look bad, if the audience perceives that there is no evidence to support the argument. It will look like the proponent himself has bad character, because he is lowering himself by using sleazy smear tactics. But if there is even only a small amount of evidence supporting the character attack, that may be enough to fuel the suspicions of the audience. In such a case, the character attack argument can be devastatingly powerful in rhetorical persuasion. Part of the reason is that in typical political and legal cases, the audience or jury does not have direct access to the facts of a case. They arrive at a decision on what to do under conditions of inexactness and uncertainty. The question is who to believe, the one side or the other. There is a conflict of opinions and there are arguments on both sides. To appreciate how the character attack can be such a powerfully persuasive device, you have to look at it from the viewpoint of the political audience or the jury who must make a decision based on a balance of considerations.

3.9 Evidence for Judgments of Integrity and Hypocrisy

Integrity is a quality of character that needs to be judged as relatively stable over a long period — perhaps even a lifetime. But how firmly qualities of character are fixed is a subject of some controversy in ethics. According to Nagel (1979, pp. 32–33), qualities like cowardice, conceit or envy are "beyond the control of the will" (p. 33), so a person cannot change or revise his character. But according to Moody-Adams (1990, p. 117), "it is at least intuitively plausible that people can change or revise their characters". There has to be some middle ground on this question. While qualities of character do have to be relatively stable and enduring, they should not be regarded as entirely fixed or closed to revision. Surely growing to maturity involves, and is even based on, changes in character. And improvement of one's character is surely possible in some cases, even though certain basic elements of a person's character are so natural or ingrained that working with the character you already have is bound to impose limitations on changes that can be made. There are many examples where a person's character has been changed for the rest of his life — for example by some traumatic event like being a front line soldier in a war. It would seem that in studying a person's life and personal development, it is possible in many cases to see evidence of changes in character.

A person's integrity, for example, may be studied and evaluated in a biography. But that doesn't mean that integrity has to be such that commitments never change, or never admit of exceptions. A biography might show, for example, that a person changed his basic ethical convictions over his lifetime. For example, he may have come from humble beginnings, and developed a conservative political philosophy in his youth. But in later life, he may have undergone a profound change in thinking, and became a socialist. Or a person may have had all kinds of problems in her youth, and gotten into trouble, but then led an outstandingly altruistic life, after a religious conversion.

Generally, however, integrity is based on a consistency in living up to commitments based on an ethical position over a prolonged period of time. When there are changes of commitments or apparent inconsistencies of commitment, it should be possible to explain them so that the person's position can be seen as having had the required stability. Integrity is likely to be achieved only after a struggle. And a person should be able to question his ethical convictions. So judging integrity, in any given case, is likely to be a far from simple consideration of logical consistency over a whole lifetime. What is at stake is a kind of consistency of commitment that tends to be stable but can change under certain conditions. The problem is to give an account of these conditions.

Ethical convictions are not absolute. They can change, or be subject to exceptions. There may be all sorts of reasons why one cannot follow one's ethical principles in some cases. Or although possible, it might be just too much of a hardship to demand that she to follow her principles without exceptions. Ethics is full of morally problematic situations. Ethical principles can even conflict in some situations, a fact well known in ethics. Ethical dilemmas involve a person's commitment to two ethical principles, in a case where following the one principle amounts to violating the other one. For a person to have integrity, it would not be appropriate to demand a rigid following of ethical principles, nor would it be right to require an absolute logical consistency in acts and deeds that never varies.

Judging integrity is a tricky business. Two parties are involved — the person whose integrity is being judged and the person who is doing the judging. The act of judgment takes place by the one person using empathy to try to put himself into the mind of the other person, and to reconstruct the rationale behind what the other person did and said. Such an act of mental transference seems highly subjective, and in a way, it is. In many cases, the judgment tells us as much about the integrity of the person doing the judging as it does about the integrity of the person being judged. But there can be definite objective evidence to verify or falsify a hypothesis put forward when a judgment about integrity is made. This evidence consists of reports of the person's actions, and records of what he said in talking about them. The problem is to determine how to assess such evidence, and to judge what conclusions should or should not be arrived at on the basis of it.

Some would say that it is imperious to think that we could ever make such moralistic judgments about our fellow human beings. But, in fact, we do it every day. We make judgments of a person's integrity or lack of it every day, in business, law, politics, personal relationships, and in all matters of daily life in which people deliberate and act collaboratively with others.

The basic problem is that integrity is a kind of consistency that involves sticking to one's commitments, but this is different from abstract logical consistency. It requires a certain flexibility in adapting to the specifics of a situation. In any real situation, new information may come in that may call for retracting previous commitments. Ethical principles are general rules of the kind that admit of exceptions in specific situations. In some situations — for example, in an ethical dilemma — there can be conflicts of commitments that are difficult to resolve, and that may call for compromises in a person's principles. Too rigid a consistency in dealing with such problematic situations may be more a sign of fanaticism than of real integrity. Sticking to one's commitments needs to be seen as a more flexible and elastic kind of consistency that can be tuned to the requirements of a complex situation in the real world where changing your mind isn't always a bad thing.

Three kinds of situations provide especially telling evidence that can be used to judge a person's commitments: situations where fulfilling a commitment goes against a person's interests, situations of adversity, especially where difficulty and anger are involved, and situations in which a person is confronted with temptation. These three types of situations provide hard tests of a person's commitment. So evidence drawn from one of them can be an especially high grade of evidence.

Generally speaking, the evidence against which judgments of integrity should be evaluated comes from the known or supposed facts in an actual case. This part of the reasoning is abductive. One agent can construct various possible explanations of the given facts, and then pick the most plausible explanation and use it to draw an inference about the primary agent's presumed commitment. There can be various problems at this level. One is that such a body of evidence can sometimes be interpreted and judged in radically different ways. Two biographies of the same person, for example, may use roughly the same body of facts as data, but draw directly opposed conclusions about the integrity of the person who is the subject. In one, he may be portrayed as a humanitarian who gave a lot of money to charitable causes, who was very loyal to his friends, and who was a leader in getting equal treatment for minorities. In the other, he may be portrayed as a person who associated with gangsters, who was often rude and violent, abused women, was unfaithful to his wife, was callous and unforgiving to anyone who crossed him, and was a social climber.

At this level, there can be contradictory accounts of what are supposed to be the facts of the case. The first abductive question is to ask about the data in the case. But there can also be opposed explanations arising out of the facts, even after agreement is reached on what the facts of a case really are. Cases of judgments of integrity are particularly susceptible to disagreement on what should be inferred from the facts. What one should do in judging such cases is to look at the facts and arguments on both sides, and come to some assessment. In such cases, there may be good evidence on both sides, and room for disagreement. This kind of case may prompt skeptics to throw up their hands and say, "Well, there you go. You can't decide personal matters like this in an objective way anyway. It's all subjective". But what this chapter has shown is that a primary agent can use abductive reasoning, based on factual data, in judging whether a secondary agent may rightly be said to have integrity or not, in a given case. The judgment is based on the commitment set of the secondary agent. If that commitment set is inconsistent, then the secondary agent lacks integrity. If consistency can be proved, the primary agent has integrity. Leaping to the conclusion that all is subjective is a fallacy, if meant to apply to all cases. Hard cases must be expected, where the evidence does not go clearly and decisively one way or the other. It does not follow that there are no cases where a person may be rightly judged to have integrity or not. But deciding such cases, as shown above, is not just a matter of assembling the facts. It is a matter of using these facts to draw conclusions about what a person's commitments may rightly be taken to be in the given case. Such judgments are always inferential, because they involve conclusions about what a person's commitments really are, or may be taken to be on the basis of the evidence, and conclusions about whether the person has lived up to them or not, from what we can tell from the given evidence.

When a person's integrity is attacked by alleging that his commitments are inconsistent, the argument can be incredibly powerful. Such an argument can destroy the credibility of the person attacked. It can not only destroy the person's argument, but it can also destroy his capability for taking part in a discussion, or any sort of argumentation. For if he has no credibility, if he might be a liar or deceiver, then an audience will tend to discount everything he says. Thus attacking a person's character is called argument against the person or *ad hominem* argument. It has been shown above how such attacks on a person's integrity can be evaluated on the basis of evidence. The argument will be abductive, as we have seen, and will be based on supposed facts. In chapter 6, more precise details of how to evaluate *ad hominem* arguments will be given. There, we will return to a consideration of the attack against Gore, and more carefully analyze whether it should properly be classified as a species of *ad hominem* argument.

3.10 The Defeasibility of Character Judgments

The cases studied in this chapter have shown that although the process of reasoning that stands behind a character judgment is inherently fallible and conjectural in nature, it is based on a kind of logical reasoning from a set of given data in a case. Of course, the data are themselves subject to challenge and correction, and the conclusions drawn from them are subject to critical questioning. But even when there is basic agreement on the data concerning what was said and done in a case, the conclusion drawn can be subject to defeat as new evidence comes in. Character judgments are based on a kind of indirect reasoning that can be supported or criticized by factual evidence, but that tends to be inconclusive. The basic problem, as pointed out in chapter 1, is that one person cannot see directly into the mind of another.

In simulative reasoning, a kind currently studied in psychology and artificial intelligence, one reasoner reasons about the reasoning of another reasoner. The one reasoning agent uses his reasoning capability to understand the reasoning of the other agent. He forms a hypothesis about the acts and goals of the other agent, and uses the given (supposedly) factual information of a case to support this hypothesis. This kind of reasoning is abductive. It results in a hypothesis that is only a plausible conjecture at best. But it can be a supposition based on good evidence, in some cases. Character judgments are nevertheless fallible. The plausibility of the judgment is limited by the extent to which such an act of empathy is possible from the shared contexts and the known data in a case. The conclusion drawn from the data, according to the new theory, is based on a plausible inference to the best explanation of the data as appearances that are presumed to be true and accurate in the given case. The case studies in this and the previous chapters have shown how this form of evidence takes the form of an inference to the best explanation based on contextual frameworks, called scripts in artificial intelligence, shared by the two parties. The second party relies on this shared context to simulate the reasoning of the first, and to draw conclusions by inference to the best explanation from observations or reported facts about what the first party did, and how he reacted to events. The support for the conclusion drawn is judged within an evidential network of abductive inferences forming a chain of reasoning in which one inference leads to another.

The theory that will be defended in chapter 4 is that the inference is an abductive one, based on a relation of empathy in which the second person by an act of the imagination inserts himself into what he presumes to be the situation confronted by the first person. According to the theory, one person judges the character of another person by trying to figure out the sequence of actions and goals of that other person as he reacted to the circumstances of his situation. This view appears to be a new, or at least innovative one, for ethics. But it was proposed as early as 1946 by the British archaeologist and philosopher R. G. Collingwood. Collingwood used the notion of "reenactment", in his book, *The Idea of History*, as the basis for his famous theory of historical explanation. This notion has proved puzzling and even mysterious to some commentators. But it has been a source of considerable interest and encouragement to others who wanted to seek out some alternative to the views of positivistic philosophers who tried to reduce historical explanation to deductive and inductive reasoning based on general laws. The main problem is that reenactment still seems (especially to its positivistic critics) to be a highly subjective process. It has remained hard to determine how judgments based on it could be verifiable on the basis of objective evidence and clear reproducible logical reasoning. This empathetic kind of judgment is admittedly imperfect, and is typically one of hindsight in which the evaluator does not have complete access to the original situation. It seems highly subjective, because it requires an act of empathy where one person tries to put herself into the past situation confronted by the other, and second-guess what the other thought.

Collingwood hoped that his theory of reenactment would be the basis of a new science of human studies, showing that the humanities, including history, can be based on a distinctive process of logical reasoning that uses verifiable evidence to support its conclusions. By revealing the logical process of reasoning behind empathy judgments, this book moves Collingwood's theory to a higher level, where it needs to be taken much more seriously by its critics. The new theory of character judgment set out in chapter 4 is based on what is called simulative multi-agent reasoning. In this kind of reasoning one agent, who is familiar with his or her own ways of thinking about practical deliberations, uses this same way of thinking when trying to figure out how and why another agent acted in a certain way. The kind of reasoning used, it is argued, is best seen as abductive, hypothesizing another's internal states of mind by evidence given as data in her external actions and words. The judgment is accomplished by choosing the hypothesis that best explains a person's actions and words in a given case, as far as the reporting of these words and deeds, properly tested, can be presumed to be true and accurate by another person.

Judging another person's character is often useful, and even necessary for activities like writing a biography, writing history, or evaluating legal and ethical arguments about a person's allegedly good or bad character. But it is also filled with all kinds of problems and limitations, often leading to errors, wrong judgments, bias, slander, and rhetorically persuasive but logically weak character attacks. As shown in chapter 1, character judgment is often abused, resulting in character assassination, and idealized, flattering portrayals of heroes in propaganda whose worst qualities of character are hidden or minimized. What the case studies examined so far mainly reveal is limitations in our ability to avoid prejudice and error. What has been shown is that in many cases we are not as good at judging character as we seem to think.

Chapter 4

SIMULATIVE REASONING AND PLAN RECOGNITION

In chapter 3, character was defined as a relationship between the two agents involved. The primary agent is the person whose character is being judged. The secondary agent is the person who is doing the judging. The imperfection in the reasoning used by the latter to arrive at a conclusion about the character of the former derives from several factors. One is that the two agents are not in the same situation. The situation confronted by the primary agent is now a thing of the past. The secondary agent cannot insert herself into that same situation to test herself out, and see what she would do. This imperfection is especially notable in historical judgments of character, where a historian or biographer attempts to reach conclusions about the character of a person who lived in a different age or culture.

A skeptic might use this failure of match to argue that all judgments of character are meaningless, because the judge is simply not in the situation, and is therefore prone to making all kinds of simplistic and erroneous assumptions. And, to be sure, the dangers of bias, or even intentional misrepresentation are all too real. Especially prominent of late are the postmodernists who say that all historical and ethical judgments are subjective, and the secondary agent simply imposes her own bias on a situation by seeing it through her own preconceptions and interests. But rather than being a reason for giving up, this recognition of limitations could be an important first step towards recognizing the empathetic nature of character judgments.

It is fairly clear, from the previous chapters, that making any kind of judgment about the character of a person requires a kind of empathy in which the one agent can make sense of the actions and thinking of another. The one agent has to reason backwards from the given evidence of what took place in a case, and then try to give some sort of explanation of what happened, how it came about, and why the other agent acted the way it did. In order to perform this act of empathy, the one agent has to be able to reenact or simulate the actions and thinking of the other agent. This reasoning about reasoning is now called simulative reasoning in recent studies in artificial intelligence and psychology. In simulative reasoning one person draws conclusions about how another person is (presumably) thinking, based on external observations of what this other person says or does. But what exactly is simulative reasoning, and how is it used where one person calls upon evidence to arrive at a judgment of the character of another? Philosophers have advocated something like the notion of simulative reasoning in the past, and it is best to begin with a review of some of these prior notions.

4.1 Collingwood's Theory of Reenactment

Collingwood (1946, pp. 282–283) introduced his theory of history as the reenactment of past experience in order to answer the question of how the historian can know the past. In order to answer this question, he (p. 282) ruled out several preliminary hypotheses. First, he ruled out the hypothesis that the historian is an eyewitness to the facts he wishes to know about. Second, he ruled out the hypothesis that the historian knows the past simply in virtue of witness testimony. Collingwood argued that the historian does not come to know the past just by believing an eyewitness of the given historical events. He must often compare accounts of witnesses and sometimes even criticize them — this pointing to a third hypothesis. According to this third hypothesis the historian comes to know the past by reenacting it in his own mind.

Collingwood gave the example of a historian reading a document about the past (p. 283). The latter, he says, must "discover what the person who wrote those words meant by them" (p. 282). A specific case he offered (p. 283) was that of a historian reading the Theodosian code, an edict of a Roman emperor. According to Collingwood's account, what the historian must do is to imagine the ancient situation in which the emperor was trying to deal with a given problem. He must see this problem as the emperor saw it himself, just as if he were in the emperor's situation. Of course, it is difficult to make such a mental leap. One would have to know something about the ancient world, and how things were different from the way they are now. So how would such a mental leap take place? According to Collingwood's theory, the process is one of reenactment. The historian must imagine himself as confronting the same problem that the past person saw himself as facing, and must try to formulate solutions to that problem. In Collingwood's words, the historian must see the possible alternatives and the reasons for choosing one possible solution rather than another, just as the historical person did. The historian must duplicate his process of problem solving in order to interpret the document written by the emperor. In Collingwood's view, the historian must go through roughly the same process which the Roman emperor went through in order to understand the reasons why he came to the particular solution of the problem that he came to. This process of reenactment is Collingwood's solution to the epistemological problem of how the historian can come to know the past. The historian must use the process of empathy, or putting himself in the mind of someone who carried out some particular actions in the past. The historian must use this process of empathy in reconstructing the experience of the person in the past and follow through the thinking this past person presumably went through in his process of deliberation.

Collingwood opposed his view of history to the view of it as a mere collection and arrangement of facts. The latter he often called the "scissors-and-paste" view. As he wrote in his autobiography (1939, p. 114), "the scissors-and-paste" exponents think that "people get into the habit of reading books, and then the books put questions into their heads". Collingwood had a different paradigm of historical research. In his view, historical problems arise from practical problems: "We study history in order to see more clearly into the situation in which we are called upon to act" (p. 114). Thus he saw the process of historical investigation as going through several stages. First, the historian faces a practical problem confronted by people in the era in which he writes. He expresses this problem in the form of a question. To answer the question, he looks to history, and to some person in a past era who confronted a similar problem. But the person in the past tried to solve the problem by deliberating on it, and then taking action of some sort. The action taken may have solved the problem or it may have failed. The current situation will not be exactly the same as the past one. The context will be different in many respects. But even so, the past actions taken to solve the past problem may throw light on the current problem. But what is this process of problem-solving that Collingwood alludes to in this theory of reenactment of past events?

Dray (1964, pp. 11–12) explained it as one of goal-directed deliberation.

> Clearly the kinds of thoughts which Collingwood's theory requires are those which could enter the practical deliberations of an agent trying to decide what his line of actions should be. These would include such things as the agent's conceptions of the facts of his situation, the purposes he wishes to achieve in acting, (and) his knowledge of means that might be adopted . . .

Dray (p. 12) described Collingwood's theory of reenactment as essentially resting on a process of "vicarious practical reasoning on the part of the historian". The historical agent is engaged in a process of practical deliberation in trying to decide on a course of action. What appears to be involved is goal-directed practical reasoning. But the historian himself is also an agent who goes through the same process of practical reasoning in his daily life as the historical agent. The two have something in common. It is this common basis of practical reasoning that enables reenactment to take place.

A basic difficulty for Collingwood's theory is that the situation of the historical agent will never be the same as that of the reenacting historian. Hence the best the latter can do is to try to guess what the historical agent was thinking. The historian is in a different era. It is hard for us to imagine, for example, the situation of an ancient Roman emperor. We are apt to make mistakes, and we can never make the guess a perfect fit. As Dray pointed out, this difficulty often made Collingwood's theory appear unattractive. The logical positivists saw historical explanation as a process of logical deduction from historical laws. As Dray (1995, pp. 102–104) described this reaction, the positivists argued that we don't really know why one action was performed rather than another unless the doing of the action follows necessarily from the reasons given. But in Collingwood's theory, the reenactment is a guess. There is a logical leap from deliberations in the original situation to the historian's reconstructed explanation of them based on reenactment. Surely history has to be more than just a process of guessing, the positivist critics say. So, to make Collingwood's theory worth pursuing, there must be understanding of the process of logical reasoning underlying the process of reenactment. How does the historian arrive at a conclusion from given data, taken as evidence, based on some structure of reasoning that can be retraced and evaluated? To try to address the problem, Collingwood (1939, pp. 29–43) proposed his famous theory of historical investigation as a process of question and answer. But this, of course, did not satisfy the positivists, who saw it as just as bad as saying that history is based on a subjective process of guessing. Collingwood's theory of history as reenactment, although boldly imaginative, did not appear to go very far. What was lacking was a systematic and objective analysis of the structure of the logical reasoning used to get from the premises to the conclusions of a reenactment.

4.2 Simulative and Autoepistemic Reasoning

What Collingwood called reenactment in historical explanations, and what is sometimes called empathy, involves a form of reasoning often called "attachment" or "simulation" in artificial intelligence and cognitive science. Typically, simulative reasoning involves two agents. It is a form of meta-reasoning in which an agent reasons about another agent's reasoning. Agent *Y* uses simulative reasoning about agent *X* when *Y*'s reasoning about *X*'s reasoning depends on *Y*'s own reasoning. Simulative reasoning can have more than one stage. For example, consider the statement, "Helen thinks that Bob thinks that she is courageous", or the statement, "Helen thinks that Bob thinks that Hector is courageous". In such cases, several individuals can be involved. But simulative reasoning can also occur within a single agent, in which case, it is a reflexive kind of meta-reasoning. For example, an agent may reconsider the reasoning that it carried out in the past, and reason about that reasoning. Or an agent may question his own beliefs. In so doing, he may have beliefs about his own beliefs.

Simulative reasoning is associated with what are called iterated modalities in modal logic. For example, in the statement "It is possible that it is possible that *A*" (where *A* is a proposition), the modality "it is possible that" is iterated. Doxastic modal logic studies reasoning about beliefs. Iterations of belief of the kind studied in doxastic modal logic occur in formulas of the following form, where *a* is an agent, *p* is a proposition, and *B* is the belief operator.

Formula 1: $B_a B_b p$

The English rendering of this formula is "*a* believes that *b* believes that *p*". Such a formula can be extended through further iterations. For example, suppose we want to express the following sort of statement: *a* believes that *b* believes that *a* believes that snow is white. This statement can be expressed by formula 2, where *p* stands for the statement "Snow is white".

Formula 2: $B_a B_b B_a p$

One thing that has often seemed problematic about such iterations is that they can be expanded to create formulas that are hard to make much sense of, intuitively. For example, consider formula 3 below.

Formula 3: $B_a B_b B_c B_a p$

This formula put into English reads, "*a* believes that *b* believes that *c* believes that *a* believes that *p*'. It may be possible to imagine an interpersonal scenario in which this statement is true: for example, a poker game. But the scenario is so complex that it makes one wonder whether iterated belief modalities can be grasped in any clear way that would systematically make sense. This question leads to another. What practical use, if any, could be made of iterated belief modalities?

One use may be in connection with dialogue systems that are currently being employed to model different aspects of rational argumentation. Quite often, contexts of dialogue occur that involve several participants engaged in group argumentation. Of course, in the simplest case a dialogue involves two participants called the proponent or the respondent. These take turns asking questions and putting forward arguments to each other. But many of the real examples we want to study in dialogue theory involve more than two interacting participants. Consider a trial. The prosecution puts forward arguments that counter or address the arguments of the defense. Similarly, the defense puts forward arguments directed to those of the prosecution. Both employ such arguments to try to persuade the so-called "finder of fact", the judge or the jury. Let's call the finder the judge for ease of exposition. It is impossible to grasp what is going on in such argumentation without being able to grasp expressions like "the prosecution believes that the defense believes that the judge believes that p". This kind of belief iteration might come into play, for example, when one is trying to grasp the prosecution's strategy to counter what it thinks to be a weak argument of the defense.

Another use of iterated modalities is with reference to political argumentation in parliamentary or legislative debates where two opposed parties appear to be arguing against each other's positions. And, in a sense, they are, but if you view what is going on in another way, both will be seen as really trying to impress the voters, who may be watching the debate on television. Here the same kinds of iterations permeate the argumentation.

A notion that has been shown to be very important in argumentation is that of sincerity. An arguer may assert a statement as true, but does he really believe that it is true? There may be no way to know directly, but his sincerity may be tested indirectly. For example, suppose he asserts that a particular policy is a good one, but there is evidence that his own actions in the past appear to have been contrary to that policy. If he is merely a hypocrite, not practicing what he preaches, his argument for the policy might be discounted. In evaluating this kind of argumentation, iterated beliefs could be very important. This can be shown as follows. Assume that the arguer advocating the policy is a and that the agent his argument is addressed to is b. For a's argument to be credible to b, it is necessary that b should believe that a believes that the policy is a good one. Let p represent the statement "The policy is a good one". The doxastic modality underlying the argument can then be expressed in formula 4.

Formula 4: $B_b B_a p$

If b doesn't think that a really believes p, given the evidence of a's past actions, then b could attack a's argument using the circumstantial type of *ad hominem* argument.

Epistemic modal logic studies propositional attitudes of knowing. The basic operator is "a knows that p". This too is a kind of modality that can be self-applied. Such self-applied single-agent simulative reasoning is called autoepistemic reasoning in AI. For example, Socrates was said to be wise because he knew the limitations of his knowledge. He knew that he did not know anything. In contrast, many experts know that they know everything about their field, or think they do. Autoepistemic reasoning is used, in such cases, because the agent is claiming knowledge about his own knowledge. He may claim to know, or not to know, that he knows something, or doesn't know it. An example of iterated autoepistemic reasoning is the following pattern (where *a* is an agent): *a* knows that *a* does not know that *A*. This example shows the characteristic pattern of iteration, because knowing is applied by an agent to his own knowing. Interpersonal agent simulative reasoning also often has this iterated epistemic form. For example, in the statement, "*a* knows that *b* knows that *A*", the knowing is iterated. In interpersonal simulative reasoning, the one agent reasons about the reasoning of a different agent. As noted above, interpersonal simulative reasoning can be complex, as in the statement, "*a* knows that *b* knows that *a* knows that *A*". Even though statements like these seem abstruse, they could apply to real cases. For example, reasoning in espionage often depends on what one spy knows another spy knows. It might even depend on what one spy knows another spy knows that the first spy knows.

Moore (1985, pp. 78–79) illustrated autoepistemic reasoning using the example of his reasons for believing that he does not have an older brother. The reasoning is based on the following inference.

If I did have an older brother, I would know about it.

I don't know of any older brothers.

Therefore, I must not have any older brothers.

This inference appears to have the form *modus tollens*, and as such, is deductively valid. It also has the form of argument commonly known in logic as argument from ignorance (*argumentum ad ignorantiam*). Once thought to be fallacious, this form of argumentation is extremely common in everyday reasoning, and even in science, and is often quite a reasonable form of argument (Walton, 1996). The argument from ignorance is a form of autoepistemic reasoning, and hence a form of simulative reasoning, in which an agent reasons from his own lack of knowledge to a conclusion. What is shown is that simulative reasoning is probably a lot more common in everyday argumentation than you might initially think. We often reason from a basis of what we don't know. And one agent often reasons from a basis of what she believes another agent believes. These simulative arguments are not only reasonable, but have a distinctive logical form. This form is illustrated by Moore's example, above. In it, an agent reasons about its own lack of knowledge, drawing a conclusion as follows.

Form of Argument from Ignorance

If *A* is true, I would know that it is true.

I don't know that *A* is true.

Therefore, *A* is false.

This form of reasoning commonly appears in expert systems. An example from Collins *et al.* (1975, p. 398) illustrates a typical case. Suppose a machine database (an expert system) is highly expert in some domain of knowledge, like rubber production in South America. A user poses the following question to the database: "Is Guyana a major rubber producer?" The machine scans through its database on rubber production in South America, but finds no information at all about Guyana. It reasons that if Guyana were a major rubber producer, it would know that. Since it does not, the machine answers: "Guyana is not a major rubber producer in South America". The autoepistemic reasoning carried out by the machine has the form of the typical argument from ignorance outlined above. Of course, you could say that the machine is just guessing. Argument from ignorance is different from a positive kind of verification in which the fact questioned is actually found in the database. What is shown is that autoepistemic reasoning of the argument from ignorance type is typically plausible reasoning. Its force depends on how complete the database is. Thus, since it is rare that a database is known to be absolutely complete and closed, argument from ignorance is typically a form of guesswork. Based on these kinds of observations, Moore (1985) concluded that autoepistemic reasoning is a species of what is called nonmonotonic reasoning in logic. Nonmonotonic reasoning is reasoning that can default, or turn out to be wrong, when new information is added to a database. Generally, simulative reasoning tends to be a kind of guesswork that can default as new information comes into a case.

4.3 Strategic Use of Simulative Reasoning

There is quite an interest in simulation in the fields of psychology and philosophy of mind. So-called simulation theory has been developed by its exponents as providing a theoretical model to explain human and animal behavior. An early experiment of Premack and Woodruff (1978) will give the reader an idea of how this research developed. In this experiment, a chimp was shown a film of an actor trying to reach for some bananas dangling overhead. The actor was not successful in reaching the bananas. The chimp was then asked to select from various pictures that supposedly represented the actor's next move. The chimp (correctly) selected the picture of the actor moving some crates underneath the bananas. Now the problem is to interpret how the chimp (presumably) reasoned to the (right) conclusion of moving the crates solution. One obvious answer to the question is provided by simulation theory. According to this, the chimp can understand how the actor should solve the problem by putting itself in the actor's place (simulatively), and then imagining how it would solve the problem. The chimp would imagine itself trying to reach for the bananas, and then calling upon its own experience, see itself dragging some crates under the bananas. The other answer to the question is called the theory-theory. According to this, the chimp might not need to simulate anything, but may simply have a general grasp of how practical reasoning works. According to the theory-theory, the chimp reasons that if you want bananas that are out of reach in the way pictured in the film, then the means of achieving that goal is to drag something underneath, to extend your reach by standing on it. According to the theory-theory, no simulation is required, because the chimp is already "hard-wired" to grasp how goal-directed action works, at least in simple situations of the kind it is familiar with.

What exactly is simulation supposed to be, according to the literature in psychology and philosophy of mind? According to the account given by Goldman (1995, p. 189), "simulation" means "pretending to have the same initial desires, beliefs, or other mental states that the attributor's background information suggests the agent has". Goldman (1995, p. 187) cited a psychology experiment in which respondents were asked to judge the state of annoyance or "upsetness" that a person feels in a situation in which she is delayed in traffic and misses her flight departure at the airport. It seems fair to say that simulation theory of the kind typically advocated in the psychological and philosophical literature involves one agent imagining the beliefs and feelings of another agent. This approach seems quite appropriate, of course, for psychology, because the aim there is to explain behavior, including the actual motives, needs, wants and beliefs of subjects, whether human or animal.

The approach in this monograph is different, however. This difference has been explained and referred to several times, but it is worth repeating and emphasizing, because readers, so familiar with the social science viewpoint, keep imposing this viewpoint, or confusing it with the normative and ethical viewpoint adopted here. From the latter viewpoint, one agent tries to judge the ethical qualities of character of another, in a given case, typically a text of discourse describing the facts and actions supposedly true in the case. For this purpose, it is not necessary to judge, or even to determine the actual beliefs, desires or motives of the person in the case. What is necessary is to try to judge the commitments of the agent in the case, as far as one can infer them from the given data in the case. Though commitments do act as a kind of profile of the *persona* or character of the agent, they are not necessarily identical to the actual beliefs of the agent. Agents can be committed to policies, actions or propositions that they do not necessarily believe to be true (Hamblin, 1970; Walton and Krabbe, 1995). What you are committed to is (roughly) what you have gone on record as advocating in the past, according to what can be inferred from your past words and deeds, insofar as these are known (or not known) in a given case.

In this context, simulation means something more modest than it does in the psychology literature on simulation theory. It does not mean trying to recreate or imagine the actual beliefs, feelings or motives of another agent. It only means using your familiarity with kinds of reasoning that you use yourself, like practical reasoning, to draw abductive inferences about the commitments of another agent from the observed or recorded actions of that agent.

Gordon (1986, p. 162) presented an interesting example to show that simulative reasoning is used when one person tries to predict the actions of another person. Chess players report that they often visualize the chessboard from the opponent's point of view. In such an act of the imagination, the chess player sees her pieces as her opponent's pieces, and vice versa. This reversal also entails a reversal of strategy, as noted by Gordon (1986, p. 162): "whereas previously the fact that a move would make White's Queen vulnerable would constitute a reason *for* making the move, it now becomes a reason *against*." This kind of case is interesting, because it shows the strategic or procedural use of simulative reasoning. The chess player performing the simulative reasoning is not trying to duplicate in imagination the actual beliefs or feelings of the other player. All she is trying to do is to put herself strategically into the position of the other player, to see how she herself would develop strategies for planning out future moves in that position. In such a case, the simulative reasoning consists in trying to figure out the reasoning of the other agent. It does not consist in trying to figure out the actual beliefs of the other player, or in trying to imagine how the other player feels, whether he is dejected or elated, for example.

Simulative reasoning depends on a kind of rationality assumption. The secondary agent generally assumes that the primary agent is engaging in the kind of reasoning the secondary agent is familiar with. But the rationality assumption is far from total or perfect. In some cases, the secondary agent may use simulative reasoning to judge that the primary agent is illogical, or irrational, or is committing a logical fallacy. In some cases, the secondary agent may even use simulative reasoning to arrive at the conclusion that the primary agent is contradicting itself. So while simulative reasoning does rest to some extent on a kind of rationality assumption, that assumption is less than perfect or complete. When a secondary agent simulates the reasoning of a primary agent, the former will generally assume that the latter is using

a structurally correct chain of reasoning. But simulative reasoning is often abductive. The secondary agent is seeking a best explanation of the words and deeds of the primary agent in a given case. The best explanation of the data that can be given may be that the primary agent has reasoned illogically, committing a fallacy, or reasoning on the basis of a contradiction. So simulative reasoning does not always require a strict rationality assumption.

When one agent reasons from the reasoning of another agent, the secondary agent may not know everything that the primary agent knows or believes. Quite the contrary, for example, in attempted judgment about the qualities of character of another person, perhaps even someone who may have died a long time ago. In such a case the secondary agent may not in fact be in a good position to know what the primary agent knew or believed about many things. Because of the gap between the situations of the two agents, the secondary agent needs to be aware that his hypothesis is a guess that could turn out to be wrong or inadequate. It doesn't follow, however, that simulative reasoning is useless or inherently erroneous. It is sometimes the best form of reasoning we have, and it can result in an intelligent hypothesis that is based on the factual evidence, as known in a case. Simulative reasoning should be looked at in a balanced way. It can be good reasoning, even if an inherently tentative form of it, subject to correction and improvement as new facts come into a database. What is important is to avoid the extremes of either rejecting it entirely as subjective, or clinging to it dogmatically without being open to critical questioning and new facts found in a case.

4.4 Scripts and Stories

In chapter 2, section 7, it was shown how legal evidence is often presented by witness testimony in the form of a connected account or story (Pennington and Hastie, 1993). Typically, in evaluating the character of a person in biography or history, the body of evidence comes from witness testimony from persons who were familiar with the person. Such evidence consists primarily of a "story", or connected account that purports to describe some actions of the primary agent whose character is being evaluated. This set of data is more than just a set of random facts. It is an account of some incident that hangs together (Pennington and Hastie, 1991). The secondary agent, or evaluator, is presented with this story, which may tell, for example, how the primary agent coped in some difficult situation, and overcame many obstacles. The secondary agent can follow this story, and can appreciate how difficult it would have been for him to cope, if he had been presented with the same difficulties in the same situation. Thus understanding is possible in history because the secondary agent can imagine the problem faced by the first agent, as indicated by Collingwood's theory of reenactment. But the story could be true or fictional. Even if its constituent statements are not true, the secondary agent can follow the story as long as it hangs together as an account of some incident in which action was taken to solve a problem. The important thing is that the secondary agent must be able to "identify" with the actions, situation, and problem of the primary agent. What does it mean to "identify"? It means that the second agent must place himself in the situation of the first, in the way postulated by Collingwood's theory. This process of interpersonal identification between agents requires what is now widely called the property of empathy. The second agent needs to perform an imaginative mental leap, to place himself in the situation confronted by the first agent. Such empathy is the basis not only of historical understanding, but also of fictional literature and character judgments.

For example, suppose the primary agent in the story is the protagonist in an adventure movie. He is shown as being in a mine cave-in. The entrance to the mine has collapsed, and the only way out is by climbing up a narrow claustrophobic passage way full of rats. The other people stuck in the cave are injured or dying, and badly need help. But help is not on the way. Nobody outside the cave knows about the disaster. The agent is injured, and the cave is dark. The obstacles to his saving the others by climbing out are formidable. Nor is it certain that climbing the narrow passageway will get the agent out. But his torch indicates that there is some source of oxygen in the direction, suggesting a possible way out of the cave. Portrayal of this kind of situation is common enough in disaster movies. A good example is *The Poseidon Adventure*. A huge ship overturns, and a small group of survivors is trapped in an air pocket inside the hull. To get out, they must climb over a series of obstacles. A minister, played by Gene Hackman, keeps urging them on, even though they all find it easy to give up hope. In the end, despite many dangerous and difficult obstacles, some of them manage to survive and escape. Others die along the way, trying to help in the escape process.

Let's get back to the case of the agent in the cave — a simpler example. The viewer is presented with the situation in the form of what we are calling a story — a connected account of a sequence of events and actions in which the agent is the central character or protagonist. The agent is shown as persevering against difficult obstacles as he climbs over the racks through the dim and claustrophobic passageway. Despite his injuries, his fears, and his discouragement in an apparently hopeless situation, he manages to get out, and save the other people. What is the reaction of the viewer? Different viewers will react in different ways, but many viewers may be stimulated emotionally and inspired by the story — especially because of the perceived character of the agent in the story. The latter is perceived as having qualities of character that are admirable. The basis for this perception is to be found in two things. First, the story shows the agent as carrying out actions. Second the viewer places herself imaginatively in the situation confronted by the agent, and she realizes how hard it would be for her to go through the same sequence of actions to get out of the cave.

In some cases, such a story may be true, or the viewer may think the incident was real. In other cases, the story may be fictional and the viewer may know this. The figures in the story could even be bizarre, perhaps from other planets. In such a fictional type of case, it may be very evident that the story does not represent real persons or events. The two types of cases need to be judged differently, but it is not the actual truth of the story that is the main ingredient. What the story needs to have is a quality of plausibility or believability so that it hangs together in such a way that it seems to the evaluator as though it could be real. Or at least it should represent events that are somewhat similar to the kinds of situations she finds herself in, or could find herself in. The story must hang together so that connections between actions and events follow normal patterns (Wagenaar *et al.*, 1993). For example, if the agent in the cave slips on a rock and falls, the viewer presumes that the outcome is painful for him, just as it would be if the viewer herself fell on a slippery rock. Some events in the story can be bizarre or unexpected. But over the fabric of the story as a whole, the sequences of events and actions must follow each other and fit together in fairly normal patterns that the viewer is familiar with. In this sense, the story must be coherent.

Evaluations of an agent's character are based on what a person says and does. What a person says can be viewed as speech acts carried out with a partner in dialogue. From this viewpoint then, a person's character is judged by his actions. But a person's intentions — which correspond to an agent's goals in the model of practical reasoning outlined above — are also vitally important. Actions and intentions are bound up together in the practical reasoning carried out by an agent. But how do these observations help in telling us how to properly evaluate a person's character in a given instance?

The answer is that the person's actions in a given case are given to us as a body of data in the form of a story that relates an account of some incident that supposedly took place. The story is seen as a text of discourse that describes what happened. There are typically gaps in the story, or bits of relevant information that are missing, or not known. Once the evaluator gets the story in focus, she reads through it, and understands what she is being told, or not told, in the account. There will be a number of persons or agents who took part in what happened. Let's designate one as the principal agent — the person whose character is at issue. Let's say that in the story, the principal agent was confronted by some problem, say an ethical problem, and the story tells us how he tried to deal with it by taking a number of actions. The evaluator must make sense of this story — that is, she must understand it as a coherent account — before she can evaluate the character of the principal agent. How should this understanding (*verstehen*, as it is often called in the literature on historical explanation) be achieved?

What the evaluator must do is to try to understand the problem faced by the primary agent, and also the actions that he/she took (presumably) in order to try to solve that problem. How can she do this? Simulative reasoning is based on practical reasoning. Collingwood's theory of history as reenactment was advanced further by Martin (1977), who showed that the reenactment requires practical reasoning. The one agent can understand the actions of the other agent because both are practical reasoners. The evaluator is an agent herself. Therefore she understands how the situation in the story was perceived as a problem by the principal agent, and she can understand the various normal steps that can be taken to deal with that kind of problem. Collingwood's theory was much strengthened by its extension by Martin. The reenactment is shown to be possible because the secondary agent can make sense of the actions of the primary agent as goal-directed. The secondary agent can then make abductive inferences from the primary agent's actions to the primary agent's goals. But even more is needed to make the theory of reenactment adequate to explain interpersonal agent judgments. How can one agent understand enough about the situation of another to grasp a problem, and how the other agent tried to solve it?

The answer lies in what are called "scripts" in artificial intelligence — background blocks of contextual shared information of a kind not explicitly stated in a story, but which speaker and hearer both take as part of the information given by it (Schank, 1986). The classic example is the restaurant story, in which a person, let's call him Bob, went into a restaurant, ate a hamburger, and then left. Let's say that's all we are told in this story. We can all easily fill in a lot of gaps, or quite plausible missing steps, in the sequence of actions said to have taken place. For example, we can infer that Bob probably sat down, that he probably ordered the hamburger before he ate it, that he paid something for it, and that he got up and walked to the exit after he had finished eating. Now in fact, it is possible that none of the unstated actions actually took place. But we can guess that they probably did, and it would be a good guess — a reasonable presumption, in the absence of any evidence to the contrary. What is the basis for drawing such probable inferences to fill in the gaps in the story? It is that we are all familiar with the so-called restaurant script — that is, with the way things normally proceed when you go to a restaurant and eat something there. You normally sit down, then a waiter comes, or you order the food in some way, then you eat the food, then you pay for it, then you leave. Many other gaps in the sequence of actions could also be filled in; because all of us as agents are familiar with these stereotypical types of actions, we can understand what another agent is doing when we hear a story relating his actions in such a situation. The script is the tacit background information that can be filled in as plausible presumptions based on the normal ways of doing some kind of action that we are all familiar with as agents.

An abductive inference used in a historical explanation or a character judgment is not just based on a given set of facts or data, as indicated in the form of abductive reasoning presented by the Josephsons. It is also based on a script attached to the explicitly given set of statements. The script itself is not explicitly stated. It is an element common to the primary agent and the secondary agent that can be used by the latter to fill in gaps in the explicitly stated account. Missing premises in the chain of abductive reasoning are derived from the script. The script is the common nonexplicit knowledge shared by the primary agent and the secondary agent.

There are limits on reenactment in historical judgments, because the primary agent may be acting in a different historical period, or in a different culture from that of the secondary agent (Martin, 1977, pp. 215–240). The script may be thinner in such cases. Reenactment becomes more speculative in such cases, the possibility of bias and errors of abductive inference are greater, and the conclusions drawn tend to be weaker. On the other hand, historical objectivity is likely to be greater if the secondary agent is somewhat removed from the situation and historical period of the primary agent. Despite these differences, a secondary agent will always share some common understanding with a primary agent, in virtue of the fact that both are agents. Also, there will be many other common elements. Even in very different historical periods or cultures, many kinds of actions and routines are the same or very similar.

4.5 Simulative Practical Reasoning

The normal and familiar way of carrying out certain types of actions is called a routine (Segerberg, 1985). A routine is an orderly sequence of actions that hang together as the normal way of carrying out some task that an agent is familiar with. For example, when I get up in the morning, I have a normal shaving routine that is so familiar I hardly have to think much about it. I put some lather on my lower face, and then scrape it off with a razor. But if you break the routine down into all of its small steps, it is a fairly complicated and lengthy process. First, I have to wash my face with hot water, to prepare the skin. In order to do that I have to turn the tap on. To turn the tap on I have to manipulate the faucet handle a certain way. To do that, I have to put my hand on the faucet handle, and move my fingers. Then after the whole washing routine, I have to go into the lather routine. I have to reach into the medicine cabinet and get out the can of lather. And so on and so forth. Telling all of the little details of the routine is quite a lengthy story. This complexity of everyday actions came as quite a shock at first to those who designed robots to carry out tasks normally carried out by human agents. The actions seem very simple, on the surface, because we are all so intimately familiar with them as agents. But when you have to make a machine carry out such actions, you start to realize all the small intervening steps, since the machine must be programmed to carry them out. As shown below, AI has dealt with the problem, in fields like robotics and planning, by breaking the sequence of actions down into a so-called hierarchy.

When confronted with a story, or account of some actions in a particular case, some information is explicitly given in the story, but then other information needs to be filled in on the basis of scripts and plausible reasoning. Intentions and character qualities are generally more difficult to reconstruct than actions. Actions are spatio-temporal events that can be observed by witnesses, and can be verified by empirical evidence. Intentions are internal to a person. The best another person can do is to make guesses or assumptions about what a given person intended to do when he carried out a certain action. Reenactment is really a process of guessing. As has so often been emphasized in philosophy by the so-called "problem of other minds", you can't directly see what is going on in another person's mind. You can only infer what his thoughts are, or in particular, what his intention presumably was, in a given case. The process of inference is abductive, but as shown above, even though abduction is guessing, it can be based on verifiable or falsifiable evidence. Judging the presumed intentions of another party is a form of guessing. But there can be good evidence about intentions. There are hard cases, but there are also easy cases. A person may declare his intentions, for example, or may act in a way that makes his intentions very clear. If a person goes through all the normal motions of cutting down a tree with his chain saw, for example, it may be reasonable to assume that his intention was to cut down the tree. That conclusion could turn out to be wrong, but there could be a lot of very good evidence in favor of it as a reasonable hypothesis.

Still, even though drawing conclusions about what somebody intended to do in a given case can be based on good evidence, inferring about what somebody else was thinking has often been portrayed as a subjective and even mysterious process. The oft-repeated question is always there. How can you know what is really going on inside someone else's mind? Despite the apparent mystery, though, it is a kind of reasoning we perform all the time in everyday life and in practical matters. In fact, we could not have any kind of really collaborative teamwork in daily activities of many kinds without constantly engaging in this process. It's something we are fairly good at. But how does it really work? To get closer to understanding the process of reasoning involved, the notion of empathy has to be even more carefully analyzed.

How does simulative practical reasoning work? First of all, in line with the previous analysis of the concept of an agent, this can be seen as based on a relation between two agents. One agent is familiar with the routines of the other. The concepts of routines and scripts also introduce elements important for such shared understanding. But for positivists, who want to base all reasoning on empirical data, reasoning based on reenactments and scripts still seems mysterious, because one person can never, directly at least, have the same experiences, or share the same thoughts as another. The problem is how we can communicate at all, or have a common basis of experience, if each of us sees things differently. If the skeptic is right, and if our own individual experiences are, in some important sense, private, and unique to each individual, how can one mind grasp the thoughts that are private to another mind?

Any analysis of simulative reasoning must begin from this skeptical premise. The truth is that we can't see or feel directly what another person is seeing or feeling. Experiences, thoughts and feelings are individual. But we can make assumptions about how another party would also react. One reason is that we are similar, to some extent, to other persons in how we see things and in what we know and think. Another reason is that we find ourselves in similar kinds of situations. Still another reason is that we react to these situations, based on what we know and think, in similar ways. Of course, these assumptions about similarity are just guesses or hypotheses that could be wrong in some cases. But they can also be highly plausible in some cases, and therefore tenable enough to warrant drawing logically reasonable conclusions from them. The conclusion drawn on a basis of simulative reasoning is only an assumption or hypothesis. But it can be useful because it has explanatory power as a hypothesis. Such reasoning is typically based on what is called an abductive inference, or inference to the best explanation.

It is generally assumed that empathy is a mysterious and subjective process that is highly intuitive and emotional in nature. It seems to follow from this assumption that it is not based on any kind of logical reasoning. The assumption is that emotion and logical reasoning are separate realms. It is true that when one person makes a character judgment, or tries to explain the intentions of another person, the process of reasoning is only a guess or hypothesis, that cannot be proved beyond doubt. But as the structure of abductive and simulative reasoning comes to be better and better understood, inferences based on empathy will begin to seem much less mysterious.

4.6 Plan Recognition

The theory of planning in AI is built around practical reasoning used in a projective manner. In the theory, it is assumed that there exists an agent who has a goal. The goal is represented by an abstract proposition of the kind that could be made true by some actions. In planning, the agent assesses a given situation to look for one or more sequences of possible actions that could lead to the goal (Wilensky, 1983, p. 5). For example, the STRIPS planner (Fikes and Nilsson, 1971) viewed planning as having three stages. The first stage is an initial state of the world, the second stage is a set of operators that transform one state into another, and the third stage is the ultimate goal state to be achieved. The problem was to figure out what sort of operators and transformations could lead sequentially from the initial state to the goal state. Early planning systems attempted to use sequences of deductive inferences, familiar from traditional methods of theorem-proving in logic. But this early work was not very successful because it encountered the frame problem. The frame problem is that the planner must not only formulate all the changes in the world at any given point as the plan proceeds, but must also formulate all the factors that remain unchanged (Carberry, 1990, p. 23). Such a formulation is impossible, because there are endless lists of things that must remain unchanged. It needs to be assumed that in each step taken in carrying out a plan, the world must be closed temporarily by provisional fiat. But once an action is carried out, things may change. So the inference at that stage must be open to reconsideration. The future is uncertain, and as a plan is put into action, the world changes. It seems then that some kind of reasoning more flexible than deductive logic is required in planning.

Another central problem in planning in AI arises from the necessity for a planning agent to collaborate with other agents in group plans requiring teamwork. To plan together, one agent must be able to share a plan with another agent. It is extremely useful for this purpose that one agent should be able to recognize the plan of another. Typically this problem of plan recognition arises where one agent sees or is informed about the actions carried out by another agent. The first agent must then try to infer, from the given data, what the plan of the second agent is. Carberry (1990, p. 17), defined the central task of plan recognition as one agent having to attempt "to reconstruct from the available evidence a plan that was previously constructed by another agent". The word "attempts" here is significant. In plan recognition in any realistic case, the one agent draws a plausible conclusion form the observed data. The conclusion could turn out to be wrong, as more data come in. But even though it should not be regarded as conclusive, the inference to that conclusion could be reasonable. Carberry presented the example of a motorist who sees an empty car with a missing tire parked on the highway. As she drives further, she sees a man rolling a tire, carrying a baby, and leading three small children. Based on this data, the motorist could plausibly infer that the stranded car belonged to this man.

Furthermore, she might infer that the man was taking the tire to be fixed. Thus the motorist would impute a certain intention to the man rolling the tire. She might impute other intentions to him as well. For example, she might infer that the man was afraid to leave the children alone in the car. This inference could be drawn by abductive inference. She sees the children following the man, and hypothesizes that he has told them to follow him. What is especially interesting about plan recognition is that one agent draws inferences about the presumed goals and other internal states of a second agent. And it would appear that, in order to deal with the frames problem, such inferences should often be seen as abductive rather than deductive.

Research on expert systems and intelligent tutoring systems in computer science has made it necessary to deal with plan recognition. An experiment with question-answering systems (Cohen *et al*., 1981, p. 247) showed that users "expect the system to infer and to respond to their apparent but unstated goals". But how could an automated system be programmed to draw such inferences and base responses on them? The method recommended by Schmidt *et al.* (1978) was to draw the inferences by making warranted assumptions based on scripts, or normal expectations in familiar situations. For example, if the agent enters a store, the system infers that the agent intended to buy something. However, their method also contained "wait and see strategy" that could activate a "revision critic". Suppose, for example, that the agent went into the store, went to the washroom, and left the store without buying anything. This data suggests retracting the inference to the conclusion that the agent had a goal of buying something. What an automated system needs, then, is an abductive inference engine for drawing defeasible inferences about the goals of an agent. By this means it can respond to questions based on plausible hypotheses about the user's assumed goals, but can then cancel such a hypothesis when the user inputs information that indicates his goal was not what it initially appeared to be. Automated question-answering systems also have the feature of allowing a user or the system to ask questions for clarification. If there is doubt or apparent ambiguity about a user's goals, the system can be prompted to ask for clarification. It can simply ask the user what his goal is. Thus resources are available for carrying out systematic techniques of plan recognition for computer systems using natural language dialogue. The system can use practical reasoning to derive goals from the given data regarding how the user speaks and acts. By practical reasoning, the system can track a user's known actions back to his assumed goals, based on scripts and normal expectations of how things go in familiar situations. The system can also ask questions if confronted with problems or apparent contradictions in these data. It would appear then that simulative practical reasoning is not only possible, but can also be realized in automated systems using plan recognition.

4.7 Characteristics of Simulative Practical Reasoning

Simulative practical reasoning has six distinctive characteristics, each of which represents an identifiable aspect of the reasoning used in the process whereby one party draws a conclusion based on observing the actions (and possibly also the speech actions) of another party. First of all such reasoning is based on a distinctive kind of premise. This premise describes or cites appearances — how things seem to be in the situation of one agent, as seen and interpreted by a second. The premise describes things not necessarily the way they really are, but rather as they seem to an observer. This observer is one participant in the process of reasoning. But a second party is necessarily involved as well.

A second characteristic of the reasoning is that it is based on plausible inferences drawn by the secondary agent. These inferences are used by the latter to draw conclusions about what is going on in the situation, and how this may be assumed to be affecting the deliberations of the primary agent. The first characteristic of the reasoning comprises the situation the primary agent is seen to be in, how he acts in that situation, and what other events are observed to occur. This factor is the external given data observed by or known to the secondary agent. The second characteristic of the reasoning comprises the conclusions drawn by abductive reasoning by the secondary agent, based on the given data. The premises of the abductive reasoning are representations of propositions that seem to be true. The abductive inferences are drawn to conclusions from these premises or given data. But such inferences rest on another basis as well, which now needs to be recognized.

A third characteristic of the reasoning is that the first party is typically in a kind of situation that the second party recognizes as familiar in certain respects. What this implies is that the second party can generally expect things to occur in patterns that are normal and familiar to both him and the first party. When the second party draws plausible inferences from observing a situation in which a first party is acting, much use is made of expectations about the way things can normally be expected to go. For example, suppose that I drive past and see you beside your car at a parking meter, fishing around in your pocket with an exasperated look on your face. I know that when anyone parks their car in a downtown area, they normally have to put coins in the meter. I know from familiar experience that there may be uncertainty about whether you have the required coins when you need to park your car. Because it is such a familiar situation, I can understand what you are trying to do, and I can appreciate your reaction to the situation. This part of the premissary base of the reasoning is not given in explicitly stated propositions. It is not observed directly. It is inferred by the shared knowledge called a script.

A fourth characteristic of simulative practical reasoning is that the process typically goes backwards (abductive reasoning) from the observed actions of an agent to presumed goals of that agent. If I see you fishing around for coins in your pocket, in the parking situation above, I assume that your goal is to get the coins and to put them in the meter. I assume that your goal is to park your car without getting a parking ticket. Of course, your goal might be something else altogether, and the hypothesis I make about your likely or plausible goal is just a guess. But given your actions, and the situation, I can infer from what I see that it is reasonable to assume that your goal is to park your car without getting a ticket. This kind of inference is possible because practical reasoning connects goals with actions taken to be the means to attain these goals. Each of us grasps practical reasoning individually, in carrying out actions ourselves. So we can also apply this skill to understanding the actions of another party who, we presume, is engaged in the same kind of process of practical reasoning.

The fifth characteristic of a simulative practical reasoning process is that of analogy, or the closeness of one situation to that of another familiar type. All of us can empathize with some person, for example, who is stuck in a dilemma or difficult situation, to the extent that we ourselves have been in a similar situation. For example, when I see the situation of a teenager who has difficulty sticking to his studies when there are many distractions, I can empathize very well, because I can easily recall my own problems with studying for exams during that difficult period of my life. So empathy is based on analogy — on the similarity between one situation and another.

It follows that there are degrees of empathy, depending on the closeness of match between one situation and another. Degree of empathy will also be dependent on the similarity of one person to another. In historical explanations, conclusions drawn by a primary agent about a secondary agent from a different historical period will be more open to failure. According to Schank (1986, pp. 6–11), there is a spectrum of empathy, and what he calls "complete empathy" is at one end of it. Complete empathy is defined by Schank (p. 6) as "the kind of understanding that might obtain between twins, very close brothers, very old friends, and other such combinations of very similar people". At the other end of the spectrum is a point Schank calls "making sense", where the situation of one party can be interpreted by another "in terms of a coherent (although probably incomplete) picture of how those events came to pass" (p. 6). Complete empathy exists when two individuals have many shared experiences already in memory (p. 9). But there will be many cases where empathy is less than complete, and where, therefore, the conclusions drawn by one party about how the other party thinks or feels are more conjectural in nature.

What these observations reveal is that conclusions drawn on the basis of simulative reasoning are always conjectures based on assumptions of various kinds, and the form of reasoning is based on how well the second agent can grasp the situation faced by the first. But it does not follow that such arguments are always weak and untrustworthy. In some cases, empathetic inferences may be very weak as arguments, because the basis for comparison and shared experiences between two persons or two situations is slim. In other cases, however, a simulative inference can be quite strong. It can be a basis of support that provides an argument that is more than just a guess or mere assumption. The reasoning can be evaluated as weaker or stronger in different cases depending on how well the premises are supported by the appearances in the case, and on how strong the reasoning is from these premises to the conclusion drawn.

The sixth characteristic of simulative practical reasoning is that it can be reflexive or autoepistemic. In such a case, a single agent reasons about his own thinking. Such single-agent cases may seem to refute the hypothesis that simulative reasoning is interpersonal and dialogical in nature. But in autoepistemic simulative reasoning, a single agent is really taking on two dialectical roles. At one level he is engaged in deliberation. At a higher level, when he tries to think about his own practical reasoning, he is moving to a different dialogue. Thus special advantage of reflexivity may be more of an obstacle than a benefit to making character judgments. For example, it is quite difficult for someone to make the claim "I am courageous", and try to prove it objectively. Even making the claim seems to present evidence that undercuts its plausibility. On balance, then, it is best to see cases of autoepistemic reasoning as cases where a single agent is performing two roles in two different dialogues. It's not as different from multi-agent simulative reasoning as it may appear to be. At any rate, subsequent chapters will bear out this approach to autoepistemic reasoning. According to the analysis in this book it is not just an iteration of beliefs, but a nesting of dialogues.

4.8 Combination of Simulative and Abductive Reasoning

How simulative reasoning is combined with abductive reasoning can be shown by considering any case of character judgment. The secondary agent is confronted with a set of data in the form of an account of some actions carried out by the primary agent. The primary agent is said to be in a kind of situation requiring action, or a decision to act, in order to solve some problem or carry out some goal. The secondary agent may recognize some pattern of reasoning evidently being used to solve the problem the primary agent confronts in the given situation. For example, the primary agent is standing in front of a burning house, and has just been told there is a baby inside. How can the secondary agent grasp the nature of the decision problem in this case? He can do it by simulation. He can place himself in the position of the primary agent in that situation. The dilemma is evident to him. In that situation, he would face a choice. Should he rush into the house and try to perform the worthy act of saving the baby alleged to be in there? Or should he stay where he is, with no risk of injury or death? The consequences could be pretty bad, for himself or for the baby, either way. By seeing himself in this dilemma, the secondary agent can grasp the problem faced by the primary agent. He does not need to know, or try to estimate how she feels or what she believes. Just by grasping the practical parameters of the situation conveyed by the facts of the case, he understands the problem she faces. This understanding is achieved by simulative reasoning. Because the secondary agent is an agent, he can grasp the problem faced by the primary agent.

Suppose the facts of the case are extended. The primary agent, Mary, runs into the house and, in fact, saves the baby. The secondary agent, Mike, can now offer a highly plausible explanation of what happened. That explanation is based on practical reasoning. The explanation is that Mary went into the burning house in order to save the baby, and was successful in carrying out that presumed goal. There could be other explanations of what happened, but all else being equal, this one may be the one that best fits the known facts of the case. In such a case, Mike can put forward the hypothesis that Mary is courageous. This hypothesis may be supported or undermined by other new facts that may enter the case. For example, suppose Mike finds out that Mary may have fled a dangerous scene in other cases. Or suppose Mike learns that Mary bragged that she went into the house to get publicity. Any new information of this sort entering the case would be relevant to the claim that Mary is courageous. It might be evidence counting against the claim that she is courageous (or it might not be, depending on the whole mass of evidence in the case). But in the absence of such countervailing evidence, the single act of entering the burning house to save the baby would count towards showing that Mary is courageous.

The secondary agent uses simulative reasoning to grasp the problem faced by the primary agent. He understands the choice she faces. Once she acts, he can use inference to the best explanation. He attributes a certain goal to her. He concludes that the best explanation of her conduct is that she went into the burning house to save the baby. Maybe this hypothesis is false. Maybe Mary went into the burning house to try to win a bravery award, and didn't really care about the baby at all. But in the absence of evidence indicating that explanation, Mike can infer that it is plausible that she went into the burning house to save the baby. By abduction, he can then draw

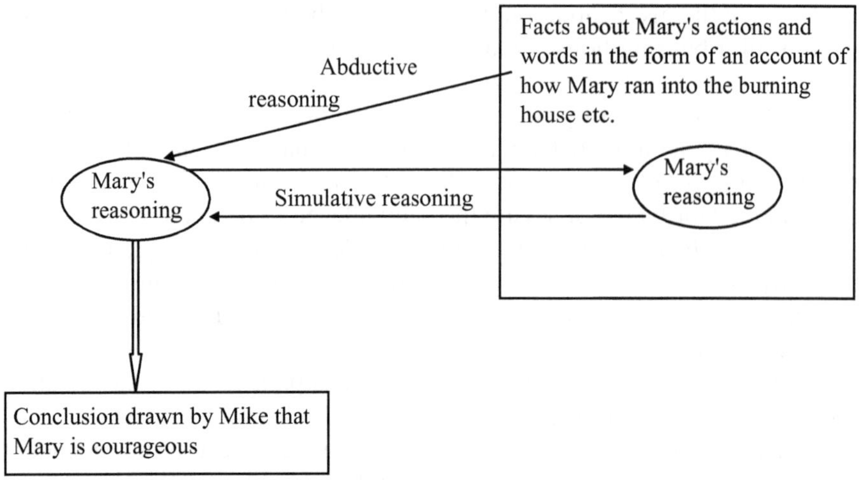

Figure 4.1. Mike's abductive and simulative reasoning concluding that Mary is courageous.

a plausible conclusion about her goal, judging by the evidence of her actions in the given situation. So it can be seen that the kind of reasoning used by the secondary agent in a case like this one is both simulative and abductive. An outline of the structure of Mike's reasoning is given in Figure 4.1.

The reasoning represented in Figure 4.1 combines simulative reasoning with abductive reasoning in the same case. This case may be taken as typical of the way simulative and abductive reasoning are often combined in many cases where an ethical quality of character is attributed to one agent by another. There is a clearly defined pathway of reasoning, in such cases, from the given set of facts in the case to the ultimate conclusion. It is a kind of backwards reasoning from the given facts to a best explanation of those facts, based on the secondary agent's ability to place himself in the situation faced by the primary agent, and to duplicate the practical reasoning that she (presumably) went through.

Simulative reasoning can have various uses. One of these, stressed by Gordon (1986, pp. 161–163), is predicting the behavior of another person. Another is taking the known past behavior of another person, and drawing a plausible conclusion about it, based on abduction or inference to the best explanation. Quite often, in such a case, the data are the observed or recorded actions of the other person, and the conclusion drawn is to some presumed intention or goal of that other person. To distinguish between these two uses of simulative reasoning, the terms "prediction" and "retrodiction" could be used. Prediction involves inference from the past to the future. Retrodiction involves inference from the past facts to propositions that are presumptions about what took place, and that may help to explain it. Retrodiction is very important both in history and in criminal law, where the event that allegedly took place is in the past. The problem is then to try to assign responsibility, or to impute a motive, for an act that may have happened a long time ago. What one does is to try to assemble a body of facts. In law this process is called fact-finding. One must then try to draw inferences from the facts. Although this distinction between fact-finding and inferring is more familiar in law and history, it is also characteristic of ethical reasoning. It is especially significant in cases of character judgments in ethics. But it is also used in cases of trying to judge responsibility for individual actions.

4.9 Abstraction and Chaining

To make simulative and abductive reasoning work in a given case of character judgment, some other features of the reasoning are required. One is the notion of levels of abstraction. Take the case of Mary and Mike. Mike concludes, using simulative and abductive reasoning from the given data, that Mary is courageous. But, to carry out the reasoning required to get from the data to the conclusion, Mike needs to start with some sort of abstract definition of "courage". Let's say that he adopts a definition like the following: an agent is courageous if that agent persists in carrying out, or trying to carry out a worthy goal in the face of obstacles that pose danger for her, or at any rate of something that would be highly painful or difficult, like likelihood of personal injury or even death. It might be added that courageous action typically involves altruism, so that the worthy goal is not just selfish, and involves giving up selfish interests to help others. This definition is abstract. Fitting it onto a specific instance might be straightforward in some cases (so-called easy cases), but highly problematic and contentious in others (so-called hard cases). Also, as noted in the chapter on courage, there can be controversy about exactly how courage should be defined as a cardinal virtue. But whatever definition is adopted, some sort of abstract definition is required if the abductive and simulative reasoning used in a particular case is to arrive at a character judgment based on clear evidence.

In the theory of planning in AI, the complexity of actions is dealt with by specifying a plan at varying levels of abstraction. For example, at an abstract level, Bob's goal may be to find something to eat. But then suppose he sees a diner. He may now form a more specific goal of trying to find something to eat in the diner. To achieve this goal, he enters the diner. In order to do this he must move his feet. A plan can thus be seen as a hierarchy of goals, subgoals and actions, all connected in a sequence. Representing plans in a hierarchical structure, with the most abstract goals at the top and the most specific actions at the bottom, is a common technique in AI. Russell and Norvig, (1995, p. 368) give the example of launching a spacecraft, quite an abstract goal. There might be many intermediate levels of subgoals, like preparing the booster rocket, preparing the capsule, and loading the cargo. At the bottom of the hierarchy are specific actions, like inserting a bolt into a hole and fastening it with a nut. The hierarchy is seen as moving forward from abstract goals to specific actions. As noted above, plan recognition uses the same hierarchy, but in a reverse order. The notions of forward and backward reasoning have been important since the beginning of recent work in AI. Reasoning forward was explained by Barr and Feigenbaum (1981, p. 23) as bringing a "situation, or problem state, forward from its initial configuration to one satisfying a goal condition". They gave the example of a game of chess (p. 23). The initial situation is the placement of the chessmen before the game starts. The abstract goal is winning the game by producing a checkmate. But specific moves transforming the initial configuration of the chess pieces are the actions that can lead to the fulfillment of this goal. In reasoning backwards, the abstract goal statement is converted into specific subgoals that may be easier to solve (p. 23). In reasoning backwards, a player might consider a particular move, and try to see how it links up with the goal of winning. When one agent draws an inference about the character of another agent, a simulative kind of reasoning backwards is used.

In any given case of character judgment, there will be the given data of the case, in the form of an account, or set of empirical statements, describing some actions and events that supposedly occurred. These will be relatively specific, not highly abstract. At the other end, there will be the abstract definition of the quality of character at issue in the case. What is then required is a chaining of inferences connecting up the abstract definition to the specific data of the case. Inferences like the following are used to fill this gap.

If someone runs into a burning house, this person is taking a strong risk that he or she will be painfully and badly injured, and might even die.

Mary ran into the burning house (in this case).

Therefore, Mary was taking a strong risk (in this case) that she would be painfully injured, or might even die.

The first premise is a relatively abstract statement that is linked to the definition of courage in a clear way (because courage is defined in terms of taking risks of painful injury or even death). On the other hand, it is a partially concrete statement that links to the facts of the given case (by containing the fairly specific action of running into a burning house in the antecedent of the conditional). The inference links the abstract to the specific or concrete data of the case. A chain of inferences of this sort links the given data of the case, at one end, to the abstract definition of the term "courage" at the other end of the chain. Without working out all the intervening steps, it is not hard to visualize how the chain works.

4.10 Defeasible Reasoning

One factor that requires comment is the defeasible nature of the reasoning used in such a chain. The first premise in the above inference is a conditional. But it is not what we might call an absolute conditional. It is more like a rule of thumb that is subject to qualifications and exceptions in particular cases. To see why, consider a qualified form of the conditional, as expressed below.

If someone runs into a burning house, and that person is not wearing protective fireproof gear, including breathing equipment, he or she is taking a strong risk that he or she will be painfully and badly injured, and might even die.

Various qualifications, like the one inserted above, are ways of linking the abstract parts of the chain of reasoning to the specific data of a given case. The chain of reasoning is not made up of deductive inferences containing universal quantifiers or absolute conditionals. An absolute conditional is one where it is logically impossible for the antecedent to be true and the consequent false. A universal quantifier, of the kind used in deductive logic, forms a generalization that is falsified by one contrary instance. Very often at least, the conditional and quantifiers used in chains of abductive and simulative reasoning in character judgments are not of that form. They are subject to qualifications linking the abstract generalizations and conditional to the specific data of a case. They are defeasible conditionals that hold generally, but are subject to exceptions.

There is quite a bit of evidence that Aristotle was well aware of the distinctive status of such conditionals, and was aware, too, that the plausibilistic reasoning based on them is different from deductive reasoning. There is evidence that what Aristotle called the enthymeme (*enthymema*) has been systematically misinterpreted in logic textbooks for over two thousand years. A most convincing case has been made by Burnyeat (1994). A typical modern logic textbook will define an enthymeme as a syllogism with one or more missing premises. The example given by Sir William Hamilton is the argument, "Cassius is a liar, therefore Cassius is a coward".[1] The

[1]The example is from Burnyeat (1994, p. 3), who cited Sir William Hamilton's *Lectures on Logic*, Lecture XX.

implicit premise is supposedly the universal statement, "All liars are cowards". Once completed by filling in this premise, the syllogism is valid. To say it is valid means that it is logically impossible for the premises to be true and the conclusion false. But is this a good interpretation of Hamilton's example? Possibly not, because it is not very plausible to contend that all liars, without exception, are cowards. The most one could say is that generally one can expect liars to be cowards, subject to exceptions. The suspicion raised by such examples is that Aristotle did not define an enthymeme as a syllogism with an unstated premise or premises, and that he meant something else by it. Burnyeat argues convincingly that what Aristotle really meant by enthymeme is a defeasible sort of argument that is not intended to be deductively valid, but only plausible. Much of the controversy turns on the famous sentence in the Prior Analytics (70a10): "An enthymeme is an incomplete (*ateles*) argument (*syllogismos*) from likelihoods or signs".[2] The term *syllogismos* does not just mean syllogism, but can refer to any sort of reasoning. Arguments from "likelihood" can be taken to refer to plausible arguments, and not to probability in the modern statistical sense. The controversy is whether the term "incomplete" was really written by Aristotle or written in by subsequent commentators. If the latter is true, as Burnyeat argues, Aristotle may have meant something quite different by "enthymeme" than what logical tradition has held for so long. The implications of this for the history of logic are sweeping, and the implications for the study of character evidence are fundamental.

Aristotle gave a number of examples of inferences based on a major premise that is a generalization that is true, or held to be true, not universally but only "for the most part". One of the most interesting examples of such an enthymeme presented by Aristotle, and cited by Burnyeat (1994, p. 25), concerns the following kind of inference: if an agent wished to carry out a certain action, and there was no external obstacle, then the agent carried out that action. This particular inference could be categorized in modern AI as a simple instance of forward reasoning in planning. The agent has a goal of carrying out a certain action. There is no obstacle to the agent's carrying out this goal. Therefore he carries it out. It is a simple instance of practical reasoning. But once this example has been presented, and analyzed as a forward-moving inference from goal to action, it could also be turned around. It could be used to suggest how backward reasoning from action to goal has the same plausibilistic structure. Burnyeat (1994, p. 25) maintained that Aristotle did not give a syllogistic reconstruction of this inference, or see it as based on logical necessity. Instead, he saw it (p. 24) as a plausible inference based on a generalization that is subject to exceptions and true

[2] This account is a paraphrase of the translation given by Burnyeat (1994, p. 6).

"only for the most part". If Burnyeat is right, Aristotle was aware that when one agent reasons about how another agent reasons from a goal to carrying out an action, the second agent uses a special kind of reasoning that is plausible and defeasible in nature, and is distinctively different from deductive reasoning. If this interpretation is right, defeasible, plausible reasoning is not a modern invention of AI, but it had roots in Aristotle. Or at least the defeasible nature of simulative reasoning was recognized as being distinct from deductive reasoning based on logical necessity. Of course, such reasoning only concludes in a hypothesis or suggestion on what an agent's internal states or goals might be. Its fallibility may be the reason why it was long marginalized, ignored, and even discredited throughout the history of logic.

Barnden (1995, p. 248) has indicated how findings in AI have tended to confirm that simulative reasoning "comes up merely with suggestions about what an agent might conclude". According to Barnden, it is characteristic of recent work in AI to link simulative reasoning with common sense models of reasoning that put a strong emphasis on its defeasibilty. It seems fair to say that much recent work in AI sees simulative reasoning as a kind of plausible reasoning in which the secondary agent arrives at a conclusion that is no more than a plausible hypothesis or guess about what the primary agent is thinking. However, the fact that the conclusion is treated as a hypothesis that might be wrong, does not mean that it has been arrived at by pure blind luck, or that it is just an unintelligent guess, not based on evidence and logical reasoning. With abductive reasoning, there are generally several hypotheses that can fit the data of a case, but some will be more plausible than others. This kind of reasoning can default, but it can also be based on good evidence that supports tentative acceptance of a conclusion.

Plausible reasoning is now widely accepted in AI as a legitimate type of reasoning, different from deductive and inductive reasoning. But in ethics, there has long been an unfortunate tendency to reject anything that does fit deductive or inductive models as "subjective" and therefore worthless. This sort of assumption strongly supports the noncognivist viewpoint in ethics. Stevenson, for example, assumes a sharp separation between facts and values. Disagreement about facts, it is assumed, can be resolved by evidence while disagreements about values are merely emotional. If I like chocolate ice cream and you don't, on Stevenson's view, then no factual evidence is relevant to our disagreement, and that's the end of the matter. Someone with the Stevenson view would conclude that disagreements about judgments of character are not based on factual evidence, and are mere disagreements of subjective opinion. But once it has been revealed how to link the reasoning from an ethical character judgment to a set of facts or given data in a case, the noncognivist viewpoint is refuted. Character judgments are verifiable and falsifiable by a chain of reasoning based on the facts of a given case.

Of course, they are only hypotheses. And they are based on simulative reasoning that is only a form of plausible conjecturing or guessing. But so is most of our common sense reasoning that we rely on all the time in practical affairs of life, in disciplines like law and history, and even in a good deal of scientific reasoning (at the discovery stage). With the acceptance of modes of plausible reasoning, like simulative reasoning and abductive reasoning, much of logical positivism tends to fade into implausibility. But the key point here is that character judgment is shown to be based on a chain of logical reasoning combining factual data with abstract definitions and rules that can be clearly formulated. It is not subjective in the way that so many noncognivists, emotivists, relativists, and other vocal critics have so often claimed in the past.

Chapter 5

MULTI-AGENT DIALOGUE

This chapter sets out a multi-agent dialogue structure for evaluating judgments of character using abductive reasoning. A first agent puts forward a hypothesis to explain the actions and other relevant facts concerning the character of a second agent. This agent then engages in a dialogue with other agents who critically question his abductive argumentation. As the dialogue proceeds, further evidence can come in that may defeat the reasoning that has been put forward up to that point. Relevant evidence could include reputation for qualities like honesty. Defeasible reasoning about character judgments is evaluated using a dialogue model that has been applied to legal argumentation in the new field of computational dialectics (Gordon, 1995; Prakken and Sartor, 1996; Bench-Capon, 1997; Hage, 2000; Lodder, 2000; Verheij, 2003). In this model, argumentation is evaluated as data is collected in a dialogue in which one party asks questions and the other replies appropriately (Lodder, 1999). When an arguer puts forward a claim, she is supposed to support it with evidence if the respondent raises critical questions or puts forward an opposed argument.

In a case where a character issue is being discussed, the dialogue will take place at two levels. At the first level, a primary agent is engaged in deliberations on what to do in a given situation. The primary agent uses practical reasoning to seek and find the means to arrive at a prudent line of action. But once such an action has been deliberated upon and carried out in a given case, at a second level a secondary agent takes on the role of evaluator of the case, using simulative reasoning to judge the character of the first agent. When inferences are drawn from the given data at the first level, these inferences depend on what the secondary agent takes the primary agent's goals and values to be. The basic kind of reasoning used by the primary agent is goal-directed practical reasoning, which concludes in a practical ought-statement — a kind of directive stating what the person ought to do in that situation, given her values or goals. The 'ought' in the conclusion is not purely prudential in the sense of representing only the interests of the single person who is involved. It expresses how the person ought to react in line with long term values and goals that are ethical in nature. It is at the second level that Collingwood's theory of reenactment explains how the secondary agent uses simulative reasoning to judge the character of the primary agent. Both are agents. The second agent also uses practical reasoning, following the footsteps of the actions and practical reasoning of the first agent. The primary agent is presumed by the secondary agent to be trying to reason out the mean, or best course of action. The secondary agent uses abductive reasoning to draw out plausible inferences about the character of the primary agent. At the second level, the reasoning is based on simulative or practical reasoning, applied to the practical reasoning supposedly used at the first level by the primary agent.

5.1 Plausible Reasoning

The kind of reasoning used in drawing such tentative conclusions is called plausible reasoning. The function of plausible reasoning in argumentation is to shift a weight of evidence to one side or the other in a dialogue in which there is a conflict of opinions on whether a particular proposition should be judged to be acceptable or not. A plausible argument shifts a weight of evidence to one side of a balance, thus supporting a conclusion that was previously in doubt. But, as the dialogue continues, such a weight can be shifted back to the other side. Therefore, plausible reasoning should always be regarded as subject to default. Its conclusions should be regarded as tentatively acceptable, but one should be prepared to give it up in the future, should new evidence come in.

Plausible reasoning is based on generalizations that state how one can usually expect a familiar kind of situation to normally go. Such a generalization is inherently subject to defeat in any real case, because the case may not turn out to be normal in the relevant respects. In other words, the generalization only says that this is the way that things normally go, and so as soon as information comes in saying that the given situation is not normal or routine, the generalization is defeated in that case. In deductive quantificational logic, the universal quantifier is used to stand for an absolute kind of generalization of the following form: "For all x, if x has property F then x has property G". A single counter-example defeats the absolute generalization. An absolute generalization is equivalent to the following negative form: "There is (absolutely) no x such that x has F, but does not have G". This negative form reveals its absolutistic nature more clearly.

In contrast, inductive generalizations have the form "Most, many, or a certain percentage (expressed numerically as a fraction between zero and one) of things that have property F also have property G". This kind of generalization is not absolute, but does allow for exceptions. If new information comes into a case, an inductive generalization can be defeated in that case. Inductive generalizations are based on the collection of statistical data that support or go against the generalization with a strength of evidence measured by the probability calculus and other methods of statistics. As with absolute generalizations, inductive generalizations have a positive burden of proof attached. In other words, if you assert one of these generalizations in a dialogue, you are obliged to either back it up by evidence, or give it up. If counter-examples are shown in sufficient quantity to refute the generalization, you must give it up. Plausible reasoning is different, because it is more tentative in nature.

Plausible reasoning is based on a type of generalization of the form, "Normally, but subject to exceptional cases, if something has property *F*, it may also be expected to have property *G*". This kind of conditional is subject to defeat in situations that are not what one would normally expect. Our confidence in it is tentative, because, as we find more out about a situation, it can come to be known that it differs from the normal type. The classical example in computer science is the case of Tweety, who we know is a bird. We know that birds generally fly, and we can put this knowledge in the form of a generalization, "Birds fly". Such a generalization can also be expressed in the form of a conditional: if something is a bird, then (normally, but subject to exceptions) it flies. Suppose that in a particular case, we find out that Tweety, although he is a bird, is a penguin. Or in another kind of case, we may find out that Tweety has a broken wing. This new information will defeat the inference based on the normal situation that Tweety, since he is bird, is an individual that flies. Plausibilistic reasoning is based on generalizations that are subject to defeat should information come in that shows that the particular case we are dealing with is different from what one would generally expect.

The problem with the literature on explanation in philosophy of history is that the generalizations that historical laws are supposedly based on have always been taken to be either universal or inductive. Once this new form of generalization is allowed as a third alternative, it becomes clear how Collingwood's theory of reenactment can form the basis of a new approach to historical explanation of human action. The general problem in the past, or at least in the recent past, is that philosophers have assumed that deductive and inductive reasoning are the only kinds worth their attention. They have ignored plausible reasoning, thinking that it is "subjective". Such reasoning was recognized in ancient Greek philosophy, but then seems to have fallen into oblivion with the rise of deductive logic.

Plausible reasoning was a well-known form of argumentation in the ancient world, especially to the sophists, early philosophers who also worked as rhetoricians. The classic case used to illustrate this form of argument, was identified by two sophists, Corax and Tisias, around the middle of the fifth century B.C. (Gagarin, 1994, p. 50). Nothing survives of their writings; but the classic case, which concerned a trial for assault, was attributed by Aristotle (*Rhetoric* 1402a17–1402a28) to Corax. The trial was about a fight that took place between a weaker, and visibly smaller man and a stronger, and visibly bigger man. The smaller man appealed to the jury, asking them whether it appears likely to them that he would have assaulted this much bigger and stronger man. The argument is based on plausibility. The basis of the argument is that such an attack would be implausible, and everyone in the jury would know it. They could put themselves in the place of the smaller man in the given situation. Would they attack the bigger man? Not likely. How could the jury arrive at such a judgment? Clearly they put themselves vicariously into the situation confronted by the smaller man. In other words, the basis of the plausible inference was simulative reasoning, of the kind described in this chapter.

Another interesting aspect of this ancient case is how it illustrates the provisional nature of the conclusion drawn by the jury. To counter the initial plausible argument that was put forward by the smaller man, the bigger man presented a reverse plausibilistic argument. The bigger man asked the jury whether he, the visibly stronger and larger man, would assault the smaller and weaker man, knowing how bad that would look in court. The jury can also appreciate the force of that argument by placing themselves in the situation of the bigger man, and imagining how they would think that the situation would look. Once again, the basis of the arguments was simulative reasoning.

Plausible simulative reasoning is important for understanding legal argumentation. When a lawyer is arguing before a jury in court, she is trying to persuade the jury to accept a certain point of view. The jury members are not legal experts. Their way of seeing the evidence in the trial may be quite different from the way the lawyer sees it. She needs to persuade them based on their own commitments. In order to carry out this task successfully, she must use empathy to put herself into the jury's way of thinking about the evidence in the trial. In doing this, she reasons about the reasoning of the jury. In short, the reasoning done by an advocate in court is simulative reasoning.

Plausible reasoning is highly familiar in computer science, where it is frequently identified as the kind that is the outcome of abductive inference, as noted above in connection with the account given by Josephson and Josephson. Abductive argument, as noted many times above, is also called "inference to the best explanation". It can now be appreciated how such argument, although it is a logical form of reasoning, results in a conclusion that is supported by standards of plausible reasoning. By these standards, it can still be a strong argument, even if subject to critical questioning. For example, suppose we see some marks on the trail that look like grizzly bear tracks and we draw the conclusion that a grizzly bear was there just recently. This is an argument. The conclusion is the proposition that a bear was there. Of course it is only a guess, or hypothesis. But it could be quite a strong argument, and it might be prudent to act in accord with it, and get out of the area. On the theory of abductive argument presented above, it could be a rational argument, if the evidence in the case is there. The premise is the observation of what appear to be grizzly bear tracks on the trail. From this set of data an inference to the best explanation can be drawn. The best explanation of the tracks on the trail, depending on their appearance, and all else being equal, is that a grizzly bear passed that way. There could be other explanations, but in the given context, it may be that the bear hypothesis is the best explanation. Reason: the trail may be in a location where we know that bears generally pass that way. If the same imprints were on the floor of a university seminar room, there may be a better explanation of them. The argument is contextual. It should be judged by asking the appropriate critical questions. But it can be reasonable. In this case, it can be seen how practical reasoning can be combined with abductive reasoning. Suppose the implicit premise that grizzly bears are dangerous is added. The conclusion to be derived is that getting out of the area is a prudent course of action.

Abduction was anticipated by the challenge-response view of ethical reasoning proposed by the American ethical philosopher Carl Wellman. Curiously, although Wellman's theory of ethical reasoning has not been all that popular within the field of ethics, and was not developed further by any philosophical school of ethics, it fits in extremely well with recent developments in artificial intelligence research. Wellman (1971) propounded the thesis that ethical argumentation is based on a kind of reasoning different from deduction and induction. He called it conductive reasoning. Conductive reasoning (Wellman, 1971, p. 53), if the premises are "close to the truth", draws a conclusion that is still only an approximation to the truth. As Wellman saw it, conductive reasoning is a kind of guesswork that draws a tentative conclusion, subject to correction in the future, from what are assumed to be the given facts of a case. There is an element of uncertainty in it. One reason for this, according to Wellman (p. 53), is that the given premises describing the facts of a case may not quite fit the case to which they are applied. Conductive reasoning is a kind of case-based reasoning that is relative to the presumed facts of the case. Thus any finding of new facts, or any alteration of the given case, may call for a withdrawing of a conclusion based on conductive reasoning. Conductive arguments tend to be weak and tentative. But when enough of them are collected together in a given case, the full impact can be significant. Conductive arguments usually need to be evaluated with reference to a larger body of evidence, in which other arguments give additional weights of evidence. Using a highly significant metaphor, Wellman (p. 58) described the weighing of the comparative merits of conductive arguments in a case as comparable to the task of trying to judge which of two small piles of pebbles is heavier without a scale, or other exact method of measuring. A rough method of doing this is to take one pile in one hand, and the other pile in the other hand, and then get the "heft" of both piles. But what about ethical arguments, like character judgments? How could these arguments be "hefted", or weighed one against another? Wellman's answer (1971, p. 138) is that such arguments can be evaluated in a dialogue between the two parties who have made the respective claims. He called this dialogue framework a challenge-response model (p. 138) for ethical justification. An argument is justified in this model when all the relevant challenges to it have been made in a dialogue exchange between the supporter and the challenger. What Wellman calls conductive reasoning appears to be very similar, or even identical to the kind of reasoning now widely called abductive.

Are conductive inference and abductive inference the same? Or if not, how is the one related to the other? Could conductive inference be a special kind of abductive inference that is used in ethical reasoning, and especially in making character judgments? Can it provide a new model of the reasoning for cases where one person arrives at a reasoned judgment about the character of another person? There does seem to be potential in taking an abductive approach to the problem of character judgments. When one person arrives at a conclusion in the form of a judgment about the presumed character of another person, typically there is a given body of data or presumed facts making up the so-called case. In any actual case, there will be a body of data, sometimes quite a large one, in which the facts of the case are reported or recorded in some way. Using that body of presumed facts of the case, the first person will draw a conclusion that takes the form of a hypothesis about the other person's character. This hypothesis can easily be seen as a sort of explanation of the given facts and reported actions of the other person, selected from alternative possible explanations. Even though it is a kind of guess, and potentially subject to defeat by new information that might come into a case, still this process of reasoning does at least appear to have a structure. Josephson and Josephson (1994) have been able to present abductive inference as having a distinctive form, as shown in chapter 2. And they have cited the various factors that need to be considered in judging the worth of such an inference in a given case. This structure casts new light on character judgment, showing it to be based on evidence, and to have a structure of reasoning in the argumentation used to support a claim.

In judging character, the simulative and abductive reasoning used tends, for the most part, to be plausibilistic in nature. At the first level, a primary agent tries to hit the mean, using intelligent guessing based on the balance of evidential considerations in the case. At the second level, another agent is presented with some sort of account of what the first agent did, and what he said about what she did, and how she felt about the situation. The second agent is confronted with some kind of story, or collection of facts or allegations about the first agent's words and deeds. What the second agent must do, then, is to try to make sense of the given data by offering some kind of judgment that appears to be the best explanation, given what we know of the context of the case. Much of what is known, or taken to be plausible, according to the interpersonal agent theory, is in the form of scripts. The situation is one that the secondary agent is familiar with, or it is similar to others that she is familiar with. Based on this familiarity with how things can normally be expected to go in that kind of situation, the secondary agent puts herself in the situation supposedly confronted by the primary agent whose character is being evaluated. She can then attempt to judge by simulative reasoning how appropriate her actions were, given how she conjectures that any agent would be likely to normally react in that situation. She makes inferences to a best explanation, based on what she knows of the particulars of the case. She forms hypotheses and draws conclusions on the basis of them. Such reasoning is plausibilistic, simulative and abductive in nature. It is a kind of guesswork that is fallible, and can be subject to defeat and reversal if new information comes in that alters the specifics of the case. It is based on a process of question and answer. Of course, such reasoning is based on factual evidence of the given data in a case, of a kind that can be collected and verified, and that can be used to support or undermine a hypothesis. The scheme of abductive argument presented in chapter 2 shows how this kind of reasoning is best represented as subject to challenge by the asking of appropriate critical questions.

But understanding plausible reasoning comprises only part of the problem. It is also necessary to understand how one agent reasons and acts in relation to the actions and perceived impressions of another. How can one agent judge what effects its actions have on another agent? How can one agent use empathy to try to figure out what the action of another agent means, or what the intentions of the other agent might be? How can one agent judge that another agent is trustworthy, or willing to cooperate? How can agents communicate with each other, so that they can engage in teamwork actions? How can what an agent says in such communications with other agents be used as evidence in judging the qualities of character of the first agent? These questions are more difficult to answer. To throw light on them, some new developments in multi-agent systems used in computer science need to be introduced.

5.2 Plan Recognition and Dialogue

Recent research in AI has been concerned with agents collaborating to develop and implement a shared plan. In order to be able to plan together, the agents must communicate with each other. For this purpose, they need to monitor each other's actions, to interpret those actions, and to ask questions of each other. Thus agents need to enter into in some kind of dialogue with each other in planning. The general framework that is used in AI is called SharedPlan theory: "According to SharedPlan theory, a key component of the mental state of each participant in a collaboration is a set of beliefs about the mutually believed goals and actions to be performed, and about the mutually believed capabilities, intentions and commitments of each participant" (Lesh *et al.*, 2001, p. 4). There is also another requirement if SharedPlan theory is to work. Each agent must have a set of methods for decomposing actions and goals into other actions and goals. In other words, each agent must be able to grasp how common sequences of actions and goals normally work in practical reasoning in a familiar context. If one agent knows that the other has a particular goal, then it must be able to infer that the other agent will have other goals related to that first goal. But how can one agent draw such inferences if it has no direct access to the goals or commitments of the other? How plan recognition works can be explained as follows. Suppose one agent sees another agent perform a certain action. The second agent then consults its list of standard routines, and uses this to extend the action into a standard sequence of actions that would normally fit with this action in the given context. If there is one goal that would fit with the given action, then the second agent draws the defeasible inference that the first agent is committed to this goal. If the fit is uncertain, problematic or dubious, the first agent asks the second agent to confirm or refute the hypothesis.

A common example often used to illustrate SharedPlan theory in AI has been presented by Schmidt (1985). It concerns a case in which a person has just acquired a framed picture, and wants to hang it on a wall in the living room in his house. He knows that the standard way of hanging a picture is to string wire through supports provided on the back of the frame. Schmidt (pp. 227–228) outlined various elements in the plan as follows (the list given by Schmidt is longer and more detailed).

> Goal: A recently acquired print, already framed in an aluminum frame, is to be hung on the north wall of my living room between the left corner of the wall and the window.
>
> Planned Action: Hang the framed picture in the aforementioned general location.
>
> Subgoal: Picture wire is needed across the back of the picture to support it when hung.

Planned Action: String the wire through supports on the frame and wrap the wire.
Default Assumption: This type of metallic frame already has supports provided for the wire.
Subgoal: A support embedded in the wall is needed.
Default Assumption: This house was built within the past ten years; therefore the wall material is probably wallboard.

The rest of the plan involves subgoals like obtaining a screw, a plastic anchor, and some tools. The example could be extended further by imagining two agents collaborating to hang the picture, and having a dialogue for this purpose. One might ask the other where screws and tools are likely to be found, for example. The other might reply that screws and tools are normally kept in the tool bench in the basement. One might tell the other that a plastic anchor is the normal way to insert a screw into wallboard to hang a picture. The other might ask where a plastic anchor can be acquired. The reply might be that they can be bought at the hardware store. He might then offer the car keys, since both know that taking the car is the normal way to get to the hardware store. This example of a collaborative plan is highly familiar to common sense. But to implement it as a computer program so that it could be carried out by two automated agents is not as easy as it might initially appear. The reason is that we take familiar routines for granted, and we assume that any agents we might collaborate with are familiar with them too. And such routine can be quite lengthy and complex. Even so, it is quite possible to devise automated systems in which two or more agents can collaborate to carry out actions by devising a joint plan. As noted in this chapter, section 5, the key is plan recognition. But plan recognition in turn depends on plausible inferences that can be drawn by one agent about the assumed internal states of the other. The key to understanding how such inferences should work is to be sought in the dialogue between the agents.

Carberry (1990) devised a computer system for plan inference called TRACK. The system works within a dialogue framework of a kind that is common in computing. Carberry (p. 3) describes it as an information-seeking dialogue with two participants. One is seeking information and the other is trying to provide it. More specifically (p. 75), it is a task-related information dialogue: "one participant is motivated by a task he wants to perform and is seeking information to construct a plan for accomplishing that task". In the language of Walton and Krabbe (1995), this framework is called an embedding of deliberation dialogue within information-seeking dialogue. It is the framework of deliberation dialogue that not only makes sense of planning as a collaborative enterprise, but also of the kind of reasoning used when two agents reason together. Within this framework,

Carberry (p. 75) described how TRACK works as follows: "TRACK assimilates utterances from an ongoing dialogue and incrementally updates and expands the system's beliefs about the underlying task-related plan motivating the information-seeker's queries". A simplified example can be used to illustrate in rough outline what the system is designed to do, and the importance of questions in the dialogue structure. Suppose a university student known to be majoring in science approaches a professor who is counseling students at registration time. The student asks her, "Does Introduction to Logic count as a course meeting the basic arts requirement?" From the student's having asked this question, the professor can infer, in the context, that the student has a goal of taking a degree. She can also infer some other conclusions — for example, that the student needs to fulfil the basic arts requirement in order to graduate. Of course, these inferences could turn out to be wrong. But they are fairly reasonable assumptions, given the context of the dialogue and what the student has said in it so far.

In order to devise an automated dialogue system that would draw these kinds of inference from what a speaker says and from other contextual information in a regulated way, TRACK uses several techniques. One is the semantic representation of the speaker's utterance. TRACK can recognize different kinds of speech acts. For example, it can recognize different kinds of questions. It can tell just from the form of the question that the asker has certain commitments or implied beliefs that are presumptions implied in the act of asking the question. For example, just by asking the question above, the student implies that he believes that there are courses meeting the basic arts requirement. But even beyond semantic representation, TRACK uses a technique called focussing. It has a library of goals and plans, based on scripts of routines, or familiar ways of doing things, as applicable to the domain of the local dialogue. For example, if the question at this point in the dialogue is one about basic arts requirements, TRACK is programmed with some scripts about how basic arts requirements work generally. These are called "plan identification heuristics", and they "relate the speaker's immediate goal to the system's domain-dependent library of goals and plans" (Carberry, 1990, p. 75). They represent standard routines indicating how things are normally done in some domain that is familiar to a group of agents collaborating in a plan. TRACK applies these tools to a local question or reply segment that is part of a longer dialogue, and uses them to extract the speaker's focused goals and plans. The method of plan recognition works the same way that it would in the example of hanging the picture. There is a dialogue between the two agents and, based on familiar routines known to both of them, each draws inferences about the presumed goals and commitments of the other.

Plan identification technology makes it possible for one agent to draw plausible inferences about the presumed goals of another agent in a process of collaborative planning. But how does it make this process useful? After all, suppose the one agent makes a mistake and wrongly infers that the other agent has some particular goal. Such mistakes are surely possible. So aren't we back to the fundamental problem of other minds? If the one agent cannot see directly into the commitments and goals of the other, how can it tell objectively or reasonably whether the other agent is committed to some goal or not? The answer indicated by the way plan recognition has developed is that the one agent can draw defeasible inferences about the goals or internal states of the other by plausible reasoning. It can use the hypothesis derived by such an inference as part of a collaborative plan undertaken with the other agent. What is important is that the agent has to realize that such an inference is defeasible. It is a basis for carrying on a dialogue with the other agent and acting collaboratively with him. But it only has status as an inference within the dialogue framework. The purpose of drawing the inference and acting on it is to help the collaboration move forward. As the dialogue continues, the inference may be secured as more plausible, depending on how the other agent reacts, or it may be defeated. So drawing plausible inferences about the goals or internal states of another agent can be rational as a form of reasoning, but it has a special epistemic status. It is a kind of inference drawn by abductive plausible reasoning, based on shared knowledge of standard routines in a domain that both agents are familiar with. The conclusion drawn has a probative weight in the dialogue framework. In other words, it indicates the right way to proceed now in a collaborative dialogue in which two agents are trying to collaborate on a practical task, even though what appears now to be the right way may have to be given up as the dialogue proceeds.

5.3 Sources of Dialogue Evidence

According to Uviller (1982, p. 849), a character trait is normally proved by one of three means. One is reputation evidence, collected by "asking a witness acquainted with the community view of the subject to report on the general regard". Using a second kind of evidence, a witness recounts incidents showing the subject exhibiting the character trait at issue. By a third kind of evidence, Uviller (p. 850) refers to the kind of case in which "a witness may recite his own opinion of the subject's character as to the relevant trait". Note that all three forms of evidence, on Uviller's account of them, are collected through witness testimony. Note also that the first and third forms of character evidence seem especially fallible. The first depends on popular opinion, a source of argumentation often associated with fallacious reasoning. The third represents mere opinion, a person simply saying that something is so, again a very weak form of argument that can often go wrong. The second kind of character evidence seems the strongest, as it is based on direct observations or factual evidence of behavior. But even it seems fallible in certain respects. For one thing, it, too, depends on witness testimony. For another, it depends on how a trait is defined or understood, and how it is judged to fit the circumstances of a case. This too seems to be appealing to a kind of inference that could go wrong.

Such complications are especially evident where a person is struggling with a choice by balancing many factors, and trying to make a best guess. To answer questions about ethical deliberation and character, a discussion of all the pros and cons of the case need to be looked at. Critical questions need to be asked. There are generally two sides to such a discussion, and the case should not be judged until all the relevant factors have been examined on both sides. In order to judge whether the captain acted with integrity or not in such a case, we as evaluators of his actions have to use simulative reasoning to enter into his thinking. To do this, it is necessary to engage in an ethical discussion, looking at all the relevant evidence in the case, and considering the arguments on both sides. One needs to evaluate the best explanations of the actions envisaged. In such an ethical case, justification requires what Audi (1997, p. 51) calls the method of ethical reflection. This consists of a judicious discussion of moral questions and what these questions involve in relation to a moral issue. An example would be a general reflection on the nature of promising as a source of duty, and how duties can conflict (p. 51). Ethical reflection might not only consist in abstract consideration of moral questions. It could also centre on a conflict between abstract principles and issues arising out of a specific case. At the first level, there is all the evidence concerning what someone did or said in a specific case. At the second level, there is ethical reflection on the virtues and vices, or ethical qualities of character that seem to be exhibited. Collingwood (1946, p. 215) saw the process of reenactment in historical explanation as not just "a passive surrender to the spell of another's mind". He described it instead as "a labour of active and therefore critical thinking". The historian not only collects and observes past thought, but also "criticizes it, (and) forms his own judgment of its value" (p. 215). The relationship of the second level explanation to the first level data is one of critical question and answer.

At the first level, the principal agent strives to use practical reasoning to hit the mean, using a form of reasoning that is intelligent guessing. Then at a second level, an attempt is made to reconstruct that agent's practical reasoning and his commitments, and to use this to build up a body of evidence that allows conclusions to be drawn in the form of ethical judgments. But getting from the first level to the second requires a technical apparatus of multi-agent dialogue. The agent, at the first level, has some quality of character, like courage or integrity, that presumably plays some role in his actions. A quality of character like courage cannot be directly observed.

But it can be inferred indirectly from what an agent does in a given set of circumstances.

But how, in some kind of technical apparatus, does the evidence track abductively from the particular circumstances of the case to hypotheses about the agent's character? As new information comes in, an agent can act accordingly, and can exhibit a kind of rationality in how it acts. Thus Wooldridge (2000, p. 3) writes of such software entities as rational agents that possess properties of autonomy, proactiveness, reactivity and social ability. A limitation of early systems is that the agent had no automatic use of memory of previous connections, and could not improve performance based on this information (Maximilien and Singh, 2002, p. 25). One obvious instance of such a limitation is that it would be helpful in collecting information to weed out messages of dubious value collected on the internet. To perform such a task the collecting agent must be able to judge whether another agent is a reliable source of information. For example, if the one agent is a trusted expert source, it might make sense for the other to treat the information received from this agent as comparatively reliable. The solution was to build a distributed trust system that contains information about the reputation of other agents with which an agent communicates that these other agents can access and use. Reputation mechanisms are now commonly used in web sites like *Amazon* and *e-bay* (Maximilien and Singh, 2002, p. 26).

An interesting new development in multi-agent systems is that agents have shown themselves capable of deceptive communication (Castelfranchi and Tan, 2001, p. xxvi). To cite a common kind of example, in a security system, the system may misinform an authorized user in order to protect confidential information. Or to cite another increasingly common kind of example, a software agent for electronic commerce may be programmed to make a profit, but then in negotiating with other agents on the net it may decide to use bluffing to get the best price. The agent may make a threat to another agent, saying, "I will quit the conversation if you don't take my last offer". The interesting aspect of this is that the agent has not been programmed to make such deceptive moves, or to try to get the best of another agent by committing fallacies. An agent is autonomous, and it learns by its experience of engaging in negotiations what kinds of moves work best to achieve its goal of getting the best deal.

One source of data for building a reputation management system is to collect and save referrals from other agents (Yu *et al.*, 2002, p. 1). To deal with referrals among agents, Yu and Singh (2000) have developed a system in which agent *a* assigns a reputation rating to an agent *b* based on three kinds of evidence: *a*'s direct observations of *b*, the ratings of *b* given by *b*'s neighbors, and *a*'s ratings of these neighbors (Yu and Singh, 2000, p. 4).

These data are used to set up a trust rating measure that is updated as new information is collected. Such a reputation rating represents a measure of the trust *a* should have in *b* as a source of reliable information, according to the evidence that *a* has. The trust rating should be regarded as provisional. It can be updated as new information comes in. Suppose that *a* finds out from *c* that *b* has behaved badly to *c* in the past, giving *c* bad information. *a* can then penalize *b* by decreasing *b*'s rating and informing its neighbors. The "neighbors" are the other agents that an agent would normally be in communication with (Yu and Singh, 2002, p. 2). But then suppose that *a* finds out that *c* has lied in the past, and given false reports of other agents behaving badly. Then *a* could update the rating of *b* by deleting his former bad rating, and *a* could now give a bad rating to *c*.

This new technology not only shows the importance of ethical character ratings in web commerce, but also offers a mechanism for reputation management that yields insights into the important role that character can and should play in multi-agent argumentation. It shows how the communication of information in a multi-agent dialogue structure can be based on an inferential link between a character judgment, based on factual evidence, and integrated into the evaluation of source-based argumentation.

Reputation is one kind of evidence that can be relevant to making intelligent and informed character judgments, especially in relation to honesty and integrity, but judgments about qualities of character like courage and cowardice seem to be based more on other kinds of evidence. Courage as a quality of character is best seen as a kind of commitment expressed in the practical reasoning of an agent in a given case. The agent is seen as having a descriptor that contains a definition of courage that has been agreed upon as relatively objective by all parties. When a certain act is attributed to the agent, and its description triggers all the right requirements to fit the general definition in the descriptor, the conclusion is drawn (defeasibly) by the evaluator that the agent has a courageous character. The evaluator can then carry the case forward by fitting the conclusion triggered by the descriptor into a complex equation that balances all the relevant factors in the case. If this judgment sounds complicated, it is. The problem is that making a judgment that somebody has a courageous character is a subtle business, often subject to misrepresentation and corruption in propaganda used to manipulate public opinion with emotional appeals by those who have some political or ideological end in mind. As was argued in (Walton, 1986), it would be better to stick with the relatively simpler situation in which a single action is judged courageous or not in a given case. But, as conceded in chapter 2, since courage typically is a matter of habit, character, commitment and caring, character cannot be left out of it.

The solution is that an agent may be said to have certain general qualities of character, and each agent will have, in addition to her commitment set, a set of these character qualities, each with its own descriptor. When a case develops in which the agent is taking part, and a set of actions and goals, as expressed in the practical reasoning of that agent, fits the descriptor, then there is a presumption that the agent has that quality. Such a presumption is defeasible, however, subject to further considerations in the case.

5.4 Commitment in Dialogue

As indicated in the last chapter, inferring a conclusion about a primary agent's character is based on empathy. The secondary agent tries to insert herself into the mind of the primary agent. But the secondary agent can never know, by directly observable evidence, what the primary agent thinks, or what her goals and intentions are. The whole process of abductive reasoning is by inference to a plausible hypothesis or supposition. Yet evidence is available in the form of verifiable facts, or at least data of some reproducible sort. The whole structure of reasoning is not based on knowledge or belief. It is based on a construct made by the secondary agent about the state of mind of the primary agent. This construct is called commitment. Commitments of a primary agent can be inferred indirectly by a secondary agent on the basis of the secondary agent's access to data on what the primary agent has said and done in relation to a problem confronted by the primary agent.

Character involves commitment of some sort. That much has already been made clear in the previous chapters. The kind of commitment at issue is often altruistic in nature. The courageous person, for example, is committed to caring for others, and for putting the safety or lives of others before those of herself. But commitment is subject to retraction as new information comes in. The reasoning on which a commitment is based is plausibilistic and abductive in nature. An agent's commitment to an action, based on practical reasoning, is inherently subject to critical questioning. A conclusion about a prudent line of action is rarely fixed, because in any realistic case, the information on the circumstances of the case is imperfectly known, and is constantly subject to change. Hence ethical commitment to a policy, goal, or action should be seen as subject to discussion, instead of being fixed and absolute, beyond all critical questioning or rational doubt.

The kind of framework needed in ethics to study judgments of character in given cases has to be a kind that takes ethically significant questions into account, and that permits examination of the leading arguments on both sides of a case to be evaluated. As Collingwood theorized, the process of evaluation is one of question and answer. Such a framework for the analysis and evaluation of practical reasoning used in particular cases involving ethical thinking should be dialectical, in the ancient sense referring to a collaborative goal-directed dialogue. Hamblin (1971), and following his system, Mackenzie (1987, 1990) and Walton and Krabbe (1995), define a dialogue as a set of orderly moves made by two participants, typically called the proponent and the respondent. The moves are made according to a set of rules appropriate for the type of dialogue, and for contributing to its collaborative goal. The rules, according to the system in (Walton and Krabbe, 1995) are of four kinds. *Locution Rules* define the specific types of moves allowed and forbidden, like the asking of questions or the making of assertions (p. 149). *Structural Rules* define the kinds of moves a participant may make at any particular point in the dialogue, depending on the prior move of the other party (p. 150). *Commitment Rules* determine which propositions are inserted into or deleted from a participant's commitment store after each move (p. 149). *Win and Loss Rules* not only define the goal of the dialogue, but also make it clear what constitutes successful realization of the goal. The kind of dialogue analyzed by Walton and Krabbe (1995) is called the persuasion dialogue. In such a dialogue, each participant has the aim of proving her thesis from extracted commitments of the other participant. The goal of the type of dialogue called the critical discussion — a subtype of persuasion dialogue — is to resolve a conflict of opinions. But the goal of persuasion dialogue generally is less ambitious. It is to throw light on the issue discussed by considering the strongest arguments on both sides of the issue, and seeing how they fare against each other. This goal is often called *the maieutic function*, meaning that the dialogue should reveal the reasons both participants have for their positions. A participant's position is revealed more fully, not only by presenting the strongest arguments that can be used to support it, but also by introducing refinements in that position necessitated by critical objections made against it.

What is the commitment store of a participant? How can we model it formally? Each participant is seen as having a kind of storehouse or memory bank, or more simply, a set of propositions ascribed to that participant and recorded somewhere. A list, for example, could be made on a blackboard. As the dialogue proceeds, propositions (statements) are inserted into that set, or are deleted, depending on what a participant says at any particular move. If a participant asserts a proposition at some point, then that proposition should be inserted into her commitment set. The commitment set of a participant functions approximately like a *persona* of her beliefs. But as Hamblin (1970, p. 257) emphasized, commitments should not be seen as being the same as beliefs. A commitment may be described as something you have gone on record as accepting. You may actually believe it, but then again you may not. Van Eemeren and Grootendorst (1984, 1992) have also emphasized that there is an important distinction to be drawn between belief and acceptance. To say that you believe something is to say something about your inner mental state. In contrast, to say that you are committed to some proposition is to say that you are willing to defend it, if challenged to give your supporting reasons for undertaking to accept it. You may not believe it, but since you have gone on record as accepting or supporting it, you are at least tentatively committed to it. That does not mean, of course, that you can't change your mind. Commitments can be retracted in a persuasion dialogue.

In fact, the problem of just when commitments may or should be retracted is shown in (Walton and Krabbe, 1995) to be the central problem for the study of formal dialogue. There is no simple answer. Commitment rules are different for different types of dialogue. In a persuasion dialogue, retraction needs to be allowed fairly freely, but it should not be allowed automatically. In some cases, there needs to be a penalty, or some restrictions on what you can retract, and how you can retract it. For details of this complex problem, the reader should turn to the treatment of the different types of dialogue in (Walton and Krabbe, 1995). Commitment, in the relevant sense, is a contextual notion. It represents the idea that an arguer can be held accountable for having gone on record in the past as having taken a certain stand, or as having advocated a particular argument in support of some thesis or proposition.

But is this sense of commitment the same as the ethical sense of the word? It does seem to be up to a point. Commitment in ethics has to do with practical reasoning, and with what values and presumed goals are expressed in or communicated by a person's words and actions. There is an aspect here of going on record as standing for certain values, especially as expressed by how one has acted in ethical test situations. This ethical notion of commitment does seem to be comparable to the logical idea. But, in ethics, commitment has more overtones of standing up to one's expressed moral values by actually carrying out actions that embody them, even at some cost to one's own self-interest. In ethics, commitment often has overtones of altruism, caring for others, and even of personal sacrifice, where that shows evidence of such qualities.

In ethical judgment of character, the primary agent goes on record about commitment in a deliberation type of dialogue, by carrying out actions, by making choices and by making verbal comments on situations that give evidence about what he stands for. But at the second level, the evaluator of the case must assemble the relevant evidence, and try to arrive at some sort of judgment in line with that evidence. This level, too, can be seen as a kind of dialogue in which different opinions are examined and questioned critically.

5.5 Legal Evidence and Examination Dialogue

As noted in chapter 2, legal evidence of the kind used in trials is presented in the form of witness testimony. Although appeal to witness testimony is a form of argument that carries probative weight as evidence in a trial, this kind of evidence is defeasible. Witnesses sometimes lie. And they often make mistakes in the identification of a suspect, and in other kinds of testimony that depend on human memory (Loftus, 1979). How does the law deal with this problem of the fallibility and occasional untrustworthiness of witness testimony as evidence? The answer is basically that the witness is questioned in a probing and revealing interview. In a trial, both sides get to examine the witness. Cross-examination, or questioning an opposed witness, is often quite a critical form of questioning. The story presented by the witness may be examined, and apparent contradictions in it cited by the questioner. The character of the witness may even be attacked in a process called impeachment. For example, if it can be shown that the witness has a bad character for honesty, that argument against him can be used to attack his testimony. If a witness is not credible, the story he tells will not be found to be plausible. Or if a witness is shown to be biased, his testimony will tend to not carry so much weight in the eyes of a jury.

Classifying the context of dialogue of legal argumentation in a trial is complex. The main dialogue would seem to be a critical discussion (Feteris, 1999, chapter 10). The goal of a critical discussion is to resolve a conflict of opinions by means of rational argumentation (van Eemeren and Grootendorst, 1992). Each side has an opinion, the opinion of the one opposed to the opinion of the other. And the purpose of each side is to persuade the other to come to accept its opinion. The trial fits this model, according to Feteris, because opinions are opposed in a trial, and each side has an advocate to plead for the one represented by its contention. But when a witness is being examined in a trial, you could see this dialogue as embedded within a larger critical discussion that is taking place. The questioning of a witness by an attorney could be seen as a form of information-seeking dialogue. A trial lawyer would probably not see it that way, because her goal as advocate is to win. But a judge or jury, called a trier, could very well do so. From the point of view of the trier, the purpose of the dialogue when a witness is interviewed, is to get information that can be used as premises for the argumentation in the critical discussion in the case.

In the classification of types of dialogue given in (Walton and Krabbe, 1995), there is a type of dialogue called information-seeking. The goal is for the questioner to get information from the respondent. The assumption is that the respondent has the information that the questioner wants to get. For example, a man in a foreign city may ask a shopkeeper where a certain building is. But information-seeking dialogue is not always this simple. Sometimes it also has an examination aspect. In an examination of the educational type, the teacher asks questions to the student in order to test the student's knowledge of specific subjects. In this type of dialogue, the questioner already knows the answer. She already possesses the information. The goal is to see whether the student also has it. In examination of a witness in a trial by an attorney, the attorney, too, often already possesses the information, and knows the answer to the question before it is asked. An old maxim tells a lawyer never to ask a question that he does not already know the answer to. Legal examination, therefore, evidently represents a special kind of information-seeking dialogue. The aim is not only to get information from a witness to present it before the trier, but also to probe into the witness's story critically. The goal is not only to present the witness's account, but also to question it critically, and bring out its weak or unclear parts. Depending on how the examination goes, the account given by the witness may be made to seem more plausible, or it may be made to seem quite implausible. The questioning in a trial can often have a critical edge. According to Sinclair (1985, p. 384), legal cross-examination is "a probing, prying, pressing form of inquiry".

According to Collingwood's theory, the dialogical method of question and answer that a historian uses to critically evaluate historical evidence can be seen as a process of testing the evidence. The legal method of examining the testimony of a witness in a trial can be seen as based on the same kind of examination dialogue. The goal is not only to obtain information by a process of questioning, but also to test the reliability of that information by a process of critically examining it. The various critical questions matching the appeal to witness testimony (chapter 2, section 7) are used for this purpose. The technique of questioning often has a hard critical edge, and the character of the witness may even be attacked as part of the process.

Suppose the witness gives an answer to a question that contradicts one of his previous statements. The examiner has choices in how to proceed. She can point out the contradiction. A contradiction in the story of the witness means that the story, as a whole, cannot be true. But the witness may be able to explain the apparent contradiction, showing that it was based on a misunderstanding that can be resolved satisfactorily. Here the importance of dialogue as a way of testing testimony is apparent. But the examiner has another option. If she sees that the witness may contradict his own testimony in answer to a question, she can lay a foundation for that question by planning a sequence of dialogue in advance. She can refresh the memory of the court by asking a question that may get the witness to re-affirm his earlier commitment. That way, when the contradiction is revealed, it is harder for the witness to explain it away by retracting his earlier commitment. The skill of cross-examination is to lead up to such a contradiction by laying a foundation in a planned sequence of question-answer dialogue that reveals a clear contradiction in the testimony of the witness. Such a sequence of argumentation can even be used to impeach the witness, for if he is contradictory in his commitments, this may show to the jury that he is a hypocrite or is confused. In either case, his credibility as a witness will be destroyed, or cast into doubt, and his testimony will begin to seem implausible.

What is shown is that legal examination dialogue is a way of testing argumentation based on witness testimony. Testimony can either pass or fail the test. In other words, the dialogue of probing question and answer is a way of evaluating the worth of witness testimony. Cross-examination is particularly revealing as a test for evidence. According to Davies (1993, p. xxxi), cross-examination is the single most important means of determining the truth in a trial. The same kind of process of evidence evaluation is used in history when a historian examines the testimony of a primary or secondary source. The historian needs to ask the right critical questions in a probing dialogue in just the right sequence, by laying a foundation. If the source seems to contradict his own story at some point, that is evidence. If what he said or wrote is in conflict with other evidence, like physical or archeological evidence, then that is evidence. If the source exhibits a bias by continually favoring one side over the other on a disputed issue, that is evidence. In both law and history, the facts may be about something that happened in the past, and cannot be re-lived. The only sources of evidence the historian or the legal examiner have are the accounts given by witnesses. Although these accounts are in a way subjective, because they are mediated from the witness as agent to the examiner as agent in a dialogue, they can be tested as plausible or implausible. Indirect access to the evidence of the facts can be gotten by questioning the witness in a critical and probing examination dialogue. The testimony can pass or fail the test. Hence the method of examination by question and answer.

The theory advocated here is that abductive argumentation, of the kind used so much in law and history especially, can be evaluated as based on evidence in a dialogue format. Such evidence, however, is in many cases not conclusive. It is based on a set of supposed facts. But there is no direct access to these facts, because the event in question is typically in the past. What we have is a story, or a plausible, connected account of the event, as told by a witness. But in history as well as law, there are hard cases, of the kind that are controversial, or come to trial. In a hard case, there are typically two conflicting stories, one on each side. The evidence needs to be strong enough to resolve this conflict of opinions by meeting the appropriate burden of proof. Abductive argumentation is also typically defeasible. There are exceptions to the rule. Thus with respect to any given argument, there are reasons both for and against it. The argument could be the best explanation at any given point in an investigation, but then later, a better explanation could be revealed by a sequence of questioning and collection of new evidence. Recent research in law and artificial intelligence shows the usefulness of viewing legal argumentation as evidence best evaluated by the dialogue method. Hage *et al.*, (1994) advocated the use of a dialogue reason-based logic as the best method for evaluating legal evidence in hard cases. Gordon (1995) put forward the pleadings game, a form of dialogue game, as an artificial intelligence model of procedural justice that can be used to evaluate defeasible legal arguments. Hage (1997) investigated typical legal arguments based on a Toulmin-style warrant expressing a generalization that is open to exceptions, concluding that such arguments need to be seen as subject to questioning, even though they can be acceptable on a tentative basis. Prakken (1997) conducted an exhaustive study of defeasible legal arguments, and came to the conclusion that the best method for evaluating them is a dialogue model in which reasons for a claim are put in a dialogue sequence with reasons against it. Lodder (1999) explicitly adopted a dialogical method of modeling legal argumentation that evaluates legal evidence as a pro-contra dialogue. Feteris (1999) advocates modeling the argumentation in a trial as a critical discussion that resolves a conflict of opinions by a dialogue process of argumentation.

5.6 Examination Dialogue and Conversational Postulates

Grice (1975) built his theory of implicature around what are called conversational postulates or conversational maxims. His theory was that human conversation is goal-directed and collaborative. His most basic conversational postulate (p. 65) was the cooperative principle: "Make your conversational contribution such as is required, at the stage at which it occurs, by the accepted purpose or direction of the talk exchange in which you are engaged". Another conversational postulate is the maxim of quantity: "Make your contribution as informative as is required (for the current purposes of the exchange)" (Grice, 1975, p. 67). An example of a conversation in which the maxim of quantity is violated has been given by Sinclair (1985, p. 377).

> Suppose A arrives at the office and says to B: "I just saw a big crash on 3rd and Jordan with three cars in it." A few minutes later C arrives and joins the discussion, saying, "I just saw a big crash on 3rd and Jordan with three cars, a truck, and a motorcycle in it." B, wondering about the extra truck and motorcycle, then asks A if that was the same crash he had seen, and A replies that it was but that what he said was not false because, after all, it was true that there were three cars in the crash, and he just hadn't bothered to mention the other vehicles.

There is something very strange about A's statement that the crash has three cars in it. It wasn't false. But it was misleading because it did not give all the information that one would normally have expected. It violated the maxim of quantity. If a hearer just heard what A reported about the accident, and did not yet hear what C reported, he would think that there were only three vehicles involved in the crash. This would be a reasonable inference to draw as an implicature. For if A knew that more than three vehicles were involved then he should make an informative contribution to the conversation by saying so.

In examination of a witness in court, what the witness fails to say can be as significant as what he/she actually does say in reply to a question. The reason is that we expect a witness to answer a question by giving the amount of information that would be reasonably collaborative, according to the maxim of quantity. Thus witness examination is a form of dialogue or conversational interaction in which the seeking and giving of information takes place. And in this dialogue, plausible inferences will be drawn both on the basis of what is said and what is not said. When a witness presents a story, for example a story that contains character evidence, the story may have gaps. Some of these can only be filled if the witness can furnish more information. But some of them will be filled by drawing implicatures, even when no further information is given by the witness.

The example of the traffic incident above shows that when a witness presents an account, it can be misleading. It can prompt implicatures that are erroneous. Twining (1999, p. 359) has argued that story telling can be dangerous in legal contexts. It can even be associated with irrational means of persuasion. Twining cited dangers of ungrounded suggestions by innuendo, appealing to prejudices and stereotypes, use of emotional language to mislead, using emotional appeals that win sympathy but are irrelevant. Many of these very dangers are associated with traditional informal fallacies in logic like appeal to pity, appeal to fear, personal attack (*ad hominem*) argument, hasty generalization, the fallacy of wrong conclusion, and use of emotively loaded terms in place of evidence. The problem is that the defeasible sorts of arguments used in history and law, like appeal to witness testimony, can turn out to be wrong. They are not highly reliable and are far from conclusive. Notoriously, they can even be used as deceptive tactics of argumentation. A character judgment could have evidence in its favor, for example. A highly plausible story could be given that seems to support a character judgment that someone is a courageous or heroic person. But as new evidence comes in, it could become clear that this story is mere panegyric. Or a highly plausible story could be presented by a biographer or character witness that makes a person out to be the worst sort of villain, liar or coward. Under cross-examination, however, the story may fall apart. It may simply turn out to be a vicious character assassination attempt.

What can be said in response to these worries is that these things are legitimate. As shown in many instances in law and history, these arguments can turn out to be wrong, or at least doubts about them can be raised. The case of Francis Bacon could be cited again here. Also, there can be conflicts of opinion about an argument's worth. Notoriously, arguments used in trials can be defeated by stronger arguments posed by the opposing side. These arguments are best seen as tentative and inconclusive. And in some instances they can turn out to be misleading and deceptive. The best we can say is that they are plausible, even when supported by good evidence of the appropriate kind. But also, they can be tested by a probing critical examination. This process is not perfect, but it can destroy a story by showing that it is not as plausible as it initially seemed. Witness testimony, for example, is not a perfect form of argument. But it can be supported by evidence. Its argumentation scheme can be applied to show which premises are in need of support. It can be critically questioned by asking the appropriate critical questions. In some cases, it can be torn apart by a probing critical examination. An argument can be tested by a process of examination dialogue. It can pass or fail the test. And yet this test is normally not conclusive. Doubts may remain. The problem is that we should prefer direct empirical evidence, where it exists, but in many cases in court the outcome of the case depends on witness testimony precisely because direct empirical evidence is not available. The event in question may have happened a long time ago, and only a witness may be in a position to know what really happened. Realistically speaking, although we are wary of the fallibility of these defeasible kinds of arguments, they are often all we have to go by. Thus a middle path is the best way to treat them. We should not rely too heavily on them, and should be ready to give them up should better evidence come along. But we should give due weight to them in arriving at a decision, if the proper requirements for supporting them are met, and if that outweighs the evidence against them. Arguments in a trial are always judged legally on a basis of burden of proof. In a criminal trial, for example, the burden, or standard for successful proof, is higher than that set in a civil case. The evaluation of these arguments needs to be seen as dependent on the context of dialogue in which the argument was used. An abductive argument may be the best explanation of the facts that are known so far in a dialogue. But as the dialogue continues, the set of facts or data to be explained may grow larger. An alternative explanation may then prove to be better. The process of examination of the facts in a case can also suggest a better explanation by poking holes in the previous story.

How examination works in a trial depends on the system of law in a country, and in particular, whether in the inquisitorial or the adversarial system. The two systems have different roots (van Koppen and Penrod, 2003, p. 2), and the characteristics of the type of dialogue for each system is essentially different. In the adversarial system, the trial is taken to be a fair contest between roughly equal opponents (p. 2). In the inquisitorial system, the trial is an official and thorough inquiry (p. 3). While inquisitorial trials have a preference for documentary presentation of evidence, adversarial trials favor oral presentation of evidence by witnesses. The Netherlands is an example of an inquisitorial system of justice in Western Europe, the United States is at the opposite end of the spectrum in being an example of an adversarial one.

In the American judicial system, trial practice manuals are very conservative when giving lawyers advice on how to conduct a cross-examination, because of the danger of a "backfire" if the witness is given any latitude. The advice to never ask a question to which you do not already know the answer is often cited (Park, 2003, p. 133). The danger is that if you give the witness any latitude, he may come out with some remark that could damage your own side of the case heavily by having a large impact on the jury. In the adversarial system, there are two forces operating on cross-examination as a type of dialogue. One is fear of a backfire. The other is the power of impeaching a hostile witness by questioning, by attacking his character for honesty, sincerity and trustworthiness by using "commit and contradict tactics" (Park, 2003, p. 145). One of the most important of these tactics is to get the respondent to contradict himself. In the adversarial system an examiner will often ask tricky questions that are snares for entrapment. This makes cross-examination look like a poor tool for discovering the truth. Even so, the truth-seeking function of the dialogue has to be sought in its adversarial nature. If the witness can be shown to be dishonest or evasive by using commit and contradict tactics, his testimony is discredited. This uncovering of problems in testimony is the technique used in adversarial cross-examination to probe into testimony and get to the truth of a matter indirectly.

5.7 A Dialectical Theory of Explanation

Abductive argument is inference to the best explanation, according to the analysis presented in chapter 2 and subsequently. The criteria for evaluating an abductive argument include evaluating competing explanations of given facts. But what is an explanation, generally speaking? And what are the criteria for judging that one explanation is better than another? These questions are of enormous import, and much has been written on them, especially in the philosophy of history and the philosophy of science. Nevertheless, through inquiring into character judgments, and advocating the theory that they should be based on abductive argumentation, inevitably this book has adopted a certain viewpoint on the concept of explanation. It is one that is controversial –too controversial to be defended here with the wide generality that would be required to establish it as a well-supported theory of explanation. But since the theory of abductive argument rests so heavily on the concept of explanation, some sketch of the new view of explanation is called for to support the new theory of abductive character judgment.

The purpose of this section is to give a brief summary of how the dialogue (dialectical) model of explanation presented in (Walton, 2004, chapter 2) works. The model offers an account of how explanations are used in everyday conversational exchanges, but not excluding explanations of a technical or scientific sort, or that can occur in academic conversations. By *dialectical* is meant that explanation is viewed as a type of verbal exchange between two participants in some conventionalized type of conversation, judging from the text of discourse in a given case. In terms of Collingwood's theory of explanation in history, explanation is a matter of question and answer. In the new dialectic (Walton, 1998), arguments are evaluated differently in different contexts of dialogue. So too can explanations be evaluated contextually as used in a dialogue. A case study method of analyzing examples of explanations that occur in everyday conversation is the best way to provide evidence to support the worth of this dialectical approach. Many interesting cases of this type have been studied in (Schank, 1986). Schank has identified many different kinds of explanations, and shown they can only be properly understood when they are being used in relation to a background story or script.

Much recent work in artificial intelligence has shown how reasoning and thinking used in understanding a story are often based on assumptions about how the way things normally go not explicitly stated in the story. The implicit and explicit elements of a story fit together into a coherent body of information called a script by Schank and Abelson (1977). A script, in the sense of the word used in artificial intelligence, is a body of knowledge shared by language users concerning what typically happens in certain kinds of situations that the language users are familiar with and can be expected to know about. The script enables a hearer or reader of a story to fill in gaps left implicit in the given discourse. This notion of a script, used in the interpersonal agent theory above, can easily be seen to be applicable to understanding how it is that we can grasp everyday explanations, despite the gaps left in them — gaps in the story that both speaker and hearer can fill in, based on their common understanding of how everyday things work.

Many examples of human advisory interactions that are actual dialogues between teachers and students have been presented by Moore (1995), in order to prove her thesis that explanation is best seen as a dialogue process. According to Moore (p. 1) participants in explanatory dialogue often do not have correct or complete information about the other party. Thus explanations "often require making assumptions about the listener's beliefs, plans and goals". According to Moore's theory of explanation, this information comes in through feedback from the listener through a continuation of dialogue in which further questions are asked. Moore proposed a computational system that produces explanations for what are called expert systems in artificial intelligence. When an expert is consulted to get information or advice, typically the questioner is not himself an expert in the domain of expertise of the respondent. Therefore it is useful, and even necessary in many instances, for the questioner to ask the expert for explanations and clarifications. Sometimes the questioner should even critically probe into what the expert has said, and make objections to it, or question how it squares with common sense. This dialogical method of question and answer is not only very useful in computing, in expert systems and allied technology, but is useful also as applied to the examination of witness testimony in law, because so much witness testimony comes from expert witnesses. The main point to be made, however, is that Moore's theory of explanation, as a dialogic process, is interesting because it has potential to be applied so well to the typical kinds of explanations found in law and history.

Explanation is a kind of verbal exchange where some event or proposition is presumed to have happened or to be true by an explainer and an explainee. The explainee is unclear, or lacks understanding, about the proposition or event, and the explainer tries to clarify it by relating it to some other event or proposition that the explainer presumes the explainee to be familiar with, or already to understand. So conceived, explanation is seen as using simulative reasoning. It is by using this that the explainer relates the one proposition or event to the other in the explanation. The concept of understanding also belongs to the definition of explanation. Understanding is defined in terms of things that an individual is familiar with. For example, if Bob is a plumber, then you can presume that he is familiar with how pipes, toilets, and so forth, work. Hence if you can explain something to him by relating it to these familiar matters, he will be more likely to understand it. But if the explainee is not a plumber, or any kind of expert on pipes and toilets, then the explainer needs to take that factor into account, and must offer a somewhat different kind of explanation. Thus the explainer must try to simulate the kind of practical reasoning that would be used by the explainee, in order to get an explanation that really works.

It is a basic assumption of the new dialectical theory that both arguments and explanations use reasoning, and that the difference between them is to be found in how they use it. An argument is used to bring reasoning to bear on an unsettled issue, a proposition that is not known to be true (or false), or that expresses a conflict of opinions. An explanation is used to throw light on some proposition that is presumed to be true (or false), but is in need of clarification. The analysis of explanation given is also pragmatic in the sense that the different types of explanations are classified in virtue of their being appropriate replies to different types of questions in a dialogue exchange between two parties. For example, a how-question prompts a different type of explanation from a why-question. In general, it is shown that why-questions are ambiguous. In some cases they are requests for an explanation, while in other cases they are requests for an argument. This ambiguity has been the source of much confusion, and the logic textbooks are currently plagued by the problem of getting students to distinguish between explanations and arguments. The dialectical theory provides a solution. Another reason why there has been confusion between explanations and arguments is that the role of reasoning in both has been misconstrued. The pragmatic approach can clarify the role of reasoning in explanations — in particular, the role of practical reasoning, the kind that Aristotle identified with *phronesis*.

The dialectical analysis supports the point of view of Collingwood (1946), William Dray (1964), von Wright (1972) and Rex Martin (1977) that explanations in history should be seen as a species of practical reasoning. It also supports the new approach in computing that sees the explanation process as dialogical (Moore, 1995). This dialectical view goes against the positivistic deductive-nomological theory, which claims that explanation consists in reduction to general laws, based on deductive or inductive reasoning. However, it can also be argued from the dialectical point of view that scientific explanation is a special subtype of explanation that has its own distinctive characteristics based on its own special uses of reasoning. It can be argued that a certain type of scientific explanation does have the characteristic of reduction to scientific laws, but that this type is quite different from the kind of explanation one commonly finds in everyday conversational exchanges. The concern of this book, however, is with the argumentation used in justifying and questioning character judgments. The theory is that such arguments are based on abductive reasoning, or inference to the best explanation, as used by a pair of agents in a bi-level structure. As it has turned out, this theory is tied to a particular view of explanation. The uncovering of this new view of explanation (although it is not new in artificial intelligence, as shown by Schank's work on it), has cast new light on abductive argument. But that is about as far as a book on character evidence can go in trying to sketch a new view of explanation.

5.8 A Dialectical Argumentation Scheme for Abduction

What kind of inference is drawn when one person judges that another person has or lacks integrity from a given set of facts describing the actions of that other person? As shown above, it is often drawn from the account of a witness of the alleged facts. However, not all inferences of this sort are based on witness testimony. Both those that are and those that aren't come under a broader classification of kinds of inference, namely inference to the best explanation. The hypothesis now put forward is that these are abductive inferences of the kind described in chapter 1. As noted there, abductive inference is very similar to, and perhaps is even the same kind of reasoning as what Wellman called conductive argument. But there are several problems with trying to compare the kind of abductive inference described by Josephson and Josephson (1994) to the kind of conductive reasoning used to arrive at a conclusion that somebody is courageous. One problem is that the Josephsons' account is in terms of constructing a hypothesis to account for data, suggesting that the most likely application of this account is to scientific reasoning and hypothesis construction. When evaluating courage and other qualities of character, however, the context is generally not that of a scientific investigation. There are many other kinds of context where such judgments would normally be encountered. One is a biography, another might be an ethical discussion. Another would be a legal argumentation — in a trial, for example. Yet another might be a case where some official organization is giving a citation for bravery. Typically what happens in such cases is that there is a given set of presumed facts, in the form of a story or account of some sort, or one produced or supplemented by examining various witnesses. Then once the facts of the case have been collected, there is a discussion of the case. As the discussion proceeds, explanations of what happened, how it happened, why it happened, and so forth, may be offered. And various arguments may be formulated, perhaps praising or condemning certain actions or participants for what they did. There may be a conflict of opinions on the questions discussed. The whole point of the discussion may be to resolve such a conflict. Wellman's notion of conductive argument fits the kind of argumentation used in such cases very well, because conductive argument is evaluated within the challenge-response context of a given case. This casuistic framework for evaluating conductive argument fits the context of ethical reasoning of the kind used in judging ethical qualities of character.

To fit the requirement of such contexts, abduction needs to be seen as a form of argumentation whose conclusion can tilt the burden of proof one way or the other in such a discussion. For example, a biographer may set out a presumed set of facts and then derive the conclusion that the person in the biography was courageous. This conclusion may appear to be plausible to the extent that it explains the given set of facts better than any alternative explanation. But a critic of the biography may take the same facts and come to a very different conclusion. She might, for example, explain the person's actions by arguing that because of his lack of self-esteem, he had a need to do daring deeds that would win him power over the others. There could be good evidence and relatively persuasive arguments on both sides of the issue. How could abduction be analyzed so that it is applicable to this kind of case, and used to model the conductive reasoning on either side? The answer is given by the abduction scheme proposed below. To generalize the context of use of such an argument type beyond the context of scientific investigation, the generic term "dialogue" is used. A dialogue can be any framework of argumentation in which an issue is unsettled, so that there can be plausible arguments on both sides. In a typical case there is a body of evidence on both sides, and many abductive arguments nested within the argumentation on both sides.

The abduction scheme for abductive argument is based on two variables (Walton, 2004, p. 216). The variable *F* stands for a set of what are called facts. A set of facts is a set of statements that describe events, or report observations about these events. They are called "facts" because they are presumed to be true. It may not be known for sure that they are true, but their truth is not in doubt. For the purpose of the abductive argument, they are assumed to describe observations of what actually happened in a given case. The variable *E* stands for an explanation. The concept of explanation is dialectical. What it means to say that *E* is a satisfactory explanation of *F* is that *E* is a set of statements put forward by a participant in a dialogue that gives the other party greater understanding of *F* (Walton, 2004). An explanation is a response to a question in dialogue. The satisfactoriness of an explanation depends on the type of dialogue the two parties are engaged in, on how far the dialogue has progressed, and on what has been said in the dialogue before the explanation was attempted. Given these parameters, the argumentation scheme for abductive argument can be set out as follows.

Dialectical Argumentation Scheme for Abductive Argument

F is a finding or given set of facts.
E is a satisfactory explanation of *F*.
No alternative explanation *E′* given so far is as satisfactory as *E*.
Therefore, *E* is plausible, as a hypothesis.

The term "hypothesis" indicates that the conclusion of the abductive argument is only an assumption that is more or less plausible as a commitment. It is not "proved" by the premises, but only set in place as a plausible commitment for the time being. It has a weight of plausibility in its favor, but that weight can be dislodged merely through the asking of appropriate critical questions.

CQ1: How satisfactory is *E* itself as an explanation of *F*, apart from the alternative explanations available so far in the dialogue?

CQ2: How much better an explanation is E than the alternative explanations available so far in the dialogue?

CQ3: How far has the dialogue progressed? If the dialogue is an inquiry, how thorough has the search been in the investigation of the case?

CQ4: Would it be better to continue the dialogue further, instead of drawing a conclusion at this point?

It is typical of abductive arguments that each has only a small weight of plausibility by itself. But each is useful to move a dialogue forward in a network of argumentation containing other abductive arguments. The small weight of plausibility of each argument has a place in distributing the weight of plausibility over the mass of evidence compiled in the whole dialogue, once it is completed. In all respects, the kind of argument structured by the new dialectical argumentation scheme for abductive argument makes the latter appear to be the same as, or certainly very similar to the kind of argument that Wellman called conductive argument. Which term should be used? Either would be fine, but the term "abductive" has now become so widely accepted that it appears to be the better term to use.

This analysis of the form of abductive argument is dialectical, meaning that it is evaluated by the interactive dialogue between two parties — the proponent who put the argument forward and the respondent who questions it. Wellman quite accurately described it as the challenge-reponse model. The context is that of a dialogue in which two arguers take turns. One puts forward a claim or conclusion to be proved, and the other challenges that claim by asking critical questions. But what kind of dialogue is typically involved when judgments of character are at stake?

An account is a set of statements, $A_1, A_2, \ldots, A_n$, offered by one party in a dialogue in answer to a question put by the other party. An account may be a narrative, but more generally it could be a set of statements that links some to others by causal relations by linking an agent's presumed goals to his reported actions. An account does not have to be internally consistent. But if an inconsistency is found, questions can be asked, and the questioner should require that the account be repaired or given up. The account can then be modified to remove the inconsistency, or expanded, to fill gaps created by deletions. Thus more than one account can be given to answer a question. If one of a pair of competing accounts is better, or more plausible than the other, the better one should be accepted. Figure 5.1 below (Walton, 2004, p. 267) outlines the process of how abductive reasoning moves towards a conclusion by judging accounts comparatively by questioning and critically examining each one.

As shown in Figure 5.1, the dialogue starts with a database representing the facts so far collected in an account. The questioner asks a question to achieve a better understanding of some or all of these facts. The respondent

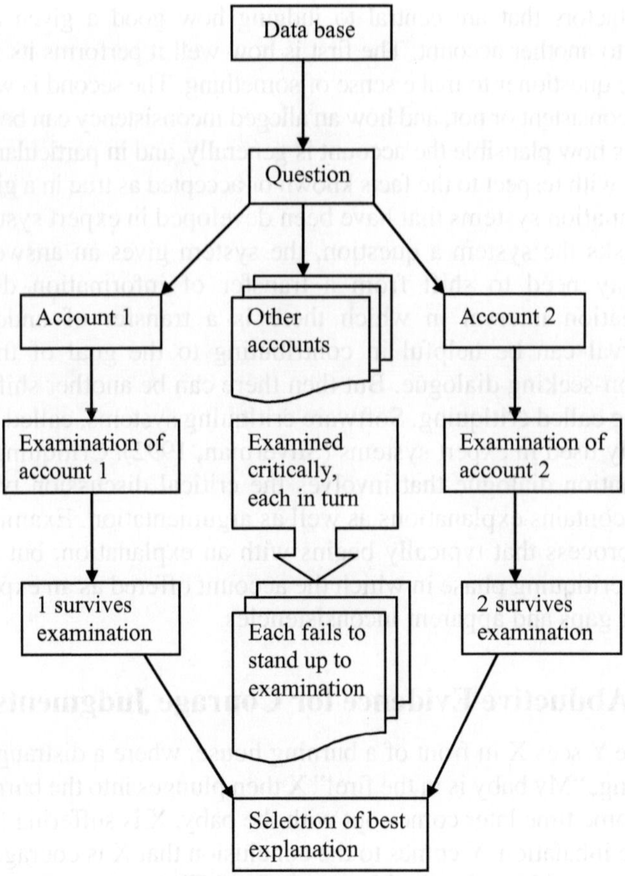

Figure 5.1. How abductive reasoning concludes to a best explanation.

replies by putting forward an account offered to explain the facts that were asked about. Alternative accounts that serve to explain the same facts may also be given. There may be two competing accounts that explain the same data in different ways, called account 1 and account 2. Which is the best or more plausible explanation? The comparative plausibility of each account is judged by how well each stands up to critical questioning.

The purpose of an account is not always to explain something. It might be offered to describe something that happened. For example, a witness in a trial may be asked to describe what she saw during a bank robbery. In cases of explanations, the purpose of offering an account is to help a questioner come to understand something that he does not now understand. In such a case, the worth or success of the account should be defined in relation to how the party who offered it understands the lack of understanding of the other party. There are three factors that are central to judging how good a given account is, compared to another account. The first is how well it performs its function of helping the questioner to make sense of something. The second is whether it is internally consistent or not, and how an alleged inconsistency can be dealt with. The third is how plausible the account is generally, and in particular, how consistent it is with respect to the facts known or accepted as true in a given case.

In explanation systems that have been developed in expert systems in AI, the user asks the system a question, the system gives an answer. But the system may need to shift from a transfer of information dialogue to an explanation interval in which there is a transfer of understanding. This interval can be helpful in contributing to the goal of the original information-seeking dialogue. But then there can be another shift to a type of dialogue called critiquing. Software critiquing systems, called critics, are now widely used in expert systems (Silverman, 1992). Critiquing is a form of examination dialogue that involves the critical discussion type of dialogue but contains explanations as well as argumentation. Examination is a complex process that typically begins with an explanation, but then often shifts to a critiquing phase in which the account offered as an explanation is probed for gaps and apparent inconsistencies.

5.9 Abductive Evidence for Courage Judgments

Suppose Y sees X in front of a burning house, where a distraught woman is screaming, "My baby is in the fire!" X then plunges into the burning building, and some time later comes out with the baby. X is suffering from burns and smoke inhalation. Y comes to the conclusion that X is courageous. How could Y reasonably arrive at this conclusion? The answer proposed in the case of Mike and Mary, in chapter 4, section 6, is based on the assumption that both X and Y are agents, and therefore one can simulate the reasoning of the other. Because Y is an agent, he uses the same kind of practical reasoning that X uses. So when Y draws a conclusion about X's quality of character based only on what he has seen about X's actions in the given case, Y's reasoning rests on his own use of practical reasoning. In using simulative reasoning to draw a conclusion about the internal qualities of character of X, Y assumes that he is using the same kind of practical reasoning that X is using.

The reasoning in the case works as follows. First of all, various data or presumed facts are evident to Y. Y sees the burning house, and judges that there would be risk of painful injury or even death for anyone who entered the house. As evidence, there are other people standing around, including the mother of the child supposedly in the house, and none of them are going into the burning house. In this situation, presumably Y drew a number of conclusions. One is that there is a chance that the baby who is supposed to be in the house is still alive. Another is that there is some chance of saving the baby if someone could run into the house and bring the baby out. When X went into the burning house, her action was presumably the outcome of deliberation based on the facts as she saw them, and the conclusions (above) she drew from these facts. This set of facts and plausible inferences is the first level, or deliberation level of the case.

At the second level, various facts are evident to Y. In addition to all the facts evident to X, Y also has some data that he sees. Y sees that X has heard what the distraught mother has said. Then Y sees X run into the burning house. Then Y sees X come out of the house with the baby. From these actions, Y infers that the reason X went into the burning house was to save the baby. These inferences are based on scripts that put all the events together into a connected story. Y also infers that X was aware of the risks of this action. Seeing X's actions, and presuming that X was aware of the risks of those actions, Y draws a conclusion about X's goal. X's goal was (Y assumes) to save the baby. Saving a human life is a worthy goal, of ethical import. Y knows that, and Y infers that X also knows that. By simulative reasoning, Y uses his own practical reasoning as an agent to draw conclusions about why X acted as he did in the given situation.

The simulative reasoning used by Y is abductive. Y observes actions of X, and then Y draws conclusions about X's presumed goals, based on the evidence of the observed actions, and Y's reconstruction of the way X presumably saw the situation. Y infers that X concluded that the only way to save the baby was to go into the burning house. Y infers that X thought that it was possible for him to save the baby by going into the burning house. Y reasons that X arrived by practical reasoning at the mean. Y reasons that X judged that the action of going into the burning house, although it was risky and would likely have painful consequences for her personally, was worth the risk, in light of what she saw as valuable and possible. Because Y is also an agent, Y can go through the same sequence of practical reasoning that X did, and can reconstruct, although imperfectly, how Y arrived at the mean. By reconsidering the form of the basic practical inference, the structure of Y's reasoning can be made evident. Y puts himself in the place of X, in the given situation, and then recreates what he takes to be X's line of reasoning. Y can reconstruct the whole story of X's actions because Y understands how the motives and actions of X are connected into a schema for human action (Pennington and Hastie, 1991). The structure of the reasoning can be shown to fit the model of practical reasoning. The variable *A* represents the state of affairs of saving the baby. The variable *B* represents the state of affairs of X's going into the burning house.

(*PInf.*) *A* is my goal (represents my general values).
To bring about *A*, it looks like I should bring about *B*.
Therefore, as far as I can tell, I ought to bring about *B*.

To simulate X's practical reasoning, Y reasons backwards, from the facts of the case, to a hypothesis about what X's goal presumably was. Y does not know what X's goal was. This question is a matter for conjecture and discussion. But Y does know some facts of the case, in virtue of what he saw. He saw X go into the burning house. In other words, he saw what X actually did. Therefore, Y can infer by simulative reasoning that X arrived at the conclusion of (*PInf.*) above. In other words, Y as an agent infers that X as an agent used practical reasoning to arrive at the judgment to act as she did, based on goals that X had, and on how X saw the given situation. Y infers that X's goal was to save the baby. And Y infers that X judged that it was necessary to go into the burning house to save the baby. Y's reasoning went backwards, from the conclusion of (*PInf.*) to the premises. By seeing the action that X actually carried out, Y as agent used simulative abductive reasoning to draw conclusions about how X saw the situation, and about what X's goals were.

In simulating X's reasoning, Y also needs to take the following critical questions into account.

CQ1: Are there alternative possible courses of action to *B*?

CQ2: Is *B* the best (or most acceptable) of the alternatives?

CQ3: Do I have goals other than *A* that ought to be taken into account?

CQ4: Is it possible to bring about *B* in the given circumstance?

CQ5: Does *B* have known bad consequences that ought to be taken into account?

Y assumed that X had gone through this list of considerations herself, prior to her action of going into the burning house. Y presumably ruled out less risky alternative means of saving the baby. Y presumably was aware of, and took into account the risks of personal injury, or even death, in his entering the burning house. Y presumably judged that it was possible to save the baby by going into the burning house. All these critical questions need to have been answered appropriately by X, in her own personal deliberations, before entering the house. Otherwise, Y's argument to the conclusion that X's action was courageous is defeated. In drawing this conclusion, Y must run through the same checklist of critical questions that X presumably did. At the first level, X must have engaged in deliberation about her own practical reasoning. At the second level, Y must use the given data of X's actions to run through the same sequence of practical reasoning, only backwards. The simulated sequence starts from X's conclusion as a new part of the given data, and then reasons backwards to a conclusion about what X's goal in so acting presumably was. Of course, it is just a guess. Y can never know by direct evidence what X's goals really were. All Y can do is to scan the evidence, and reason to a hypothesis about what X's goals presumably were, given the factual evidence in the case.

In the simple case above, Y is drawing a conclusion about X's intentions with respect to X's carrying out a single action. Drawing a conclusion about courage as a quality of X's character would be more general, and would be based on a wider set of data. For example, many incidents in X's life might be cited as evidence for the conclusion that X is a courageous person. But the compiling of this body of evidence would come from inferences drawn, as above, from several incidents known or reported about X's actions in various situations. For example, in a biography of X, many such incidents might be related. Then the conclusions drawn on the basis of all these singular incidents would be massed together into a more comprehensive body of evidence. The whole network of evidence would be based on abductive simulative reasoning in particular cases.

The sequence of simulative reasoning that led to the conclusion that X is a courageous person can be exhibited as follows.

> Y observed X go into the burning house.
>
> Y knows that going into the burning house is very dangerous.
>
> Y presumes that X knows that going into the burning house is very dangerous.
>
> Why would someone do something that is personally dangerous? The risk must have been judged to be worthwhile in order to realize some worthy goal.
>
> From observing what X did, Y infers that X came to the conclusion that it was possible for her to save the baby by going into the burning house.
>
> Y infers, therefore, that X's goal was to save the baby.
>
> Y thinks that saving the baby is a highly worthwhile goal.
>
> Y thinks that X thought that saving the baby is a worthwhile goal.
>
> Y concludes that X took the personally dangerous risk of going into the burning house in order to realize the worthwhile goal of saving the baby.

Taking a personal risk involving danger and injury, and possibly even death, in order to realize a worthy goal, like saving the life of another person, is an indicator of courage.

Therefore, Y concludes that X is courageous.

This kind of abductive, simulated reasoning is based on the given set of facts in the case. Should these facts change, through new relevant information that coming is, the conclusion could be defeated. Suppose all the above facts are true, but suppose that Y heard X say, as she entered the building, "Call the reporters. I want to get a medal for this act of heroism". In this new case, while saving the baby was still a good thing, doubts are raised about whether X is really courageous. While it still might be truly said that X's action was one of bravery, critical questions about X's goals would throw the hypothesis that she is courageous into doubt. For by simulative reasoning, Y could now draw the conclusion by abduction that X's goal was one of self-aggrandizement. This goal is not one that should be thought of as providing a good reason for risking one's life. Ethical arguments of this kind would at any rate throw doubt on the hypothesis that X is courageous.

Some would say that the whole issue in such a case is subjective, because it all depends on goals that are "in X's head". And it needs to be conceded that the reasoning, on either side of the issue, is guesswork, based on presumptions by one party about what another's party's goals are. But there are many aspects of the reasoning that are objective and can be clearly stated for analysis and evaluation. And the inferences about these missing or unstated parts of the story can be drawn out, however, by plausible reasoning. This reasoning can then be tested by critical examination. The practical reasoning is based on given data in the case that can be verified or falsified. The chain of practical reasoning from the premises to the ultimate conclusion is a sequence of inferences that can be evaluated at each step. Although the reasoning is simulative and abductive, it does have a clear structure as a sequence of argumentation.

5.10 Abductive Evidence for Integrity Judgments

Simulative reasoning is a form of guessing, because the secondary agent does not have direct access to the internal motives and goals of the primary agent. In cases where simulative reasoning is useful, there is often uncertainty about whether a hypothesis is true or whether its negation is true. Thus simulative reasoning is often most applicable to a situation in which there is a conflict of opinions. The goal of simulative argumentation is one of conflict resolution. The problem is to judge whether one proposition or its negation is the more plausible hypothesis to explain the facts of a given case. In some cases, the conflict itself prompts the problem. In a typical case where a primary agent's integrity is at issue, for example, the secondary agent perceives an apparent contradiction, or conflict of commitments, in the actions and words of the primary agent. Simulative reasoning is required in the argumentation surrounding such a case.

Suppose, for example, that Y listens to a speech given by X in which X promotes certain goals and values. X argues that smoking is a bad practice, because it is very bad for health. X counsels young people not to take up smoking. Y draws the conclusion that X is against smoking. But then later, Y sees X lighting up a cigar and smoking it. Y then has the problem of trying to reconcile two lines of argumentation he attributes to X.

1. Y thinks that X is against smoking, as a matter of general policy.
2. Y sees X smoking, and so draws the conclusion that X is really not against smoking.

The conclusions drawn from these two inferences are opposed to each other. Both can't be right. Either X is against smoking or she is not. Y must therefore try to find some way to explain the apparent contradiction. In this case, much of the problem turns on how to interpret rules and general policies. Is X really saying that smoking is always a bad action for every person? Or was she allowing for exceptions to the rule? Maybe X was only arguing that smoking was bad for young people, but that it could be OK for people whose health is not so much affected by it.

How can Y resolve the problem? If X is really preaching one thing but practicing the opposite, then X is a hypocrite. A hypocrite is a person who advocates some practice as the right conduct for everyone but then acts contrary to it (in an intentional and purposive way) in her own personal case. Such an inconsistency shows that her real goals and values are not the ones she professes in her public declarations and exhortations. In the case above, Y sees X smoking. So that side of the contradiction appears to be firmly supported. Y must then turn to the details of the speech given by X. What did X really mean to say in the speech, and what does her wording imply about her commitments?

In this case, Y must try to follow the practical reasoning of X, used when X put forward her diatribe against smoking. Why was X against smoking? The reason she gave was that smoking is bad for health. So what was X trying to say about smoking as a policy? Was she saying that no person should ever smoke? Or was she saying that smoking is generally bad, subject to exceptions? For example, if a person over thirty smokes an occasional cigar without inhaling, maybe it could be argued that smoking an occasional cigar is not really bad for health.

Another possibility is that X's action of smoking the cigar may not have implied that she is really committed to smoking as a policy that is all right for her personally. X could have had various excuses for her conduct. She might argue, for example, that although she would not normally smoke, on this occasion she was trying to save the life of an American citizen by intervening with the Cuban ambassador. She might argue that if she had refused to join with him in smoking cigars, he would have been insulted. She may have inferred that if he felt insulted, the deal to save the American citizen's life would fall through. Of course, Y does not know that any story like this one would be ventured by X. But it is possible that X would come forth with some such excuse like this one if she were confronted with the contradiction, and accused of being a hypocrite.

What Y must try to do is to reason about X's reasoning, based on the given evidence of what X said and did. But how can Y draw inferences from what X said, and from what X did, that imply conclusions about what X really thinks, or is committed to as policies? The facts themselves suggest a contradiction in X's commitments, which in turn suggests that X is a hypocrite. But the evidence is not conclusive. How can Y get more evidence? One thing that Y can do is to engage in textual interpretation of X's speech. What were X's exact words, and did they imply a universal policy against smoking, or only a more restricted kind of policy that might admit of exceptions? Another thing that Y could do would be to engage in further dialogue with X, asking X what she meant by saying that smoking is bad. At this stage, more evidence would enter the picture. Given an excuse like the one cited above, Y might then withdraw the claim that X is a hypocrite. What Y must do is to ask the right critical questions about X's words and deeds in the case, and then, if X can answer the questions, engage in dialogue with X. That is how the matter should properly be resolved.

In a case like this one, simulative reasoning is involved, because it is a matter of Y's reasoning about X's reasoning. Because both X and Y are agents, Y can draw plausible conclusions about what X is thinking from what X says and does. In particular, if there is an apparent conflict of commitments that can be inferred from what X says and does, then Y may draw the conclusion that X lacks integrity. But there is evidence, of a kind that can be verified and tested, that should be used to support or criticize such a judgment. One kind of evidence is the factual data about what X did. Another kind is the textual evidence that could be provided by a transcript of X's speech against smoking. These data can be used as an evidential basis for supporting or refuting the allegation that X lacks integrity. However, whether X can be said to lack integrity or not, as shown by this body of data, is a matter of X's commitments. All Y can do is extrapolate from the data to construct a hypothesis about X's thinking in the case. Logic, of a sort, is relevant to testing this hypothesis. For it can be argued logically from the given data of the case that an inconsistency of commitments has been shown, or not. The issue should be resolved by isolating the propositions on both sides. The one proposition is supposedly the negation of the other, and both propositions are arguably commitments of the primary agent. The case for or against integrity turns on whether there is a contradiction there or not. That is the heart of the matter.

Chapter 6

A MULTI-AGENT SYSTEM FOR CHARACTER EVIDENCE

In this chapter, a multi-agent system that can be used to assist in the management and evaluation of character evidence in law is put forward. It is based on argumentation schemes for various kinds of character-based arguments identified in the chapter, and generally on the scheme for abductive reasoning. As modeled in the system, character arguments are shown to be rationally acceptable under the right conditions as evidence. However, they are also shown to be a fallible form of evidence that should be subject to critical questioning. We already know that can be dangerous and prejudicial in some instances, as shown by the examples of character attack and assassination in chapter 1. The system will show that when one agent judges the character of another, the reasoning process is one of guesswork and estimation in a situation of incomplete knowledge. Still, it can be based on factual data furnished by the words and deeds of another, and that can be evaluated in such a way as to provide a hypothesis about an agent's character that can carry probative weight as evidence in law.

Argumentation schemes are currently being investigated as potentially useful tools in computational research on legal reasoning support systems (Bex *et al.*, 2003; Verheij, 2003, 2005; Gordon, 2005; Walton and Gordon, 2005). The PFARD system developed in this chapter is based on a set of argumentation schemes especially designed for use in managing character evidence. Each scheme has a matching set of critical questions. It is shown how this system can be applied to evidence in legal cases to confirm as well as to refute character evidence. The system displays the steps of reasoning used when one party makes a character judgment about another party in a given case. Basically, the first party considers the reported facts of a case in which a second party's actions and words are described. This body of facts making up the given case functions as the data of an abductive inference. The first party can then form a hypothesis that the second party has certain qualities of character, or not, by examining alternative explanations of the given facts in the case, and drawing an inference to the best explanation of those facts. This abductive argument can then be judged to be relevant or not, and evaluated as strong or weak in light of the mass of evidence in the case.

6.1 Character-Based Inferences

The first problem is to distinguish between forms of inference that are character-based and forms of inference that are closely related to character-based ones, but are not really character-based. The latter are easily confused with the former.[1] Let's begin with some very simple and basic forms of character-based inference that were identified in chapter 1. The first is the inference from a reported or alleged fact about an agent's action to a conclusion about the agent's character.

Inference from Lying to Dishonest Character

He lied.
Therefore he is dishonest.

This type of inference is character-based, because one of the statements in it (the conclusion) is about the agent's character. At least, it can be assumed that the statement that the agent is dishonest is about one of his character traits. More about this assumption will be discussed below, but let's accept it for the moment.

The reverse kind of inference, also cited in chapter 1, can be classified as character-based on the same grounds.

Inference from Dishonest Character to Lying

He is dishonest.
Therefore he is lying now.

In this instance the property of character appears in the premise rather than in the conclusion of the inference. Once again, the assumption that dishonesty is a property of the agent's character means that the inference is character-based.

[1]This distinction is quite important in evidence law, for the prohibition on character evidence does not apply to kinds of inferences that are based on propensity, habit, motive, or other factors, as long as they are not based on properties that can properly be called character traits. According to Park (1998, p. 719), the character evidence ban does not apply "if testimony leads to an inference that a person committed an act without any intermediate inference about general cross-situational propensity (character) . . . even if the evidence shows 'propensity' in the sense of showing a proclivity to repeat situation-specific conduct".

Both these inferences are character-based in that both depend essentially on some property (trait) of the agent's character that is being cited.

Let's now contrast such typical character-based inferences with a kind of inference that was recognized in chapter 3 as sometimes playing an important role as evidence in law. As noted in chapter 3, the form of this type of inference was identified by Park, Leonard and Goldberg (1998, p. 159) using the following example.

The Bank Robbery Inference from *Modus Operandi* to Alleged Criminal Act

Factual Premise: Defendant robbed other banks using exactly the same method.
General Premise: Defendant is a bank robber who uses that distinctive method to commit the crime.
Conclusion: Defendant is the person who committed the crime at issue.

The general form of this type of inference can be identified as follows.

Inference from *Modus Operandi* to Carrying Out an Action

Modus Operandi Premise: Agent *a* carried out a set of actions in the past using the same general method or routine (*modus operandi*).
Action in Question Premise: This particular action fits the same *modus operandi*.
Conclusion: There is reason to suspect that *a* carried out this action.

This form of argument is quite a weak one. For there may be many agents who have the same *modus operandi*, and there may be no evidence that any of them committed the act in question. The argument nevertheless can have some probative weight if a particular person is a suspect, and there is plenty of other evidence against him. By itself, however, it does not carry much weight.

The main point to be made here is that the inference from *modus operandi* to actually carrying out an action can look superficially quite similar to a character-based inference. But the *modus operandi* premise is subtly different. It is not based on a generalization about the agent's character, but on one using a repeated pattern of action or *modus operandi*, a routine way of doing something methodically. Comparable remarks can be made about other forms of argumentation commonly used in evidence law, including argument from motive, from bias, from habit (propensity), and from reputation. Each of these forms of inference can be used as evidence in law without being character-based. Much the same kinds of remarks need to be made in connection with the argument that Uviller (1996, p. 220) put in the form of a syllogism, as noted in chapter 1.

Major Premise: Racketeers coerce contracts.
Minor Premise: Delta is a racketeer.
Conclusion: Delta coerced the contract at issue.

As already noted in chapter 1, this argument is not as compelling because it could easily be wrong, in the absence of further evidence. As Uviller observed (p. 220), many racketeers do not coerce contracts, and many contracts are coerced by racketeers other than Delta (p. 220). But even though weak, it might carry some weight along with other evidence in a case. The point to be made here, however, is that it is not a character-based argument, assuming that being a racketeer is not a trait of character. It is an argument about the propensity, or perhaps the *modus operandi*, of a certain type of criminal.

In chapter 2, a particularly interesting form of inference representing a common kind of reasoning in evidence law was identified by Park *et al.*, (1998, p. 158). In chapter 2, this inference was classified as character-based.

The Armed Robbery Inference

Factual Premise: The defendant committed an armed robbery.
General Premise: The defendant is the type of person who commits armed robberies.
Conclusion: It is more likely that defendant is guilty of the present crime than would otherwise be the case.

We now need to examine this inference more closely, and raise some questions about whether it is really character-based. Does the argument depend on an implicit premise that committing armed robberies requires a certain property of character, like a trait for violence and taking risks? If so, the armed robbery inference is a character-based argument. But is it really classifiable in this category? There are grounds for doubt. It looks more like it could be an argument from habit or *modus operandi*. The ambiguity resides in the expression 'type of person who commits armed robberies'. Is this a character property attribution, or merely a claim about a pattern of actions or a disposition to carry out a certain kind of action? It is hard to say, and thus care should be taken to try to disambiguate this kind of evidence.

A main issue in evidence law is whether past convictions should be relevant in a criminal trial. The issue concerns the following type of inference.

The Past Convictions Inference

He had past convictions (typically, for a similar kind of offence).
Therefore he is guilty of the offence alleged in this trial.

The problem of relevance turns on whether this is a character-based argument or not. It could be an argument from propensity or habit, or some other kind of argument that is not character-based. On the other hand, it could be a character-based argument of the following form.

A Character-Based Chain Argument

He had past convictions (typically, for a similar kind of offence).
Therefore he has bad character.
Therefore he is guilty of the offence allowed in this trial.

In this argument, the second premise has been made explicit, showing that the argument is character-based. The previous argument was incomplete, or unclear, in this respect. What needs to be done in cases where the past convictions inference was put forward as an argument is to determine if it is a character-based argument or not.

6.2 Inferences Linking Evidence to Character

It is not hard to see why inferences from action to character have generally been taken to be inductive in nature. They are based on observed instances, which can then presumably be counted up, and thus they provide empirical evidence for a generalization expressing a probability.[2] Similarly, it is easy to see why inferences from character to action have also been generally taken to be inductive. The assumption is that they are based on some sort of probabilistic generalization, in the form of a propensity, which is then used to make a prediction or guess about the chances of a singular event happening. A propensity, presumably, is just a summing up of the positive instances of an agent's carrying out a certain kind of action. Thus the inductive model of probability as a counting up of positive instances seems to apply naturally.

[2]Probability is a hard notion to define uncontroversially, but as applied to legal reasoning, it is often associated with Bayes' theorem, which defines conditional probability as a function of the probability values of single statements or events. The Bayesian approach has been described by Allen (1997), who argued that it cannot be implemented in a typical trial because of the computational complexity of the evidence in a trial. Allen's arguments apply very well to character evidence used in trials.

The notion of character generally accepted in law and the social sciences is that character is a "disposition" or "propensity" for a person to act in a certain way, following generalized patterns of conduct or "traits". This commonly accepted notion of character is well expressed in the much-quoted definition of "character" given in McCormick's (1992) widely used handbook of evidence law: "a generalized description of one's disposition, or of one's disposition in respect to a general trait, such as honesty, temperance, or peacefulness". According to this model of character as a form of evidence, or as part of common forms of reasoning that are often taken to furnish evidence, inferences drawn to or from a person's character are inductive in nature. Some common forms of inference of this kind are illustrated by the following examples.

Inference from Action to Character

He did something that can be described as honest.
Therefore he is honest.

Inference from Character to Action (Predictive)

He is honest.
Therefore if he carries out some action in the future, it is likely to be honest (as opposed to being dishonest, in a case where honesty is an issue).

As noted in chapter 1, there is a common tendency to think that honesty can very simply be defined as a propensity to tell the truth. Thus dishonesty is a propensity to lie, or not tell the truth. Some problems with this approach were cited in chapter 1. First, a lie is more than just saying something false. Saying something false can happen through ignorance, or being misinformed. Thus lying needs to be defined as intentionally saying something false, or that one thinks is false. There has to be an intention to deceive (Bok, 1978). Another problem is that some lies are not evidence that a person is dishonest. In chapter 1 the incident of de la Riviere's lying to the Turks to cause them to attack a heavily defended fort was cited (Bradford, 1972, p. 153). In the circumstances, telling this lie was not taken as evidence of a dishonest or morally bad character. Thus for evidence of dishonesty more is required than just past incidents of having said something that was not true. It is for this reason that the inferences from action to character and certain forms of inference from character to action are abductive rather than inductive. The problem has to do with how the character trait of honesty is to be defined. Honesty is a characteristic that depends on the circumstances of the deliberations that the agent is faced with in a given situation and how he reacts ethically.

It is easy to think that all common inferences from character to action are inductive, but as Park (1998, p. 722) observed, "propensity evidence often throws more light on the past than on the future". In historical and legal reasoning, evidence of a person's character, or propensity to engage in a certain kind of behavior, may be used to draw a conclusion about whether this person carried out some action or not in the past. Such an inference is not predictive but retroductive, meaning that it goes backward in time from given assumptions to a hypothesis about a prior event.

Inference from Character to Action (Retroductive)

Bob is honest.
Therefore, if a question is raised about whether Bob performed some action in the past that could be described as dishonest, there is some probative weight in favor of the hypothesis that Bob didn't do it.

The retroductive inference from character to action seems similar to the predictive inference from character to action, except for the time directions. One goes from the present to the future while the other goes from the present to the past.

The next point that needs to be recognized is that the types of character-based inferences cited above can be combined to form chains of reasoning that function as evidence in legal cases.

The Lying Witness Chain of Reasoning

Factual Premise: The witness lied in the past.
Character Premise: The witness is dishonest.
Conclusion: It is likely that the witness is lying in this case.

This chain of reasoning combines inference from action to character with inference from character to action. The factual premise infers from specific actions to a general character trait. This conclusion is then used again as a premise (the character premise) to infer a further conclusion. Thus what we have is a chain of reasoning made up of two character inferences. The same kind of chain of reasoning can be formed by non-character-based inferences, as illustrated by the armed robbery inference. Also, one can have chains of reasoning composed partly of character-based inferences and partly of non-character-based ones.

The theory of this book is that there is an alternative to the inductive model to represent the forms of reasoning in such cases, called the abductive model. This theory posits that the generalization is not an inductive one, based on a propensity concerning probability. Instead, the generalization is seen as defeasible, that is, as open to defeat by exceptions that cannot be predicted in advance in any probabilistic way. The inference is based on a burden of proof set for a particular type of dialogue. Based on a given set of statements that both parties in the dialogue agree are factual, the one party puts forward a hypothesis to explain these facts in the form of a presumption. If it is a good (or so-called best) explanation of these facts, the other party is obliged to tentatively accept it, subject to further information that may enter the dialogue in the form of new facts.

The abductive model of character evidence at first seems to many like a poor alternative to the inductive model. In the inductive model, numbers can be attached to each statement that is a premise or conclusion in the argument, and then probabilities can be calculated to measure the probative weight of the inference, using the axioms of the probability calculus. This approach is seen to be objective and scientific. The abductive model, in contrast, brings in a context of inquiry or dialogue between two parties, and in each dialogue questions are asked, and there must be some burden of proof set for a claim. These notions, in the common opinion, seem to be subjective, perhaps because we can't calculate the strength of a given inference by attaching numbers to each statement involved and then performing a numerical calculation. Or even if we could, the assignment of the numbers would seem pretty arbitrary.

The notion of abductive reasoning is a relative newcomer to the logical scene, but there are many in the field of artificial intelligence now using and advocating it as a tool to deal with defeasible reasoning of a kind that is extremely common in AI (Josephson and Josephson, 1994). The abductive model also applies very well to trace reasoning of the kind so common in evidence law (Walton, 2004). For example, if a footprint matching the shoe of the suspect is found at the crime scene, then that trace is considered to be relevant evidence in the case. Why? On the abductive model, it is relevant evidence because a plausible explanation of how the imprint got there is that the suspect stepped there and his shoe left this trace. If so, that could link him to the crime, making the footprint relevant evidence in the case. Of course, there could be other explanations of the print, but in their absence, this evidence has a probative weight. Is the probative weight best seen as representing a kind of judgment based on probability? Perhaps, but it can also be viewed as based on an abductive judgment of what can be concluded from the facts of the case on a basis of best explanation leading to a presumption that shifts a burden of proof to one side or the other in a dialogue. In (Walton, 2004) it is shown how such inferences can be analyzed and evaluated in a dialogue-based (dialectical) model.

Prediction is a form of reasoning we associate with probabilities, and thus it is appropriate to classify the inference from character to action as an inductive form of inference. Since the retroductive form of inference from character to action appears to have the same structure, except for the time difference, it is natural to regard it too as inductive. However, it is the argument of this chapter that two of the three common forms of inference about character modeled above are better seen as abductive in nature, rather than as inductive. It may be granted that the predictive form of inference from character to action is generally best seen as inductive. But the other two forms of inference modeled above are best classified as abductive.

6.3 Generalizations and Fallacies

According to a standard classification, there are three types of generalizations. The universal generalization is absolute, meaning that it refers to all the individuals in the domain envisaged in the statement without allowing for even one exception. For example, if the generalization "All men are mortal" is an absolute one, this implies that it refers to all men without exception, and thus that it is falsified by finding a single counter-example. The familiar inference "All men are mortal, Socrates is a man, therefore Socrates is mortal" is deductively valid, because its warrant is an absolute universal generalization. This means that it is logically impossible for the premises to be true and the conclusion false. Inductive generalizations are statements like "Most lottery winners lose their winnings within ten years", or "98 per cent of lottery winners lose their winnings within ten years". These generalization express probabilities, often, or even typically, of a kind that can be measured by attaching numbers to them. The strength of an inference based on an inductive generalization can be measured by assigning numbers between zero and one to each of the statements in the inference, and calculating the strength of the inference using the axioms of the probability calculus.

Deductive and inductive reasoning, based respectively on absolute and inductive generalizations, have dominated logic in the past, especially with the rise of science in the Enlightenment period. Basing his approach on the view generally accepted in logic at the time, the great evidential theorist John H. Wigmore (1931, p. 17) operated on the assumption that there are only two types of inference, deductive and inductive. Despite this theoretical stance, Wigmore was very practical in examining the reasoning used in actual cases at trial, often adopting the language of inference to the best explanation when discussing such cases. For example, in two cases Wigmore (1931, p. 20) considered these inferences.

The Biased Witness Inference

> Last week the witness *A* had a quarrel with the defendant *B*, therefore *A* is probably biased against *B*.

The Bloody Knife Inference

> *A* was found with a bloody knife in *B*'s house, therefore *A* is probably the murderer of *B*.

Neither inference is of the deductive or inductive type. It is possible that, despite the quarrel, the witness could be telling the truth, or giving accurate testimony. And despite the use of the word 'probably' as a qualifier, the inference is not really based on numerical probabilities. Rather the fact of the quarrel raises the question of whether the witness might be biased, and unless that question can be answered, a presumption of bias throws some doubt on the reliability of the testimony of the witness as evidence. A similar analysis can be applied to the bloody knife inference. The hypothesis that *A* is the murderer explains the fact of *A* being found with a bloody knife in *B*'s house. There could be other explanations, but the hypothesis of *A* murdering *B* could be the best of the ones that fit the case. So analyzed, the generalizations in these cases could be classified as rough and subject to exceptions that can only be judged in relation to the mass of evidence in the circumstances of the case. The inference based on such generalizations is abductive. Generalizations of this kind are very common in legal evidence. For example, testimonial evidence and character evidence are both based on generalizations about how a person having general character traits, like honesty, will generally act in a given set of circumstances. This kind of evidence is best seen as resting on generalizations that are neither absolute nor probabilistic, but that warrant abductive inferences.

In recent years there has been a strong interest in this third type of reasoning in the field of artificial intelligence (Prakken, 2001; Bex and Prakken, 2004; Bex *et al.*, 2004). Previously, Alfred Sidgwick was a voice in the wilderness criticizing the narrowness of logicians who concentrated exclusively on deductive and inductive forms of reasoning. Sidgwick (1893, p. 23) argued that if you depend on an absolute universal generalization as a warrant for an inference, once it is admitted to have one exception, its value as support for the inference is lost. Legal argumentation is full of generalizations that are subject to exceptions of a kind that cannot be quantified or anticipated in advance, as new evidence comes into a case (Anderson, 1999). Inferences based on generalizations about an agent's character fit into this category.

Statements about character are often pivotal as evidence in law because they function as general statements that warrant inferences. A character statement, like "The witness is a liar" or "The defendant is a violent person", licenses the drawing of conclusions that are specific statements relevant as evidence in a case. For example, if the crime was a violent one, then the statement that the defendant is a violent person has probative weight as evidence, even if it may be only slight probative weight, that the defendant committed this crime. Anderson and Twining (1991, p. 43) classified four types of general statements that are important in reasoning about evidence in law. The first type they call the scientific generalization, like the law of gravity, for example. The second they call common sense generalization. One of their examples is the generalization that running away indicates a sense of guilt. The third type of generalization they distinguish is the commonly held belief. The example they give is that of national or ethnic stereotypes suggesting that a person of such and such origins has certain characteristics. The fourth type is what they classify as the generalization that presents general background information bearing on the present case. The example given is the generalization about a person's habits or character. It is notable that all four types of statements are two-edged as generalizations that fit into logical reasoning. The reasoning based on them is often weak, and in some cases it is even fallacious. For example, generalizations about national or ethnic stereotypes are often associated with bias, and even with a kind of prejudice that is highly antithetical to sound logical reasoning. Common sense generalizations tend to be based on commonly held beliefs and generally accepted opinions that often turn out to be wrong or superficial. They are even associated with a traditional fallacy, the *argumentum ad populum*, or appeal to popular opinion.

Using reasoning based on generalizations like those described by Anderson and Twining cannot be avoided in evidence law, but care is needed, because they can make the reasoning fallacious in some instances. Twining (1999, p. 357) expressed this ambivalence by saying that although generalizations are necessary in legal argumentation, they are also dangerous. He classified five dangers of reasoning based on these kinds of generalizations (pp. 357–358).

1. The warranting generalization may be indeterminate with respect to frequency or universality (all/most/some), level of abstraction, defeasibility (exceptions, qualifications), precision or "fuzziness", empirical base/confidence (accepted by scientific community; part of everyday firsthand or vicarious experience; speculative etc.).
2. It may be unclear as to identity (which generalization — there may be rival generalizations available to each side in a dialogue) or source (whose generalization — male/female experience in a domestic violence case).

3. There may not in fact be a "cognitive consensus" on the matter, especially in a plural society.
4. Value judgments (including prejudices, racist or gender stereotypes) may be masquerading as empirical propositions.
5. When articulated, a generalization may be expressed in value laden language or in loaded categories.

The kinds of errors cited by Twining fit under a category recognized in traditional logic called the fallacy of hasty generalization. This fallacy is also often called *secundum quid* (in a certain respect), because it involves ignoring exceptions to a generalization that does not hold in all respects, and that may fail to hold in exceptional circumstances. More confusingly, it is also called the fallacy of accident by many logic textbooks. A leading textbook (Copi and Cohen, 1994, pp. 125–126) treats one variant of the fallacy as occurring when "we apply a generalization to individual cases it does not properly govern". Another variant of the same fallacy is committed when we leap to a conclusion too hastily by applying "a principle that is true of a particular case to the great run of cases". Two examples they cite are quoted below (p. 125).

The Hearsay Example

The rule that hearsay testimony may not be accepted as evidence in court is not applicable when the party whose oral communications are reported is dead, or when the party reporting the hearsay does so in conflict with his own best interests.

The Euthydemus Example

In a dialogue with the young Euthydemus, who planned to become a statesman, Socrates drew from Euthydemus a commitment to many of the conventionally accepted moral truths: that it is wrong to deceive, unjust to steal, and so on. Then Socrates (as recounted by Xenophon in his report of the dialogue) presented a series of hypothetical cases in which Euthydemus reluctantly agreed that it would appear right to deceive (to rescue our compatriots) and just to steal (to save a friend's life), and so on.

In both of these cases, the fallacy committed arises from overlooking exceptions to a generalization that should be qualified. The fallacy could be analyzed as the error of confusing an absolute universal generalization that holds without exceptions with a qualified generalization that holds only subject to exceptions. This type of fallacy is associated with generalizations locked into prejudices and stereotypes of the very kind that Twining warned about in legal argumentation.

6.4 Character-Based Evidence Contrasted to Other Evidence

The normal kind of evidence commonly found to be so important in so many trials could be classified in terms of argumentation theory as argument from sign. For example, suppose a shoeprint matching the shoe of the suspect is found at the scene of a crime. The shoeprint is a sign pointing to the guilt of the suspect, we say. It is evidence that the suspect committed the crime. It is not conclusive proof, because it could have been planted there, or it could just happen to match the shoe found in the suspect's possession by an odd coincidence. Nevertheless, there is general agreement that this kind of finding is relevant evidence. It might often be classified as circumstantial evidence, though of course, it might be partly testimonial as well. An expert, for example, might be called in to testify that the print matches the shoe. Compared to character evidence, it seems to be much stronger and less susceptible to going wrong or being subjective. After all, it is based on hard facts, the finding of the print. It is a trace that has been left, and it can be examined, or photographs of it can be shown. Character evidence seems much more fuzzy, and based on subjective interpretation. Here we can draw a distinction between two kinds of evidence based on two underlying kinds of argumentation. One is mediated explicitly through the character of an agent, and depends on a premise about that agent's character.[3] The other is not. The first could be called character-based evidence. The second might be thought of as circumstantial or forensic evidence. To make the distinction sharper for purposes of discussion, let us call this contrasting kind of evidence non-character-based evidence.

If you try to reconstruct the argumentation structure of both kinds of evidence, there is a key difference. Let's begin with physical or circumstantial evidence, like that of the shoeprint case. It is based on a form of argument called argument from sign. But it is also based on some additional nonexplicit premises. One of these premises is the assumption that if a shoeprint matching a shoe belonging to the suspect is found at the crime scene, that would show the suspect was at the crime scene. Why? It is not easy to say exactly, but the reasons have to do with assumptions about people normally wearing shoes to get to a location, and about how the shoes can leave prints in the ground. Thus there is a chain of argumentation made

[3]The term "explicitly" is an important qualification. To make a clear distinction here is harder than it looks. For example, the normal kind of testimonial evidence, as in the case of an eyewitness to a crime, does not depend explicitly on the character of the witness. But it does depend implicitly on it, the reason being that it could be a reasonable criticism to argue that the witness has a character for dishonesty. On this basis, you could argue that all witness testimony is character-based.

up of inferences that link the suspect to the area where the crime was committed. Another way to reconstruct the evidence in the shoeprint case is as a chain of abductive reasoning. The best explanation of the observed fact of the shoeprint is that the suspect made the imprint by wearing the shoe when he was present at the crime scene. Unless there is a better explanation offered, the conclusion is drawn by plausible reasoning that the suspect himself produced the print in this way. Just as in the argumentation scheme reconstruction of the case, there is a chain of argumentation linking this conclusion to the ultimate conclusion that the suspect committed the crime. In such a case of circumstantial evidence then, even though the reasoning is abductive, and is based on a chain of argumentation requiring other assumptions that we assume to apply in a normal case, unless reasons are given to the contrary, we can often accept this kind of evidence as both relevant and reasonably reliable.

The case is quite different with character evidence. First consider predictive character evidence. A known thief and liar, even one who makes his living by deception, may, in a particular case, give a highly accurate account of some event that took place. It may turn out that his account is true, and is highly accurate even in small details, as can be confirmed by other evidence. Or a person who has proved he was highly courageous in the past, may under different circumstances act in a cowardly manner. This kind of evidence is hazardous and fallible, at least partly because any attempt to predict the future is fallible, especially one based on generalizations that are so subject to exceptions. Predictive reasoning can be contrasted with abductive reasoning. The latter kind of reasoning is normally based on facts or observations about some past event, taken as traces, and then probes even further into the past by constructing an explanation of how the event presumably came to occur. Abductive character evidence of this kind takes the following general form.

Abductive Character Inference for Identifying an Agent from a Past Action

Factual Premise: An observed event appears to have been brought about by some agent.
Character Premise: The bringing about of such an event fits a certain character quality.
Agent Trait Premise: This agent has this character quality.
Conclusion: This agent brought about this event.

This inference, too, seems highly unreliable and shaky, as compared to instances of non-character evidence of a kind often taken to be relevant evidence, like forensic evidence, for example, Suppose the crime was one of fraud, and committing this sort of fraud is consistent with the character quality of dishonesty. Suppose we round up the usual suspects, and one of them, Bob, is known to be dishonest. Does it follow that Bob committed the fraud in question? Hardly. In fact, it is just this sort of spurious reasoning that many would associate with prejudicial or fallacious reasoning. There are lots of dishonest people around. To pick on Bob is to leap to a hasty conclusion.

To sum up the discussion so far, we can say that character-based evidence is weak and unreliable, compared to non-character evidence like circumstantial evidence, of the kind commonly used and judged relevant in trials. So far, it appears that the association between this kind of argumentation and prejudice is very well founded. Small wonder that the rules of evidence have taken such pains to try to circumscribe the use of this kind of evidence in trials by excluding it as irrelevant. But there is more to be said. Suppose a mother has been charged with child abuse when her child was found beaten to death. Suppose that the circumstantial evidence suggests her guilt, but does not by itself prove it beyond a reasonable doubt. Suppose the mother has a long record of having a violent and abusive character. By itself, that record may be inconclusive and even prejudicial as evidence that she committed the crime she is presently accused of having committed. But as one piece of evidence within the larger body of evidence in the case, it may be relevant. By itself, it is inconclusive. But in conjunction with the other evidence in the case, it gives an additional reason to support the ultimate conclusion at issue. In other words, the abductive character inference to a past action is not altogether worthless as evidence in all cases. It does have some role to play in some cases as a form of evidence that is fallible, but that can lend a small weight of support to other relevant evidence that has been collected in the case.

There is also another kind of case where abductive character inference to a past action is an important kind of evidence relevant in a legal context. This concerns a negative form of character argumentation.

Negative Abductive Character Inference to a Past Action

Factual Premise: An observed event appears to have been brought about by some agent.
Character Premise: The bringing about of such an event is inconsistent with a certain character quality.
Agent Trait Premise: This agent has this character quality.
Conclusion: This agent did not bring about the event in question.

The kind of case we have in mind here is one where a defendant argues that he is not guilty of the crime alleged because committing such a crime would require the agent to have a bad character trait of some sort, and there is no evidence that the defendant has such a bad character trait. The defendant may even argue that he has the opposite good character trait, that he has a good reputation, and that character witnesses can affirm that he has an excellent character. For example in a rape case, there may be no evidence except the claims of the accuser and the defendant. The only argument the defendant may have is that it is implausible he would have committed such a crime as can be shown by his good character over his whole life. Hence this argument can be a very important form of evidence in some legal cases. The rules of evidence in the common law state that a criminal defendant has the right to put forward this kind of character-based argumentation, and that it is considered relevant. Once again, however, as in the positive form of the argument considered above, such character evidence is not by itself conclusive or even very strong. But it has an important role to play as a defense against allegations in the context of a wider body of argumentation in a case.

To sum up, character-based evidence is not that different from other kinds of trace evidence that are often rightly taken to be relevant in trials, in several respects. It can be abductive in some cases, while in other cases it is not. It depends on additional assumptions, like other kinds of evidence. It can sometimes be weaker, and in other cases, stronger, just like other kinds of evidence. What makes it distinctively different as a kind of evidence is that it is routed through explicit premises that make assumptions about the character of an agent. Thus the argumentation depends directly on an assumption about character, with all the frailties that such an assumption entails. Among the frailties are that such inferences can often be based on rumor, innuendo, popular opinion, or even deliberate character assassination. Even when based on good factual evidence it can go wrong, because it is an inherently weak and defeasible form of argumentation. Moreover, audiences easily tend to be overly impressed by such arguments, for whatever reasons. Perhaps it is because they represent a common heuristic we often use in daily thinking, where we may be less careful and critical in our reasoning than we should be in a court of law.

6.5 Argumentation Schemes

It will be recalled from chapter 2 that Uviller (1982, p. 849) distinguished three kinds of character evidence. All three kinds of evidence, it should be noted, come from witness testimony. The first is the normal kind of factual evidence in which a witness recounts an incident showing that the subject had a character trait. The second is the account in which a witness offers his own opinion of the subject's character trait. The third is reputation evidence, which comes from a witness acquainted with the general community view of the subject. To this list we now add a fourth kind of character evidence, that which comes from challenging any one of these three kinds of arguments by alleging an inconsistency. This kind of evidence was studied in chapter 3, for example, in the kind of case where evidence is offered suggesting that a person does not practice what he preaches. Finding of inconsistencies also plays an important role as argument used to raise questions about witness testimony. As shown in chapter 7, the medium for evaluating this kind of evidence in trials is the process of examining the witness. The witness may report alleged facts, or venture an opinion by drawing an inference from such facts, and the consistency and plausibility of his account may then be tested by questions asked in cross-examination.

When you put all these kinds of evidence together, you get a broad picture of how evidence is judged in a trial. A set of alleged facts is introduced as evidence, often through the medium of witness testimony. These are not "facts" in the sense that they are true propositions that cannot later be rejected or questioned. They are assumed to be factual for two reasons. First, they have been introduced into the trial as relevant evidence, meaning that they take the form of variously accepted types of arguments recognized as evidential by the trial rules, like argument from witness testimony. Second, they relate to the issue being decided in the trial — the so-called ultimate *probandum* of the case. One of the main problems is to identify each of these argumentation schemes as representing a form of inference that is commonly recognized as relevant and is commonly used in cases of character evidence.

In previous chapters, argumentation schemes for argument from witness testimony and for abductive argumentation have been presented. Each scheme has a set of critical questions, and these are used to provide standard ways of beginning the dialogue needed to properly evaluate the argument as it occurs in a given case. Another argumentation scheme that is centrally important to character evidence is the scheme for practical reasoning.

Scheme for Practical Reasoning

(*PInf.*) *A* is my goal (represents my general values).
To bring about *A*, it looks like I should bring about *B*.
Therefore, as far as I can tell, I ought to bring about *B*.

In deliberating on whether carrying out *B* is the prudent course of action to take, the primary agent engages in deliberation by asking the following questions.

Critical Questions for Practical Reasoning

CQ1. Are there alternative possible courses of action to *B*?

CQ2. Is *B* the best (or most acceptable) of the alternatives?

CQ3. Do I have goals other than *A* that ought to be taken into account?

CQ4. Is it possible to bring about *B* in the given circumstance?

CQ5. Does *B* have known bad consequences that ought to be taken into account?

This scheme is centrally important for all cases of character evidence, because of the simulative nature of this kind of evidence. It is also important to mention a modified version of it that has been developed. Atkinson, Bench-Capon and McBurney (2004, p. 88) showed that in many cases, the action in the conclusion is not only justified in relation to an agent's goals and means, but also in relation to an agent's underlying values. They hold (Atkinson *et al.*, 2004a, 2005) that three elements are premises of a rational agent's performing an action: the means of carrying out the action, the agent's goal, and the reason why the goal is desired (the value). They describe values as social interests that explain why goals are desirable. In their model, values are justifying arguments that support goals. Much more needs to be said about the application of this value-based model of practical reasoning to the study of character evidence, but there is not enough to comment further on it here. It would be a good research topic.

The next step is to recast the various inferences described in the four preceding sections of chapter 6 as argumentation schemes. Let's begin with the three simplest and most basic ones.

Scheme for Argument from Action to Character

Agent *a* did something that can be classified as fitting a particular character quality.
Therefore *a* has this character quality.

Matching Critical Questions

CQ1. What is the character quality in question?

CQ2. How is it defined?

CQ3. Does the description of the action in question actually fit the definition of the quality?

Scheme for Argument from Character to Action (Predictive)

Agent *a* has a character quality of a kind that has been defined.
Therefore if *a* carries out some action in the future, this action is likely to be classifiable as fitting under that character quality.

Matching Critical Questions

CQ1. What is the quality in question?

CQ2. How is it defined?

CQ3. Does the description of the action in question actually fit the definition of the quality?

Even though the critical questions are the same for both, the predictive scheme for argument from character to action needs to be distinguished from the retroductive scheme that reasons from character to a particular action. These two schemes in turn need to be distinguished from the argument from a past action to an agent's character.

Retroductive Scheme for Identifying an Agent from a Past Action

Factual Premise: An observed event appears to have been brought about by some agent *a*.
Character Premise: The bringing about of this event fits a certain character quality *Q*.
Agent Trait Premise: *a* has *Q*.
Conclusion: *a* brought about the event in question.

Matching Critical Questions

CQ1. What is the quality *Q* in question?

CQ2. How is *Q* defined?

CQ3. Does the description of the action in question actually fit the definition of *Q*?

CQ4. How large is the reference class of other agents who also might have brought about this event and who have the same character quality?

The predictive scheme is an inductive form of argument whereas the retroductive one is abductive. Although it is easy to mix these schemes up, it is vital from a viewpoint of character evidence to carefully distinguish between them in actual cases.

When we come to section 9 below, a general system for the analysis and evaluation of character evidence will be presented, and it will presuppose the existence of a set of argumentation schemes. One of these schemes will be that representing abductive reasoning. However, there is also a group of schemes pertaining specifically to arguments based on character, including the one identified above in this section. One special group of schemes that fall under this heading is the family representing the various species of *ad hominem* arguments.

6.6 *Ad Hominem* Arguments

The historical origin of the *ad hominem* has been something of a mystery. Its beginning as a clearly identified type of argument has generally been attributed to Locke or Galileo (Finocchiaro, 1980). However, recent historical research (Nuchelmans, 1993) has traced the roots of it back through the treatises of the middle ages to Aristotle. One root passage (Nuchelmans, p. 37) is the reference to *peirastikoi logoi*, or arguments designed to test out or probe a respondent's knowledge, by examining views held by that respondent (*On Sophistical Refutations* 165a37). Another root of the historical development of the "argument against the person" is the more often cited passage in *On Sophistical Refutations* (178b17) in which Aristotle contrasts directing a refutation at an argument with directing a refutation against the person who has put forward that argument. Because there are two roots, however, the textbook treatments of the *ad hominem* have been ambiguous and confusing.

There is already a literature on the *argumentum ad hominem*, or use of personal attack argument to try to refute an opponent's argument (Barth and Martens, 1977; Finocchiaro, 1980; Brinton, 1995; Walton, 1998). At the heart of this form of argument is the attack on a person's ethical character. The problem then is to see how what has been learned in the previous chapters about the evidence behind character judgments can throw new light on this form of argumentation. Although the various forms of *ad hominem* argument have been analyzed and classified in (Walton, 1998), there remain many questions about character evidence as a form of argument based on alleged facts about character that can be used to support or refute this type of argument.

The type of *ad hominem* argument that is the concern of this case study is the personal attack type, defined above. The other type is the Lockean type, portrayed by Locke in his *Essay*, in a neglected passage fully quoted in

Hamblin (1970, p. 160). Locke describes this type of argument as pressing "a man with consequences drawn from his own principles or concessions." This type of argumentation is called "argument from commitment" in (Walton, 1998). Barth and Martens (1977) see the *ad hominem* fallacy as best analyzed on this Lockean model, as being basically the same as argument from commitment. But these are two distinct types of arguments, and although argument from commitment is a subpart of the personal attack type of *ad hominem* argument, it is not the whole argument (Walton, 1998). The *ad hominem* argument should be seen as a character-based type of argument. It is not the same kind of argument as arguing from another party's commitments.

Nor should the *ad hominem* argument be seen as the same as arguing that another party has an inconsistent set of commitments, and that therefore her set of commitments cannot represent a consistent position. The following argumentation scheme for this type of argument was given in (Walton, 1998, pp. 252–253).

Argumentation Scheme for Argument from Inconsistent Commitment (or, You Contradict Yourself)

a is committed to proposition *A* (generally, or in virtue of what she said in the past).

a is committed to proposition ~*A*, which is the conclusion of the argument that *a* presently advocates.

Therefore *a*'s argument should not be accepted.

Argument from inconsistent commitments looks similar to the circumstantial *ad hominem* argument (see the scheme for this type of argument below). But it lacks the character premise. Thus it is not a character-based argument, and should not properly be classified as an *ad hominem* type of argument.

Another thing that is important to notice right away when initially approaching any particular case is that the circumstantial type is different from, but also related to the direct or so-called abusive type. The circumstantial type essentially involves an allegation that the party being attacked has committed a practical inconsistency, of a kind that can be characterized by the expression, "You do not practice what your preach". This allegation of inconsistency is then used as the basis for launching a direct, or personal *ad hominem* type of attack to the effect that the person attacked has a bad character, and that therefore her argument is bad, or should not be taken seriously. So the distinction is that the direct *ad hominem* does not require an allegation of circumstantial inconsistency whereas the circumstantial type does.

The subtypes of *ad hominem* arguments classified in the research cited above are the abusive (direct) *ad hominem*, the circumstantial *ad hominem*, the bias *ad hominem*, poisoning the well subtype, and the *tu quoque* subtype. Each subtype has a well-defined form (Walton, 1998). The method for identifying and evaluating *ad hominem* arguments worked out in (Walton, 1998) uses a set of argumentation schemes (forms of argument) for each distinctive subtype of *ad hominem* argument recognized, and a set of appropriate critical questions matching each scheme. The following is the argumentation scheme for the direct, or so-called abusive form of the *ad hominem* argument — called the ethotic type of *ad hominem* argument in (Brinton, 1985) and (Walton, 1998). The variable *a* stands for an arguer, the variable α stands for an argument.

Ethotic *Ad Hominem* Argument

a is a person of bad character.
Therefore, *a*'s argument α should not be accepted.

Why should this argument, at least in some cases, be seen as reasonable? The reason is that the attack on the arguer's character, if successful, undermines the arguer's credibility as a person who can be trusted. In politics, or in examination of legal testimony in court, much depends on a person's credibility. Hence *ad hominem* arguments can be very powerful in such contexts of use. The problem, for the purpose of this chapter, mainly centers on the first premise. How should the contention that a person has an ethically bad character be supported or criticized by appropriate reasoning on the basis of evidence? The answer is that such a claim should be supported or criticized by abductive reasoning, based on the given facts or data of a case.

The argumentation scheme for the circumstantial *ad hominem* argument, or "You don't practise what you preach" argument, is the following. The variable *A* stands for a proposition.

Circumstantial *Ad Hominem* Argument

1. *a* advocates argument α, showing he is committed to proposition *A*.
2. *a* has carried out an action, or set of actions, that imply *a* is personally committed to the opposite of *A*.
3. Therefore *a* is a hypocrite.
4. Therefore *a*'s argument α should not be accepted.

An *ad hominem* argument in a particular case is evaluated, in the first place, in relation to whether it meets the requirements for the scheme, and in the second place, to how critical questions are managed. The fallacious cases are the ones where critical questioning in a further dialogue exchange is suppressed. But in principle, both types of *ad hominem* arguments can be reasonable, as used in some cases. What type of reasoning should support the premise? How can it be proved or disproved that the person is a hypocrite? The answer is that such a premise should be proved by abductive reasoning from the given database allegedly describing that person's deeds and words in the given case. The circumstantial *ad hominem* can be a reasonable argument if supported by this kind of evidence, and the right kinds of evidence needed to support the other premises.

The bias subtype is distinctively different from either the direct type or the circumstantial type. The bias type is a milder form of argument than the other two, because it attacks the arguer's character in a different way. It does not allege that the arguer is an evil person or a liar, for example. It only attacks his character for good judgment skills in two-sided argumentation of a kind that requires looking at the evidence on both sides of an issue. But it is understandable why it is hard to tell in some cases whether an *ad hominem* argument should be classified as a bias type or a direct type. Both kinds of argument can attack an arguer's judgment skills. But the bias type specifically attacks the arguer's bias as a reason for discounting his argument. For example, if it can be shown in court that a witness is biased, then a jury will tend to discount the worth of his testimony, even though it may not discount it altogether. Thus there is an important distinction between character evidence of the kind found in the direct or circumstantial type of *ad hominem* argument, and evidence of the bias of a witness or arguer that shows a lack of balance in argumentation.

In chapter 3, where the case of the attack on the integrity of Al Gore was examined, the issue was considered whether the argument in this case is really an *ad hominem* argument or just a direct personal attack on Gore himself. I believe there is something more in this question than many commentators might initially be inclined to think. In a way, the editorial is a kind of pseudo *ad hominem* argument being played as much for its entertainment value as for its serious political content as an argument. On the other hand, there is enough of an element of counter-argument there to serve as a basis for justifying the classification of the editorial as containing a circumstantial *ad hominem* argument. The basis for this classification is that Gore's speech as a whole is being attacked by the argument in the editorial, even though no details of the speech are given in the editorial itself. But the speech is recent news, and readers of the editorial are presumably aware of its contents. And therefore there is some basis for classifying the *Time* segment quoted above as an *ad hominem* argument. But that basis only allows such a classification as conditional and partial. A subtler analysis of the argument is that it is used to attack Gore's personal *ethos* in a way that makes amusing material for an editorial comment, while posing as an *ad hominem* argument, thereby making the editorial seem more legitimate as a political argument. So the interesting point is that the argument is a borderline *ad hominem* that has all the elements of this type of argument except (arguably) one.

This kind of argument works in a dialogue by shifting a weight of presumption onto the respondent to reply to the attack, by denying the allegation, or by otherwise appropriately replying to the argument. In the absence of such a reply, it has a sticking power in virtue of the weight of presumption in favor of it. But if an inadequate, failed, or implausible reply is given, that will make the character attack argument much stronger. One interesting feature of this case is that the *Time* editorial actually prints a reply attributed to Gore, described in the editorial as "most nauseating spin". But the reply, expressed in a kind of political psychobabble that is all too familiar to readers, and widely felt to be ridiculous, is a kind of clincher that has the effect of giving more weight to the character attack argument rather than disarming it. The reply gives more support to the original allegations that Gore is carried away by his own emotional rhetoric, and that he is not only dishonest, but is deeply confused, and cannot be trusted to give a straight answer. Instead of replying to the argument by questioning it, the quote seals the argument in place, making any further reply to it much more difficult, the trendiness of the phrasing of the speech making it seem insincere.

6.7 Plan Recognition and Practical Inconsistency

Although the *argumentum ad hominem*, or personal attack argument, has been traditionally treated as a fallacy in logic, recent research in argumentation cited above shows that, in many cases, as used in conversational arguments — including cases in political argumentation — *ad hominem* arguments are not fallacious. This research has shown that while some personal attack arguments can definitely be judged fallacious, many others are quite reasonable (when evaluated in the appropriate context), while still others should be evaluated as weak (insufficiently supported) but not fallacious. Probably the most convincing evidence that the *ad hominem* is sometimes a reasonable argument appears in its use in law. For example, the character of a witness for honesty can be attacked in cross-examination in a trial. And as shown in chapter 1, there are other instances of legal argumentation in which a person's character can be used as evidence to attack his or her argument. Impeachment of a witness is allowed in witness examination, and is one of the most useful and important kinds of evidence in many trials. If the testimony of a witness can be shown to contradict his previous testimony, that is a very important kind of evidence that a trier needs in order to judge the probative weight of the witness's story. Of course, showing the witness to be inconsistent in his commitments can be a form of impeachment that can destroy the credibility of the witness. But even that showing can be an important form of evidence for the trier. Character can also be relevant, and vitally important, in the argumentation during the sentencing stage of a trial, for example. These instances show that *ad hominem* arguments are not inherently fallacious, and in many instances, in the right circumstances, can be reasonable, appropriate and useful, helping to resolve a conflict of opinions.

Several interesting cases of the circumstantial type of *ad hominem* argument have been studied in (Walton, 1998). One of these is called the smoking case (p. 7). In this case, a parent tells her child that smoking is a very bad thing because it is associated with chronic lung disease. The parent argues, therefore, that the child should not smoke. The child replies, "You smoke yourself. So much for your argument against smoking!" In traditional logic this type of case would be classified under the heading of the circumstantial *ad hominem* argument. On this basis, the child could be said to have committed a fallacy. The child presumably concludes wrongly from the parent's own actions that the parent's argument that smoking is unhealthy is incorrect or unbelievable. Leaping to this conclusion is fallacious, because the parent could have a good argument about smoking. It could really be true that smoking is unhealthy, and the parent could have presented good evidence to prove it. But the child also has a point worthy of some consideration. If the parent really believes that smoking is unhealthy then why does she herself smoke? The question is not a bad one to ask, given the conflict between the parent's actions and her argument. The apparent contradiction seems to demand an explanation. So there are two ways that the child's argument could be interpreted. If it is a hasty leap to rejecting the thesis that smoking is unhealthy, it is fallacious. But if it is merely the asking of a critical question about an apparent contradiction, it could be a reasonable argument.

Evaluating the *ad hominem* argument in this case may not depend only on the child's argument. It could also depend on how the parent and the child continue the dialogue. In this case there are a number of ways in which the dialogue could be continued. The parent could admit that although she smokes, she has often tried to give up. The parent could even use this as an additional reason for arguing that the child should not smoke. She could argue that smoking is addictive, and therefore it wouldn't be a good idea for the child to start smoking. But the dialogue could also be continued another way. The parent might simply accuse the child of committing the *ad hominem* fallacy and refuse to discuss the matter any further. So how can this case be resolved? Is it an example of fallacious use of the circumstantial *ad hominem* argument by the child? Or could the child's argument possibly be reasonable, at least to some extent? First of all, notice the basis of the child's argument. The child has observed the parent's actions. By using these observations, the child then constructs a plausible hypothesis about the parent's intentions or goals. Since the parent smokes, and admits that she smokes, the child draws the tentative conclusion that perhaps the parent doesn't really believe her own contention that smoking is unhealthy. After all, the child might reason, actions speak louder than words. Of course it is difficult for children to understand abstract medical evidence about the dangers of smoking. But what children see is the behavior of adults, and they are often more influenced by that. So the child is basing his argument on an apparent contradiction. The parent is not practicing what she preaches. Therefore, the child concludes, the sincerity of her argument that smoking is unhealthy is somehow dubious or questionable.

Another classic case of the circumstantial *ad hominem* argument called the sportsman's rejoinder is discussed in (Walton, 1998, p. 32). In this case, a hunter was accused of barbarity for his sacrifice of innocent animals for his own amusement in sport. The hunter replied to his critic, "Why do you feed on the flesh of harmless cattle?" Let's assume for the sake of argument that the critic is in fact nonvegetarian, and does eat meat from time to time. Now we have to ask whether the circumstantial *ad hominem* argument used by the hunter is reasonable or fallacious. First of all, notice that the hunter does appear to have trapped the critic in a kind of contradiction. For if the critic himself admits to the practice of eating meat, and yet criticizes the hunter for killing animals, he is surely being inconsistent. For there does appear to be a kind of practical inconsistency in condemning those who eat meat while at the same time admitting that one eats meat oneself. To resolve the problem in this case, one must analyze the apparent contradiction very carefully. First of all notice that the critic has not actually criticized the hunter for eating meat. The critic criticized the hunter for enjoying his sacrifice of innocent animals for his own amusement in the sport of hunting. It is logically possible for the critic to be quite consistent, provided that the critic is not himself a hunter. As DeMorgan (1847, p. 265) put the point, "The parallel will not exist until, for the person who eats meat, we substitute one who turns butcher for amusement." In this case we can see that there is some basis for arguing that the hunter has committed a fallacious circumstantial *ad hominem* argument. As long as the critic is not himself a hunter, he can deny that he enjoys the sacrifice of innocent animals in the sport of hunting. In other words, there is a basis for arguing that the critic is consistent, and therefore has not based his criticism on any kind of fallacious inconsistency.

Nevertheless, as with all these *ad hominem* arguments, there is something to be said for both sides. There is a connection between the practice of meat eating and the practice of hunting. Eating meat does normally require the prior killing of animals. So the practice of eating meat is at least indirectly related to the killing of animals. By eating meat, a certain kind of commitment is made about the practice of killing animals. Meat eating does not necessarily imply that the meat eater kills animals, or approves of the sport of hunting. And yet the practice of eating meat promotes the killing of animals because animals need to be killed in order to provide the meat. In ethics, this kind of indirect involvement is often called the problem of "dirty hands". By supporting a bad practice indirectly, even though one does not carry out the action directly oneself, one may be accused of complicity.

In all these cases of the circumstantial *ad hominem* argument, the basis of the argument is an alleged inconsistency. It is not (usually) a logical inconsistency that is alleged, but a practical inconsistency between word and deed. Thus resolving such a case depends on plan recognition. The accuser alleges that the other agent has acted in a way that goes contrary to some goal, plan or commitment that the other agent has expressed verbally. But the usual problem is to judge whether there is really a practical inconsistency there or not. In the smoking case, it can be shown that there is a practical inconsistency there. The parent advocated nonsmoking but she herself smokes. In the sportsman's rejoinder case, there was no inconsistency between eating meat and condemning hunting for sport. And yet there was a sort of connection there to be found. Once these matters concerning the alleged inconsistency are analyzed, it can be determined whether the *ad hominem* argument is strong or weak, fallacious or not. But to carry out the analysis, the connection has to be articulated between the agent's expressed goals and the actions he carried out that are supposedly related to these goals. Building up such an analysis depends on working out connections within sequences of actions based on scripts about the ways things are normally done. For example, we know that it is necessary to kill animals in order to obtain the meat that we eat. Thus the tools needed for providing an analysis that can be used to prove whether an *ad hominem* argument is strong or weak, and to pinpoint its weaknesses if it is weak or fallacious, are practical reasoning, multi-agent reasoning and plan recognition. We need to look at the two arguers in any given case as agents. One is alleging a practical inconsistency held to exist between the expressed arguments and the actions attributed to the other. But is there really a practical inconsistency there, or just the appearance of one? To resolve this issue, an evaluator of the argument in the case needs to collect the textual evidence and build up a hypothesis in the form of a plan connecting the expressed argument and the alleged actions. To carry out this task, the evaluator needs to have a stock of routines in the form of scripts showing how things are normally done in the domain of the argument. The connection can only be established or refuted by depending on these scripts. Thus, in effect, the evaluation of *ad hominem* arguments depends on plan recognition or some comparable method of determining connections between actions and goals in types of situations we are all familiar with.

Typically, the *ad hominem* argument goes by an inference from presumed data about a person's actions as premises to a conclusion about that person's presumed internal states, goals or commitments. There is also an ethical element to these arguments. As shown in the Gore case, the real function of an allegation of circumstantial inconsistency is typically to mount an attack on a person's integrity. The thrust of the argument is to make the person attacked appear to be a hypocrite. Such an attack, if successful, would show to a public audience that the person being attacked has a bad ethical character. The outcome would be to destroy the person's credibility in a blanket fashion that would make it extremely difficult for him to put forward any attempts at persuasion in the public sphere.

6.8 Simulative Reasoning in *Ad Hominem* Arguments

In simulative reasoning, a secondary agent uses his own reasoning to reason about the reasoning of a primary agent. The process of judging *ad hominem* arguments is based on a more complex form of simulative reasoning. The primary agent is the person who allegedly committed the *ad hominem* fallacy when she put forward some particular argument. The secondary agent is the arguer who attacks the primary agent, claiming she is a bad person. But such *ad hominem* arguments also generally have an audience. In a trial, for example, the audience is the trier — the judge or the jury, as the case may be. In a case of political argumentation in the media, the audience is typically the political constituency of voters. Typically, the *ad hominem* argument is put forward by the primary agent to discredit the secondary agent in the eyes of this audience. In the Gore tobacco case, for example, the attack on Gore appeared in an editorial in *Newsweek*. This magazine is read by a lot of people. The audience is comprised of all the people who read *Newsweek*. And it is to this audience that the argumentation is really directed, although Gore himself may also be such a reader. It is somewhat unclear what the purpose of the article is, in this case. It may be a political attack. But it may just be an editorial that raises questions, thereby making a comment of interest to readers. Partly also, humor or "heckling" seems to be involved.

If you look at the *ad hominem* argument in this case from the viewpoint of the audience to whom it was directed, how should the argument be evaluated? The audience uses its own reasoning to judge the reasoning of the secondary agent's reasoning in his *ad hominem* argument. But Gore's attacker is also using his (or her) reasoning about Gore's reasoning to argue that Gore is inconsistent in his commitments. The audience or readership of the editorial can be described as a tertiary agent. Of course, the audience is not a single person, but can be counted on to reason, and draw conclusions, in the same way any individual agent would. The case is one of nested triple simulative reasoning. Agent *Z* is using its reasoning to reason about the reasoning of agent *Y*, who is using its reasoning to reason about the reasoning of agent *X*. And so by transitivity of simulative reasoning, agent Z is using its reasoning to reason about the reasoning of agent *X*. The secondary agent is using his practical reasoning to put forward the argument that Gore is inconsistent in his commitments. But then the audience, because it can grasp practical reasoning very well, can understand the nature of the attack very well. The argument is effective because the audience understands very well how a person can get caught in a conflict between goals and actions. And the audience can also understand very well how such a conflict can indicate a kind of inconsistency that throws an arguer's sincerity and credibility into doubt.

The mediating factor in the simulative reasoning is the credibility of the primary agent. It is this credibility that is being attacked by the secondary agent. The credibility is that of the tertiary agent, who previously, it may be assumed, held Gore in some esteem as a government official. If Gore is shown to be inconsistent in his commitments, in a way that suggests a he is hypocrite, that conclusion will affect his credibility as a political leader. So the attack is by no means merely humorous, or meant to be only a comment on some innocent foible of Gore's behavior. It is a personal attack that could damage his credibility as a politician. Another complicating factor in the simulative reasoning in the case is that the editorial is presumably reporting an *ad hominem* argument that had been put to Gore previously by someone (we do not know who). Gore had already replied to the argument, as reported in the editorial. Gore's reply is even quoted in the editorial. So the editorial is not the originator of the attack. At least so we may presume. Yet by bringing the attack and its reply to a wider audience, the editorial can be seen as mounting an *ad hominem* argument.

There is also a fourth level to the simulative reasoning in this argumentation in this case. We as evaluators of the argument are members of the audience that read the argument in the editorial. But more than that, we are trying to adopt a critical point of view in which the argument is identified, analyzed and evaluated by objective (or at least fair) criteria. Many of the readers of the editorial, it may be assumed, will not take the trouble to analyze the argumentation in it so carefully. They will find it amusing that Gore is shown to be so hypocritical. If they were against Gore to begin with, this attack will be taken as just another reason to dislike him, or to reject his political views. But how would a critical thinker use simulative reasoning to probe more deeply into the argumentation in the *ad hominem* attack and raise critical questions about it? The answer is that, using simulative reasoning, the critical questioner must try to put herself into Gore's reasoning in the situation that presumably confronted him, at least insofar as that can be judged according to the evidence given. What are the facts of the case? We were told that Gore gave a speech and that, although details were not given, the speech implied that Gore was distraught about a person dying from smoking-induced lung cancer. Presumably then, Gore would be against any actions that would support smoking as a practice. In this part of the case, the facts (the exact wording of the claims made in the speech) are incomplete. But the inference drawn from the supposed facts seems reasonable enough. There is not much of a basis for challenging it.

But then we turn to the other side of the alleged inconsistency. What did Gore do that was presumably inconsistent with what he recommended in his speech? We are told that for some years following Gore's sister's death, his family continued to grow tobacco and he continued to accept money from tobacco interests. By simulative reasoning, what we need to do here is to try to use our reasoning to try to recreate Gore's presumed goals and plans by asking more critical questions. Who in Gore's family continued to grow tobacco? Did Gore have any control over this activity? Did he make any profits from it? Did he know about it? Did he try to do anything about it? Was it something he should not have tried to interfere with? If we, by an act of plan recognition, try to put ourselves into what was presumably Gore's situation, we can see that Gore may have had no control over this activity by some members of his family. What about the allegation that he continued to accept campaign money from tobacco interests? Once again, critical questions need to be asked about Gore's personal involvement. How direct was the link? Did Gore get direct contributions from tobacco companies in a way that it would have made it obvious that the support came from "tobacco interests"? It is probably hard to tell where all campaign money comes from, since, by law, large contributions cannot exceed a certain amount. So support comes from many small donations. It is probably not possible or useful to trace them all to identifiable interests or individuals. In other words, it is plausible that any national politician accepts money from what could be called "tobacco interests". What is important is whether, in Gore's reasoning, he saw himself as a supporter of "tobacco interests". From the data given in the case, there is only a suggestion that such is the case. There is no real evidence that Gore saw himself and his actions in this way. And hence there is no proof that Gore was inconsistent in his commitments. We have to look at the actions and goals from a point of view of Gore's practical reasoning in his plan, as we can reconstruct it by plan recognition. Of course, this act of empathy is based on hypotheses, and we can only infer indirectly on the basis of attributing a coherent plan of action to Gore. But the data given in the case provide the presumed facts from which these inferences can be drawn. It is within this framework of plan recognition that the simulative reasoning should be judged. Judging by these facts, there is no strong argument that Gore was inconsistent in his commitments, in a way that would justify the claim that he is a hypocrite. Once we try to put ourselves as evaluators into Gore's reasoning, as far as we can reconstruct it from the given facts of the case, the *ad hominem* falls short. It is merely conjecture or innuendo that suggests, but does not prove, that Gore was hypocritical.

But it is useful to take another step in simulative reasoning and look at the case from the viewpoint of the readers of the editorial. Would they have looked so closely at the wording of the argument? Would they have asked all the right critical questions? Would they have laid out the facts of the case, and then measured the *ad hominem* argument against the evidence of these facts? The presumption is that many would not. Many would quickly scan the editorial, and would see it as a good joke that would confirm their own suspicions about politicians. The suggestion and innuendo of the *ad hominem* argument in the editorial would therefore have an effect on the audience. In fact, the humor value of the editorial is that it seems to confirm widely held suspicions about the sincerity of politicians. The reason why the *ad hominem* works is the same as the reason why innuendo and slander so often work by suggestion to tarnish a person's reputation. The putting forward of a dubious claim can create a powerful suggestion that can raise suspicions in an audience. If the audience is predisposed or already committed to a certain view, even a weak argument, as long as it supports that view, may be accepted quite willingly by them. From their point of view, it is just another reason to hold the view they already hold. They add it to the supporting arguments they already accept. Character attack is both very powerful and easy to put forward, even on the basis of little or no real evidence. It is powerful because it undercuts the credibility of the person whose character is attacked. It is easy to put forward because very little evidence is required to raise the suspicions of an audience who may already be suspicious.

6.9 The PFARD Multi-Agent Dialogue System

The PFARD system of character judgment is a five-tuple $\{P, F, A, R, D\}$. P is a set of defined ethical character properties, like courage or integrity, defined precisely at a general level of abstraction. These general character qualities (properties) are codified in definitions that are agreed to independently of an evaluation of any character inference in a particular case at issue. *F* is a set of statements representing the data, the observed or documented facts given in a case. They are often called facts in law and data in science, but they are more like hypotheses or assumptions, because they are subject to retractions as new evidence comes in. *A* is a set of argumentation schemes used to infer other statements from a given set of facts *F* in a case. Among the most important forms of argument for character judgments are the schemes for practical reasoning and abductive reasoning. *R* is a set of domain-dependent routines, representing familiar ways of carrying out actions, based on scripts. *D* is a set of dialogues, of various kinds, but deliberation dialogue, persuasion dialogue and information-seeking dialogue are the most important types. The participants in the dialogue are two agents, called the primary agent and the secondary agent. Otherwise a dialogue has the kinds of rules, moves, locutions, commitment sets, and so forth, as presented in (Walton and Krabbe, 1995). The system works in the simplest kind of case as follows. The primary agent has carried out some actions, and they are observed by the secondary agent. The primary agent may say some things as well, and these statements also are treated as given data or facts. Or the secondary agent comes to know them through some source, like testimony, or reading about them. The facts are a set of statements that are presumed to be true by the secondary agent, but they might later be shown not to be true. Using *A* and *R*, the secondary agent expands the set of given facts by drawing inferences from them, producing hypotheses. The expanded set of statements made up of the facts and hypotheses are then fitted into some element of *C* using the dialogue *D* to test fit. The process is simulative, because the secondary agent is reenacting or recreating the actions and plans attributed to the primary agent.

Character judgment is possible because a secondary agent can use simulative reasoning to understand the reasoning of a primary agent as described in a given case, in a set of data presented to the secondary agent. The secondary agent uses abductive reasoning to construct plausible hypotheses about the goals and actions of that other agent by abductive reasoning, and then judges which hypothesis is the most plausible, according to the given data. The secondary agent can reconstruct the plans and actions of the primary agent because both agents have a grasp of routines that are common in everyday experience. The structure of abductive and simulative reasoning used in character judgment is summarized in Figure 6.1.

What makes simulative reasoning possible in cases of character judgment is that both reasoners are agents. As an agent, the primary agent deliberates on how to act in a given situation, facing a problem. As an agent also, the

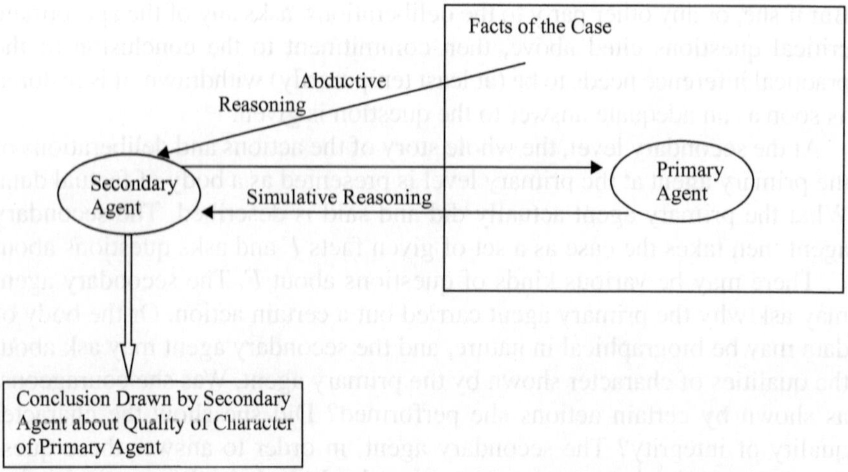

Figure 6.1. Using abductive and simulative reasoning in character judgment.

secondary agent can look at the data describing what the primary agent did, and understand how that agent was acting in trying to solve a problem in the situation presented. The secondary agent can ask the same questions the first agent did, and see how answers to these questions are plausible or implausible. Even though the situation of the primary agent may be quite different from that of the secondary agent, perhaps even in a different historical era or culture, some aspects of their situations will remain the same. These aspects compose what are called scripts, or routine ways of doing things. The process of simulative and abductive reasoning used to conclude to a character judgment takes place at two levels. At the primary level, the primary agent is engaged in deliberation on how to act by choosing among alternative courses of action in a given situation. At the secondary level, the secondary agent is engaged in a critical discussion, asking questions about what the primary agent did, and what his reasons were for doing these things. The simulative step from the one level to the other is possible because both participants are agents who can approach practical problems and seek out a solution in roughly the same way, or at least by the same process of thinking.

The primary agent is engaged in deliberation on what to do in a problematic situation. The primary agent uses practical reasoning to reason forward from her goals, and the means she is aware of that can be used to achieve these goals. Evaluating the practical reasoning of the primary agent is carried out by the secondary agent using a dialogue method of question and answer. If the two premises of the practical inference above are commitments of the primary agent, then the conclusion should become a commitment of hers.

But if she, or any other party to the deliberations, asks any of the appropriate critical questions cited above, then commitment to the conclusion of the practical inference needs to be (at least temporarily) withdrawn. It is restored as soon as an adequate answer to the question is given.

At the secondary level, the whole story of the actions and deliberations of the primary agent at the primary level is presented as a body of factual data. What the primary agent actually did and said is described. The secondary agent then takes the case as a set of given facts F and asks questions about F. There may be various kinds of questions about F. The secondary agent may ask why the primary agent carried out a certain action. Or the body of data may be biographical in nature, and the secondary agent may ask about the qualities of character shown by the primary agent. Was she courageous, as shown by certain actions she performed? Did she show the character quality of integrity? The secondary agent, in order to answer these questions, uses abductive argument to reason backwards in the practical inference above. The secondary agent takes the conclusion of the practical inference as given data at the first level. Once the events at the first level are in the past, it is known what the primary agent in fact did. The secondary agent must then reason backward from the conclusion and draw inferences about what she takes to be the premises that this conclusion was based on. To carry out this abductive task of inference, the secondary agent must try to reconstruct the deliberations of the primary agent, as they presumably took place at the primary level. For example, suppose the primary agent carried out action B. And suppose that it looks from the data at the primary level that the primary agent thought that action B was the appropriate means to carry out goal A. Then by abductive argument, using simulative reasoning, the secondary agent can infer that the primary agent had goal A in mind when he acted the way he did.[4] Of course, this conclusion is only a conjecture. But it is based on abductive reasoning from the given evidence. The primary agent was not actually there at the time the action was carried out. Nor can she know for sure what the primary agent had in mind. But the conclusion drawn can be an intelligent, plausible hypothesis, well supported by the evidence.

How can argumentation schemes like the one for abductive reasoning be implemented in computational models of legal argumentation that could be used to assist lawyers and judges in evaluating character evidence in a trial? The key problem in current research efforts is to specify how critical

[4]There also needs to be a technical apparatus for defining actions and constructing sequences of actions. There are various methods that could be used. The recommended one is the action-state semantics of Hamblin (1987) worked out in the appendix of (Walton and Krabbe, 1995, pp. 189–223). The key component is the concept of a partial strategy.

questions can be used in conjunction with schemes to manage and evaluate legal evidence in trials. Current research on this problem has led to two key developments. One is the proposal for a method of formally modeling argumentation schemes advanced by Verheij (2003), who explained that critical questions have four different roles that can be distinguished.

(1) criticizing a schemes' premises,
(2) pointing to exceptional situations in which the scheme should not be used,
(3) setting conditions for a scheme's use, and
(4) pointing to other possible arguments relevant to a scheme's conclusion.

Concerning the first role, Verheij argued that there should be no need for explicit critical questions that merely ask whether a premise of a scheme is true or not. The reason he offered (2003, section 5) is that it is "a precondition of the use of *any* (his italics) scheme that its premises are true, well supported." As Verheij showed in the case of the scheme for the *ad hominem* argument, this proposal enables us to delete some of the critical questions. When it comes to formalizing schemes, this proposal for reducing redundancy makes sense. Part of the formalization required is a general condition that an argument fitting a scheme can, and indeed always should, be evaluated by asking whether the premises are in fact true in the given case.

Verheij's differentiating these four roles of critical questions suggests that in any project of formalizing legal argumentation, it may be useful to treat some of the questions in a different way from others. Critical questions that ask whether a premise is true can be deleted, because they need to be considered in all cases anyhow. Critical questions that point to exceptions could be treated as exceptions to a rule, if the rule on which an argumentation scheme is based could be stated. Other critical questions could be seen as assumptions on which the rule rests.

These proposals led to a computational model of argument for legal reasoning support systems (Gordon, 2005) that adopted a new approach in which schemes can have a dual role. They can also be used in the traditional way in logic as devices to analyze and evaluate a given argument. But they can also act as heuristic search procedures to help find and construct legal arguments in a case in which there is an issue being disputed or investigated. This model defines an argument in a resource description framework (RDF) in the framework of the semantic web. The key to understanding how this model represents critical questions lies in the distinction between a presumption and an exception. Each argument represented in the model contains a list of exceptions and a list of presumptions. Presumptions are assumed to be true while exceptions are assumed to be false. Consider, for example, the list of the four critical questions matching the retroductive argumentation scheme for identifying an agent from a past action. The third critical question can be deleted, as it merely reiterates the character premise. The first two critical questions can be classified as presumptions, since it is assumed to be true that there is such a trait that can be identified, and that is defined in some manner. However, the fourth critical question is assumed to be false. That is, it is assumed that there is no large reference class of other agents who might also have brought about this event and who have the same trait. There might be such a class of agents, but an opponent of the argument would have to prove this claim in order to make a significant impact as a critical question that would rebut the argument from character to action.

Further work is needed on how to analyze argumentation schemes on this model by applying the distinction between a presumption and an exception. However, on the assumption that this program of research can be carried out successfully, let's go on to see how an argument is broken down into several components on this model. The basic unit is an atom, which is comparable to the traditional logical notion of an atomic proposition. Another unit is the *issue*, a record for keeping track of the arguments pro and con some claimed value of a proposition and the proof standard applicable to the case. A case is modeled as a set of issues. The notion of an issue is what defines relevance of argumentation in a case. Various proof standards applicable to cases are recognized, including the common legal ones of scintilla of evidence, preponderance of the evidence, and beyond a reasonable doubt. Any given argument contains an atom as a consequent and a list of antecedent atoms. The argument also has a type, corresponding to one of the argumentation schemes.

To show how the model works, we apply it to an example of an argument that fits the retroductive argumentation scheme for identifying an agent from a past action.

Example of a Case Using Argument Identifying an Agent from a Past Action

Bob is a corporate executive who has been accused of improperly using inside knowledge to manipulate stock trading to his advantage in a way that is illegal and lying to investors. He is accused of fraud. In his trial, the prosecution argues that Bob lacks integrity, and uses this argument to conclude that Bob lied to investors. We label this argument arg-1.

Applying the retroductive argumentation scheme for identifying an agent from a past action, the argument against Bob is shown in the model as having the following structure.

id: arg-1
direction: pro
scheme: retroductive scheme for identifying an agent from a past action
consequent: Bob lied to investors
antecedents:
(an observed event *F* was brought about by *a*)
(the bringing about of *F* fits *P*)
(*a* has *P*)
presumptions:
(there is an ethical character property *P* that can be identified: true)
(*P* is defined: true)
exceptions:
(there is a large reference class of agents with *P* that might have brought about *F*: false)

The argument in this case is presumed to be valid, meaning the premises presumptively support the conclusion, but is subject to defeat. It can be defeated in three ways. First, a rebuttal is an argument in the opposite direction with the same consequent. Second, a premise can be defeated by arguing against a presumption. Third, a premise can be defeated by arguing for an exception.

Research on argumentation schemes as tools useful in designing legal reasoning support systems is still a new field of AI in law. However, this work shows promise, not only as a tool for reconstructing argumentation found in a given text, but also as a tool that could be used to assist lawyers to invent new arguments. Much work remains to be done. One of the areas most in need of investigation is that called ontology on the semantic web, referring to systems for classifying the concepts fundamental to a domain. Thus in systems for character evidence, what is needed is an ontology of ethical character qualities like integrity and honesty. Only when such an ontology has been developed can a system for judging character evidence be implemented. We will not attempt to go this far, and remain content with having taken the first step of building a general system built on a base of argumentation schemes that is adequate to show how, in principle, it is possible to draw logical conclusions about character evidence in a rational manner. As well, the PFARD system shows how to raise critical questions about character arguments, and how to attack and refute them when they are weak and contain logical gaps.

6.10 Summary of the Method

The process of arriving at a character judgment by inserting yourself imaginatively into the mind of another person has traditionally been portrayed as subjective. But the analysis above shows that it can be carried out by a logical process of simulative and abductive reasoning based on a set of given factual premises using the PFARD system. Abductive reasoning is an objective process of constructing alternative explanations from a given set of facts, and then picking the best, or most plausible explanation as the conclusion to be inferred abductively. Consider making a character judgment about a virtue like courage or integrity. You have to begin with a definition of the virtue in question that is agreed to by all the parties to the discussion. For example, courage might be defined as the virtue of persisting with trying to carry out a worthy goal even in the face of serious difficulties and personal danger. So conceived, a courageous action is altruistic and beyond duty. This definition is then applied to a particular case made up of a set of presumed facts. For example, suppose we are presented with an account of what happened when Mary rushed into a burning building to save a child. There might be some dialogue in which Mary tries to explain why she did it, and so forth. These facts comprise the given data of the case. A secondary agent can then postulate various possible explanations of why Mary did what she did. If the facts fit the definition well enough, the conclusion may be drawn by abductive reasoning that Mary is courageous. This kind of general conclusion about Mary's character would be especially well supported if during Mary's life, her actions could also on other occasions be described as courageous. Integrity is a different virtue, and the evidence to support the hypothesis that a person has integrity is collected and processed in a somewhat different way. Integrity is a wholeness or consistency of character in acting on the basis of certain worthy goals or values. Thus an agent is thought to lack integrity if he expounds certain goals or expresses particular commitments but then acts in a way that clearly signals a departure from or a contravening of these expressed commitments. For example, suppose a person expounds the virtue of honesty, but then is found to have told a lie. In this case, the evidence is a conflict of commitments, a sort of contradiction between word and deed.

What has been generally shown by the analysis in this book is that character judgments, although they initially appear to be subjective, are based on an objective structure of logical reasoning. Character judgment is arrived at by collecting evidence drawn from a set of factual data and using it to draw a conclusion based on a chain of reasoning. The process begins with a set of statements representing the data in a case, and then uses argumentation schemes to infer new statements as conclusion from those premises. Such character judgments are based on a body of evidence. These judgments are verifiable or falsifiable because the given facts can be supported or refuted by further factual evidence. And they can also be supported or refuted by appealing to or challenging the inferences in the logical reasoning used to hypothesize from the data in a case. Of course in a way, they are subjective, because the process of reasoning involved is simulative. One agent derives conclusions about what he thinks is the thinking of another agent. The process of simulative reasoning is one of inference because, as solipsists have often maintained, you can't get direct access to the thinking processes in another person's mind. But what has been shown is that the process can be one of intelligent reconstruction based on a process of reasoning that is objective and can be supported by evidence that can be observed and recorded. The key to understanding the process is abduction. Many, especially positivists, have thought that the process of character judgment is purely subjective, because it is not based on deductive or inductive reasoning. It is based on a third kind of reasoning, abductive reasoning, or inference to the best explanation. This form of plausible reasoning is fallible, and is based on normal expectations that two agents can share in a kind of situation that both are, at least to some extent, familiar with. The best explanation is one that is good enough for the purpose of the type of dialogue an agent is engaged in. What is good enough for a practical deliberation, of course, may not be good enough for a scientific explanation. What is good enough is a function of the type of dialogue one is engaged in.

Below, the various stages the chain of reasoning goes through in order to make a character judgment according to the PFARD model are shown. The system begins with a hypothesis that explains the data in a case, and then moves forward using abductive reasoning to refine that hypothesis by testing it against relevant evidence.

1. There are two agents, a primary agent and a secondary agent. Both agents are familiar with practical reasoning. An agent has goals, can carry out actions, and has incoming information from its environment. It can monitor the actions of another agent. The two agents may share knowledge about how sequences of actions called routines normally run in a special domain.

2. The primary agent is engaged in deliberation on how to solve a problem. The secondary agent can use simulative reasoning to understand the deliberations of the primary agent as systematic attempts to solve the problem.

3. There is a given set of data or facts *F* describing the primary agent's actions and words. The secondary agent is presented with this set of

data, or facts of the case. Other presumed facts may enter the case — for example, allegations about the primary agent's actions on other occasions.

4. The secondary agent uses routines based on scripts to fill in the gaps in the data, making the story of the primary agent's deeds and words comprehensible to him as a connected and plausible account. The non-explicit premises and conclusions in the primary agent's reasoning can be filled in by the secondary agent, using argumentation schemes.

5. The secondary agent asks questions about the ethical character of the primary agent, in relation to the given data. The secondary agent constructs a hypothesis stating the primary agent possesses some clearly definable quality of character or virtue. Thus the specific issue is posed of whether the primary agent may rightly be said to have this quality or not.

6. To try to resolve this issue, the secondary agent constructs competing possible explanations of the primary agent's words and deeds. Two or more opposed hypotheses are then tested and evaluated, using the given body of data as evidence.

7. In testing these hypotheses, a dialogue in the form of a critical discussion on whether the primary agent has exhibited that quality or not, is started. Arguments are put forward by one side supporting the view that the primary agent has a certain ethical quality of character. These arguments take the form of argumentation schemes.

8. In the critical discussion, appropriate critical questions are raised concerning the practical reasoning used to support the hypothesis that the primary agent has a certain quality of character. The critical questions respond to arguments that take the form of argumentation schemes.

9. The critical questions are replied to in a multi-agent dialogue in which a questioner and respondent critically look at both sides of the argumentation in relation to the given facts of the case. Both sides bring forward arguments, based on argumentation schemes, including abductive character-based arguments, to support their claims.

10. The issue is resolved by determining which side has the more plausible chain of argumentation, offering the best explanation of the facts in the case. If the abductive arguments on both sides are equally plausible, the hypothesis is judged as acceptable or not, based on the burden of proof set at the confrontation stage.

In some cases, although the critical discussion of the character question may be ethically interesting and insightful, no firm conclusion may be reached. Even so, the arguments can be based on good evidence, and can be worthy and plausible. If it is important to reach some resolution of the case, the next step may be to collect more relevant facts, and continue the discussion later. But an ethical discussion of a quality of character can generate insight, and good evidence based on logical reasoning, even if the conflict of opinions is not resolved. What is vitally important in reconstructing how this process of evaluation of a character judgment works are the various forms of argument, along with the matching set of critical questions for each type of argumentation. The most important forms of argument for character judgment are abductive reasoning and practical reasoning. Abductive reasoning can be seen as a form of argumentation in which competing hypotheses are put forward to explain a given set of facts. Questioning in relation to the evidence of these known or presumed facts tests an abductive argument. Practical reasoning is goal directed reasoning in which an agent chooses a means from the various means available, and then concludes to a prudent line of action. In typical cases, both forms of argument are based on plausible reasoning, meaning they result in a conclusion that seems to be true, and can be taken as a commitment in relation to the burden of proof appropriate for the type of dialogue one is engaged in.

In character judgment, the simulative reasoning is plausible, because one agent can only infer what another agent is really thinking, or trying to do. Yet by such an inference an agent can draw the right conclusion. It can be based on quite good evidence in some cases. The evidence rarely tends to be conclusive, however, because of the inferential leap between the thinking of the one agent and the thinking of the other. In legal and historical reasoning, for example, the given actions and reported facts in question are typically in the past. Typically, the supposed facts are based on witness reports, and if the events happened long ago, the evidence will be incomplete. Any simulative judgment will have to be conjectural, and based on incomplete evidence. In archaeology, for example, little may be known about a past civilization, and any hypotheses drawn from the evidence provided by an excavation will take the form of plausible conjectures. Even so, such conjectures can be well supported by the given body of evidence. They can also be evaluated logically, and various explanations from the known facts can be compared. Such inferences can be drawn on the basis of a plausible conjecture from the evidence, and they can also be challenged by asking the right questions and citing evidence that counts against them. Historical explanations of past actions were thought by positivistic philosophers to be based on universal laws or inductive generalizations. But typically they are not. They are based on plausible generalizations about how things can normally be expected to go in a kind of situation familiar to an agent trying to reenact the past actions of other agents. This plausibilistic aspect is especially and most notably evident in character judgments, because of the inferential leap of simulative reasoning from the thinking of one agent to the thinking of another agent.

Redmayne (2002, pp. 693–695) has examined statistical evidence suggesting that previous convictions have considerable probative value in relation to the conclusion that an individual is more or less likely to commit the same type of crime. The statistics vary with type of crime involved. For example, the likelihood of committing robbery is much higher than the likelihood of committing a drug offense. These statistics suggest that character evidence does have some value in predicting certain types of crimes, but statistics are notoriously slippery (Redmayne, 2002, p. 700). Perhaps for this reason, the policy of excluding character evidence in criminal trials has apparently been challenged in English law. Redmayne (2002, p. 684) reported that a proposal was made to weaken the presumption of inadmissibility of character evidence in 2002. One English judge had even suggested in 2001 that revealing a defendant's previous convictions at the beginning of every trial should be considered.

Why is character evidence so heavily restricted by the rules of evidence in law, if the character-based type of argument is, in principle, a reasonable kind of argument? The answer is to be sought in how powerful character-based arguments are, and their potential for mischief as fallacies. Because this type of argument is not completely trustworthy at the best of times, and because it is such a powerful weapon of deceptive argumentation, it should be treated with care and some skepticism. It is most useful in a situation of uncertainty where harder evidence is not available, or at any rate is not conclusive, and the case rests on a balance of considerations. While a jury has to be assumed to be capable of critical argumentation in our system of law, it also has to be seen as made up of ordinary persons who can be deceived by fallacious arguments. But do we need to protect juries from fallacies, or would it better to let them have all the logically relevant evidence, and make up their own minds? Evidence law is continually struggling with this question, and it seems to swing one way or the other as the rules of evidence continue to evolve. The current trend, however, seems to be in the direction of more and more restrictions on character evidence. Perhaps if juries could be better educated about character-based arguments and could learn to identify the various types systematically, there would be less need for building in more and more restrictions to Rule 404. Rulings of inadmissibility like those in the Fisher and Chapman cases (chapter 1) seem questionable, because they drive such a wedge between logical relevance and legal admissibility of evidence.

The key to understanding the logic of character evidence lies in its abductive nature as a type of reasoning. Character judgments are based on abductive arguments. Abductive arguments are based on evidence in the form of supposed factual data in a case, but that evidence can be stronger or weaker, depending on how far the investigation in the case has gone. An abductive argument is really a form of reasoning to a hypothesis, based on best explanation. If the data base is small, or of dubious reliability, the best explanation in a case so far may be highly tentative. Thus abduction tends to be a weak form of argument, resulting in a conclusion that appears to be, or is plausible, but may later be withdrawn in favor of a better hypothesis. According to the analysis in this book, abductive argument is best seen as dialectical. It should be judged in a context of dialogue. Much depends in a given case on how far the dialogue has gone, and what critical questions have been asked and answered. The strength of an abductive argument depends on what stage of a dialogue that argument was used in, and how much evidence had been collected and evaluated at that stage. All these aspects of abductive argumentation make it susceptible to abuse. Character attack arguments, being based as they are on evidence from abductive reasoning, can be misused and exploited as tactics of rhetorical deception.

One of the most basic critical questions to ask in evaluating a character-based argument is whether the character defect that the person attacked has been alleged to possess is really shown by the facts of the case. The problem is that such a character attack can do serious damage, even if based only on innuendo, in lieu of real evidence of the kind that should be required to support an abductive argument. It is because they are so subject to this kind of abuse that character judgments are so often mistrusted. Consequently, it is fair to say that there is an ethical aspect to character judgments. One should not rush to judgment. Why? One reason is that such judgments are abductive and plausible, and you could turn out to be wrong. Another reason is that the making of character judgment in public could ruin the reputation of the person attacked, and it may be hard or even impossible to remedy this kind of unfairness.

BIBLIOGRAPHY

Allen, Ronald J., “Rationality, algorithms and judicial proof: a preliminary inquiry”, *International Journal of Evidence and Proof*, 1, 1997, 254–275.

Allen, Ronald J., Richard B. Kuhns, and Eleanor Swift”, *Evidence: Text, Cases and Problems*, New York, Aspen Law and Business, 1997.

Anderson, Terence J., “On generalizations I: a preliminary exploration”, *South Texas Law Review*, 40, 1999, 455–481.

Anderson, Terence, William, and Twining, *Analysis of Evidence: How to Do Things with Facts Based on Wigmore's Science of Judicial Proof*, Boston, Little Brown & Co., 1991.

Anscombe, G.E.M., “Modern moral philosophy”, *Philosophy*, 33, 1958, 1–19.

Aristotle, “Nicomachean ethics”, In *The Works of Aristotle Translated into English*, (ed.) W.D. Ross, Oxford, Oxford University Pess, 1928.

Aristotle, *The Complete Works of Aristotle*, Princeton, Princeton University Press, 1984.

Atkinson, Katie, Trevor Bench-Capon, and Peter McBurney, “Justifying Practical Reasoning”, *Proceedings of the Fourth Workshop on Computational Models of Natural Argument* (CMNA 2004), ECAI 2004, Valencia, Spain, pp. 87–90.

Atkinson, Katie, Trevor-Bench-Capon, and Peter McBurney, “A dialogue game protocol for multi-agent argument over proposals for action”, In *Argumentation in Multi-Agent Systems*, (eds) I. Rahwan, P. Moraitis and C. Reed, Berlin, Springer, 2004a, 149–161.

Atkinson, Katie, Trevor Bench-Capon, and Peter McBurney, “Agent Decision Making Using Argumentation About Actions”, Technical Report ULCS-05-006, University of Liverpool, Computer Science Department, 2005.

Audi, Robert, *Practical Reasoning*, London, Routledge, 1989.

Audi, Robert, *Moral Knowledge and Ethical Character*, New York, Oxford University Press, 1997.

Barnden, John A., "Simulative reasoning, common-sense psychology, and artificial intelligence", In *Mental Simulation*, (eds) Martin Davies and Tony Stone, Oxford, Blackwell, 1995, 247–273.

Barr, Avron, and Feigenbaum, Edward, *The Handbook of Artificial Intelligence*, vol.1, Los Altos, Morgan Kaufmann Inc., 1981.

Barth, E.M., and J.L., Martens, "*Argumentum Ad Hominem*: from chaos to formal dialectic", *Logique et Analyse*, 77–78, 1977, 76–96.

Barton, William E., "His character", *Abraham Lincoln: His Life, Work, and Character*, (ed.) Edward Wagenknecht, New York, Creative Age Press, 1947, 32–67.

Bench-Capon, Trevor, "Argument in artificial intelligence and law", *Artificial Intelligence and Law*, 5, 1997, 249–261.

Bex, Floris, and Henry Prakken, "Reinterpreting arguments in dialogue: an application to evidential reasoning", In *Legal Knowledge and Information Systems*, (ed.) Thomas F. Gordon, Amsterdam, IOS Press, 2004, 119–130.

Bex, Floris, Henry Prakken, Chris Reed, and Douglas Walton, "Towards a formal account of reasoning about evidence: argumentation schemes and generalizations", *Artificial Intelligence and Law*, 12, 2003, 125–165.

Bok, Sissela, *Lying: Moral Choice in Public and Private Life*, New York, Pantheon Books, 1978.

Bons, Roger W.H., Frank Dignum, Ronald M. Lee, and Yao-Hua Tan, "A formal specification of automated auditing of trustworthy trade procedures for open electronic commerce", In *Trust and Deception in Virtual Societies*, (eds) Cristiano Castelfranchi and Yao-Hua Tan, Dordrecht, Kluwer, 2001, 27–54.

Bradford, Ernle, *The Shield and the Sword: The Knights of Malta*, London, Fontana, 1972.

Bratman, Michael E., *Intentions, Plans, and Practical Reason*, Cambridge, Mass., Harvard University Press, 1987.

Brinton, Alan, "A rhetorical view of the *ad hominem", Australasian Journal of Philosophy*, 63, 1985, 50–63.

Brinton, Alan, "The *ad hominem*", In *Fallacies: Classical and Contemporary Readings*, (eds) Hans V. Hansen and Robert C. Pinto, University Park, Pa., Penn State Press, 1995, 213–222.

Burnyeat, Myles F., "Enthymeme: Aristotle on the logic of persuasion", In *Aristotle's Rhetoric: Philosophical Essays*, (eds) David J. Furley and Alexander Nehemas, Princeton, New Jersey, Princeton University Press, 1994, pp. 3–55.

Carberry, Sandra, *Plan Recognition in Natural Language Dialogue*, Cambridge, Mass., MIT Press, 1990.

Castelfranchi, Cristiano, and Yao-Hua Tan, "Introduction: why trust and deception are essential for virtual societies", *Trust and Deception in Virtual Societies*, Dordrecht, Kluwer, 2001, xvii–xxxi.

Cohen, Philip R., Raymond C., Perrault, and James F. Allen, "Beyond question answering", *Strategies for Natural Language Processing*, (ed.) W. Lehnert and M. Ringle, Hillsdale, New Jersey, Erlbaum, 1981, 245–274.

Colb, Sherry F., "When to admit character evidence in criminal cases", *North Carolina Law Review*, 79, 2001, 939–992.

Collingwood, Robin G., *An Autobiography*, Oxford, Oxford University Press, 1939.

Collingwood, Robin G., *The Idea of History*, Oxford, Clarendon Press, 1946.

Collins, Allan, Eleanor H. Warnock, Nelleke Aiello, and Mark L. Miller, "Reasoning from incomplete knowledge", *Representation and Understanding: Studies in Cognitive Science*, (ed.) Daniel G. Bobrow and Allan Collins, New York, Academic Press, 1975, 383–415.

Conte, Rosaria, and Mario Paolucci, *Reputation in Artificial Societies*, Dordrecht, Kluwer, 2002.

Copi, Irving M., and Carl Cohen, *Introduction to Logic*, 9th edn, New York, Macmillan, 1994.

Cragan, John F., and Craig W. Cutbirth, "A revisionist perspective on political *ad hominem* argument: a case study", *Central States Speech Journal*, 35, 1984, 228–237.

Cranston, Maurice, "Bacon, Francis", *The Encylopedia of Philosophy*, vol. 1, (ed.) Paul Edwards, New York, Macmillan, 1967, 235–240.

Davies, Leonard E., *Anatomy of Cross-Examination*, Englewood Cliffs, New Jersey, Prentice Hall, 1993.

DeMorgan, Augustus, *Formal Logic*, London, Taylor and Walton, 1847.

Dray, William, *Philosophy of History*, Englewood Cliffs, Prentice-Hall, 1964.

Dray, William, *History as Re-enactment: R. G. Collingwood's Idea of History*, Oxford, Oxford University Press, 1995.

Drefcinski, Shane, "Aristotle's fallible *phronimos*", *Ancient Philosophy*, 16, 1996, 139–154.

Editorial (anonymous), "Top scientist departing Canada", *CAUT Bulletin*, 49, 2002, pages A1 and A13.

Federal Rules of Evidence (FRE), A Hypertext Publication, Legal Information Institute, 1997, http:www.law.cornell.edu/rules/fre.

Feteris, Eveline T., *Fundamentals of Legal Argumentation: A Survey of Theories of the Justification of Legal Decisions*, Dordrecht, Kluwer, 1999.

Fikes, R.E., and Nilsson N.J., "STRIPS: a new approach to the application of theorem proving to problem solving", *Artificial Intelligence*, 2, 1971, 189–208.

Finocchiaro, Maurice, *Galileo and the Art of Reasoning*, Dordrecht, Reidel, 1980.

Franklin, Stan, and Art Graesser, "Is it an agent, or just a program?: a taxonomy for autonomous agents", In *Intelligent Agents III: Agent Theories, Architectures and Languages*, (eds) Jorg P. Muller, Michael J. Wooldridge and Nicholas R. Jennings, Berlin, Springer, 1996, 21–35.

Friedman, Richard D., "Minimizing the jury over-valuation concern", *Michigan State Law Review*, 4, 2003, 967–986.

Gagarin, Michael, "Probability and Persuasion: Plato and Early Greek Rhetoric", In *Persuasion: Greek Rhetoric in Action*, (ed.) Ian Worthington, London, Routledge, 1994, 47–68.

Goldman, Alvin I., "Empathy mind and morals", In *Mental Simulation: Evaluations and Applications*, (eds) Martin Davies and Tony Stone, Oxford, Blackwell, 1995, 185–208.

Gordon, Robert M., "Folk psychology as simulation", *Mind and Language*, 1, 1986, 158–171.

Gordon, Thomas F., *The Pleadings Game: An Artificial Intelligence Model of Procedural Justice*, Dordrecht, Kluwer, 1995.

Gordon, Thomas F., "A computational model of argument for legal reasoning support systems", In *Argumentation in Artificial Intelligence and Law*, (eds) Paul E. Dunne and Trevor Bench-Capon, IAAIL Workshop Series, Nijmegen, Wolf Legal Publishers, 2005, 53–64.

Grice, Paul H., "Logic and conversation", In *The Logic of Grammar*, (eds) Donald Davidson and Gilbert Harman, Encino, Dickenson, 1975, 64–75.

Hage, Jaap C., *Reasoning With Rules: An Essay on Legal Reasoning and Its Underlying Logic*, Dordrecht, Kluwer, 1997.

Hage, Jaap C., Ronald Leenes, and Arno R. Lodder, "Hard cases: a procedural approach", *Artificial Intelligence and Law*, 2, 1994, 113–167.

Hage, Jaap, "Dialectical models in artificial intelligence and law", *Artificial Intelligence and Law*, 8, 2000, 137–172.

Halfon, Mark S., *Integrity: A Philosophical Inquiry*, Philadelphia, Temple University Press, 1989.

Hamblin, Charles L., *Fallacies*, London, Methuen, 1970.

Hamblin, Charles L., "Mathematical models of dialogue", *Theoria*, 37, 1971, 130–155.

Hamblin, Charles L., *Imperatives*, New York, Blackwell, 1987.

Harman, Gilbert, "The inference to the best explanation", *Philosophical Review*, 74, 1965, 88–95.

Hastie, Reid, Steven D. Penrod, and Nancy Pennington, *Inside the Jury*, Cambridge, Mass., Harvard University Press, 1983.

Huhns, Michael H., and Munindar P. Singh, "Agents and multiagent systems: themes, approaches and challenges", In *Readings in Agents*, (eds) Michael H. Huhns and Munindar P. Singh, San Francisco, Morgan Kaufman Publishers, 1998, 1–23.

Isocrates, *Works: English and Greek*, trans. George Norlin, Loeb Classical Library, Cambridge, Harvard University Press, 1966.

Jennings, Nicholas R., and Michael Wooldridge, "Applying agent technology", *Applied Artificial Intelligence*, 9, 1995, 357–369.

Jonsen, Albert R., and Stephen Toulmin, *The Abuse of Casuistry: A History of Moral Reasoning*, Berkely, University of California Press, 1988.

Josephson, John R., and Susan G. Josephson, *Abductive Inference : Computation, Philosophy, Technology*, New York, Cambridge University Press, 1994.

Kateb, George, "Socratic integrity", In *Integrity and Conscience: Nomos XL*, (eds) Ian Shapiro and Robert Adams, New York, New York University Press, 1998, 77–112.

Kranhold, Kathryn, "Clean act: can an environmentalist hold on to his ideals and still run a utility?", *The Wall Street Journal*, January 12, 1999, 1.

Kupperman, Joel, *Character*, New York, Oxford University Press, 1991.

Landon, James, "Character evidence: getting to the root of the problem through comparison", *American Journal of Criminal Law*, 24, 1997, 581–615.

Leonard, David P.,"In defense of the character evidence prohibition: foundations of the rule against trial by character", *Indiana Law Journal*, 73, 1998, 1–59.

Lesh, Neal, Charles Rich and Candace Sidner, "Using plan recognition in human-computer collaboration", Lotus Technical Report 98-14 on Agents, Discourse Processing and User Interfaces, research@lotus.com, 2001.

Lodder, Arno R., *Dialaw: On Legal Justification and Dialogical Models of Argumentation*, Dordrecht, Kluwer, 1999.

Lodder, Arno R.,"Book review of Gordon (1995)", *Artificial Intelligence and Law*, 8, 2000, 255–264.

Loftus, Elizabeth, *Eyewitness Testimony*, Cambridge, Mass., Harvard University Press, 1979.

Loui, Ronald P., and Tomas F. Gordon, Call for papers for 1994 AAAI Seattle Workshop on Computational Dialectics, 1994: http://www.cs.wustl.edu/~loui/comectics.text

Macaulay, Thomas Babington, "Lord Bacon", In *Essays, Critical and Miscellaneous*, Boston, Phillips, Sampson and Company, 1856, 243–288.

Mackenzie, Jim, "The dialectics of logic", *Logique et Analyse*, 94, 1987, 159–177.

Mackenzie, Jim, "Four dialogue systems", *Studia Logica*, 49, 1990, 567–583.

Mans, Dieter, and Gerhard Preyer, "On contemporary developments in the theory of argumentation", *Protosociology*, 13, 1999, 3–13.

Martin, Rex, *Historical Explanation: Reenactment and Practical Inference*, Ithaca, Cornell University Press, 1977.

Mathews, Nieves, *Francis Bacon: The History of a Character Assassination*, New Haven, Yale University Press, 1996.

Maximilien, Michael E., and Munindar P. Singh, "Reputation and endorsement for web services", *SIGEcom Exchanges*, 3, 24–31, Winter 2002, ACM Special Interest Group on E-Commerce. Available in *pdf* format on the web page of Munindar P. Singh: www.csc.ncsu.edu/faculty/mpsingh/papers

McCormick, Neil, *McCormick on Evidence*, vol. 1, (ed.) John William Strong, St Paul, Minnesota, West Publishing Co., 1992.

McFall, Lynne, "Integrity", *Ethics and Personality: Essays in Moral Psychology*, (ed.) John Deigh, Chicago, University of Chicago Press, 1992, 79–94.

McKinnon, Christine, *Character, Virtue Theories, and the Vices*, Peterborough, Ontario, Broadview Press, 1999.

Moody, James, and Leellen Coacher, "A primer on methods of impeachment", *The Air Force Law Review*, 45, 1998, 161–200.

Moody-Adams, Michele, "On the old saw that character is destiny", In *Identity, Character and Morality*, (eds) Owen Flanagan and Amelie Oksenberg Rorty, Cambridge, Mass., MIT Press, 1990, 111–131.

Moore, Johanna D., *Participating in Explanatory Dialogues*, Cambridge, Mass., MIT Press, 1995.

Moore, Robert C., "Semantic considerations on nonmonotonic logic", *Artificial Intelligence*, 25, 1985, 75–94.

Morgan, Vivienne, and Trevor Mason, "MP's attack bid to allow bad character evidence", *Parliamentary News*, The Press Association Limited, April 2, 2003, 1–5.

Mueller, Christopher B., "Introduction: O.J. Simpson and the criminal justice system on trial", *University of Colorado Law Review*, 67, 1996, 727–745.

Nagel, Thomas, "Moral luck", *Mortal Questions*, Cambridge, Cambridge University Press, 1979.

Norman, Timothy J., and Chris Reed, "Delegation and responsibility", In *Intelligent Agents* VII, (eds) C. Castelfranchi and Y. Lesperance, Berlin, Springer, 2001, 136–149.

Nuchelmans, Gabriel, "On the fourfold root of the *argumentum ad hominem*", In *Empirical Logic and Public Debate*, (eds) Erik C.W. Krabbe, Renee Jose Dalitz and Pier A. Smit, Amsterdam, Rodopi, 1993, 37–47.

Park, Roger C., "Character evidence issues in the O.J. Simpson case — or rationales of the character evidence ban, with illustrations from the Simpson case", *University of Colorado Law Review*, 67, 1996, 747–776.

Park, Roger C., "Character at the crossroads", *Hastings Law Journal*, 49, 1998, 749–754.

Park, Roger C., "Adversarial influences on the interrogation of trial witnesses", *Adversarial versus Inquisitorial Justice*, (eds) Peter J. van Koppen and Steven D. Penrod, New York, Kluwer, 2003, 131–166.

Park, Roger C., David P. Leonard, and Steven H. Goldberg, *Evidence Law*, St. Paul, Minnesota, West Group, 1998.

Peirce, Charles S., "Elements of logic", In *Collected Papers of Charles Sanders Peirce*, vol. 2, (eds) Charles Hartshorne and Paul Weiss, Cambridge, Mass., Harvard University Press, 1965.

Peirce, Charles S., *Reasoning and the Logic of Things*, (ed.) Kenneth Laine Kettner, Cambridge, Mass., Harvard University Press, 1992.

Pennington, Nancy, and Reid Hastie, "A cognitive theory of juror decision making", *Cardozo Law Review*, 13, 1991, 519–557.

Pennington, Nancy, and Reid Hastie, "The story model for juror decision making", In *Inside the Juror: The Psychology of Juror Decision Making*, (ed.) Reid Hastie, Cambridge, Cambridge University Press, 1993, 192–221.

Pfau, Michael, and Michael Burgoon, "The efficacy of issue and character attack message strategies in political campaign communication", *Communication Reports*, 2, 1989, 53–61.

Prakken, Henry, *Logical Tools for Modelling Legal Argument*, Dordrecht, Kluwer, 1997.

Prakken, Henry, "Relating protocols for dynamic dispute with logics for defeasible argumentation", *Synthese*, 127, 2001, 187–219.

Prakken, Henry, and Giovanni Sartor, "A dialectical model of assessing conflicting arguments in legal reasoning", *Artificial Intelligence and Law*, 4, 1996, 331–368.

Premack, D., and G. Woodruff, "Does the chimpanzee have a theory of mind?", *Behavioral and Brain Sciences*, 1, 1978, 515–526.

Redmayne, Mike, "The relevance of bad character", *Cambridge Law Journal*, 61, 2002, 684–714.

Rewa, Michael P., *Reborn As Meaning: Panegyrical Biography From Isocrates to Walton*, Washington, DC, University Press of America, 1983.

Russell, Stuart J., and Peter Norvig, *Artificial Intelligence: A Modern Approach*, Upper Saddle River, New Jersey, Prentice Hall, 1995.

Sanchirico, Chris, "Character evidence and the object of trial", *The Columbia Law Review*, 101, 2001, 1227–1311.

Schank, Roger C., *Explanation Patterns: Understanding Mechanically and Creatively*, Hillsdale, New Jersey, Erlbaum, 1986.

Schank, Roger C., and Robert P. Abelson, *Scripts, plans, goals, and understanding: An inquiry into human knowledge structures*. Hillsdale, New Jersey, Erlbaum, 1977.

Schmidt, Charles F., "Partial provisional planning: some aspects of commonsense planning", *Formal Theories of the Commonsense World*, (ed.)

Jerry R. Hobbs and Robert C. Moore, Norwood, N. J., Ablex Publishing Corporation, 1985, 227–250.

Schmidt, C.F., Sridharan N.S., and Goodson J.L., "The plan recognition problem: an intersection of psychology and artificial intelligence", *Artificial Intelligence*, 11, 1978, 45–82.

Segerberg, Krister, "Routines", *Synthese*, 65, 1985, 185–210.

Sidgwick, Alfred, *The Process of Argument*, London, Adam and Charles Black, 1893.

Silverman, Barry G., *Critiquing Human Error*, London, Academic Press, 1992.

Sinclair, M.B.W., "Law and language: the role of pragmatics in statutory interpretation", *University of Pittsburgh Law Review*, 46, 1985, 373–420.

Stone, Julius, *Evidence: Its History and Policies*, Sydney, Butterworths, 1991.

Tillers, Peter, "What is wrong with character evidence?", Home Page of Peter Tillers: http://www.tiac.net/users/tillers/character.html, 1998 (28 pages).

Toulmin, Stephen, *The Uses of Argument*, Cambridge, Cambridge University Press, 1958.

Twining, William, "Narrative and generalizations in argumentation about questions of fact", *South Texas Law Review*, 40, 1999, 351–365.

Uviller, Richard H., "Evidence of character to prove conduct: illusion, illogic, and injustice in the courtroom", *University of Pennsylvania Law Review*, 130, 1982, 845–891.

Uviller, Richard H., *Virtual Justice: The Flawed Prosecution of Crime in America*, New Haven, Yale University Press, 1996.

van Eemeren, Frans H., and Rob Grootendorst, *Speech Acts in Communicative Discussions*, Dordrecht, Foris, 1984.

van Eemeren, Frans H., and Rob Grootendorst. *Argumentation, Communication and Fallacies*, Hillsdale, New Jersey, Erlbaum, 1992.

van Koppen, Peter, and Steven D. Penrod, "Adversarial or Inquisitorial: Comparing Systems", *Adversarial versus Inquisitorial Justice*, (eds) Peter J. van Koppen and Steven D. Penrod, New York, Kluwer, 2003, 1–19.

Verheij, Bart, "Dialectical argumentation with argumentation schemes: an approach to legal logic", *Artificial Intelligence and Law*, 11, 2003, 167–195.

Verheij, Bart, *Virtual Arguments*, The Hague, TCM Asser Press, 2005.

von Wright, Georg H., "On so-called practical inference", *Acta Sociologica*, 15, 1972, 39–53.

Wagenaar, Willem A., Peter J. van Koppen, and Hans F.M. Crombag, *Anchored Narratives: The Psychology of Criminal Evidence*, Hertfordshire, Harvester Wheatsheaf, 1993.

Walton, Douglas, *Courage: A Philosophical Investigation*, Berkeley, University of California Press, 1986.

Walton, Douglas, *Arguments from Ignorance*, University Park, The Pennsylvania State University Press, 1996.

Walton, Douglas, *Ad Hominem Arguments*, Tuscaloosa, University of Alabama Press, 1998.

Walton, Douglas, *Abductive Reasoning*, Tuscaloosa, University of Alabama Press, 2004.

Walton, Douglas N., and Erik C.W. Krabbe, *Commitment in Dialogue: Basic Concepts of Interpersonal Reasoning*, Albany, State University of New York Press, 1995.

Walton, Douglas, and Thomas F. Gordon, "Critical questions in computational models of legal argument", In *Argumentation in Artificial Intelligence and Law*, IAAIL Workshop Series, (eds) Paul E. Dunne and Trevor Bench-Capon, Nijmegen, Wolf Legal Publishers, 2005, 103–111.

Wecter, Dixon, "The democrat as hero", In *Abraham Lincoln: His Life, Work, and Character*, (ed.) Edward Wagenknecht, New York, Creative Age Press, 1947, 67–116.

Wellman, Carl, *Challenge and Response: Justification in Ethics*, Carbondale, Southern Illinois University Press, 1971.

Wigmore, John H., *The Principles of Judicial Proof*, 2nd edn, Boston, Little, Brown and Company, 1931.

Wilensky, Robert, *Planning and Understanding: A Computational Approach to Human Reasoning*, Reading, Mass., Addison-Wesley, 1983.

Wooldridge, Michael, *Reasoning about Rational Agents*, Cambridge, Mass., The MIT Press, 2000.

Wooldridge, Michael, and Nicholas R. Jennings, "Intelligent agents: theory and practice", *The Knowledge Engineering Review*, 10, 1995, 115–152.

Yearley, Lee H., *Mencius and Aquinas: Theories of Virtue and Conceptions of Courage*, Albany, State University of New York Press, 1990.

Yu, Bin, and Munindar P. Singh, "A social mechanism of reputation management in electronic communities", *Proceedings of the 4th International Workshop on Cooperative Information Agents*, Berlin, Springer-Verlag, 2000. Available in *pdf* format on the web page of Munindar P. Singh: www.csc.ncsu.edu/faculty/mpsingh/papers

Yu, Bin, and Munindar P. Singh, "An evidential model of distributed reputation management", *Proceedings of the 1st International Joint Conference on Autonomous Agents and Multi-Agent Systems*, July 2002. Available in *pdf* format on the web page of Munindar P. Singh: www.csc.ncsu.edu/faculty/mpsingh/papers

Yu, Bin, Mahadevan Venkatraman, and Munindar P. Singh, "An adaptive social network for information access: theoretical and experimental results", *Applied Artificial Intelligence*, 2002, to appear. Available in *pdf* format on the web page of Munindar P. Singh: www.csc.ncsu.edu/faculty/mpsingh/papers

INDEX

Abduction, 56, 72–73, 143, 166
  artificial intelligence, 57, 59
  defined, 58
  scientific, 57
Abductive argumentation, 68, 142, 158, 161
  dialectical argumentation scheme for, 167
  strength of, 219
Abductive character inference for identifying an agent from a past action, 190–91, 212–13
  critical questions, 195
  scheme for argument, 195, 213
Abductive evaluation, 69, 73
Abductive model, 184
Abductive theory of character evidence, 35
Abelson, Robert P., 163
Abstract episode schema, 53
Ad hominem argument, 99, 104
  abusive, 197
  bias, 198–99
  circumstantial, 197, 201
  evaluating, 26, 201–202
  historical origin, 196
  schemes for argument, 198–99, 211
  simulative reasoning in, 204
  two-sided nature of, 26–27
Ad hominem attack, 206
  Lincoln, Abraham, 25
Ad hominem fallacy, 197
Adversity, 81, 92–93, 103
Agent,
  abstract concept, 46
  actions of, 203
  assumptions of, 49
  bias, 74
  characteristics, 50
  collaboration, 146
  computer science, 33, 35
  defined, 40, 46–47, 63
  deliberations of, 35
  goal, 48, 63, 74, 126, 136, 203
  interpersonal relationship between, 78
  primary, 63, 109, 204, 208
    credibility of, 205
  properties of, 50–51
  rational, 151
  reasoning, 48
  research, 50
  secondary, 63, 109, 204, 208–209
  values, 194
Agent architecture, 49
Agent in a cave example, 120–21
Agent technology, 47
Akrasia, 93
Aiello, Nelleke, 116
Allegations,
  false, 21
Allen, Ronald J. 40–41, n181
Altruism, 93
Analogy, 129
Anchoring, 54–55
  safe, 54

Anderson, Terence, 187
Anscombe, Gertrude Elizabeth Margaret, 33
Antidosis, 16
Appeal to fear, 160
Appeal to pity, 160
Appeal to witness testimony, 52–53, 55–56, 77, 155–56, 160
Argument, 165
  relevance, 10
Argument from character, 16
Argument from character evidence, 13
Argument from commitment, 197
Argument from habit, 180
Argument from ignorance, 115–16
Argument from inconsistent commitment
  scheme for argument, 197
Argument from sign, 189
Argumentation schemes, 24, 53
Argumentum ad hominem, 196, 200
Argumentum ad ignorantiam, 157
Argumentum ad populum, 187
Aristotle, 47, 135–37, 142
  definition of excellent character, 74
  ethos, 1
  panegyric discourse, 19
  phronesis, 165
  practical wisdom, 47, 66
Armed robbery inference, 180
Aspersions, 22
Assertions, 8
Assumptions, 19, 58, 208
  rationality, 118
Atkinson, Katie, 194
Attachment, 112
Attack ads, 26
Attributions, 22, 62, 66, 67
Audi, Robert, 150
Automated question-answering system, 127

Backfire, 101, 162
Bacon, Francis case, 1, 15, 17–18, 94, 160
Bank robbery inference from modus operandi to alleged criminal act, 179
Barnden, John A., 137
Barr, Avron, 134
Barth, Else.M., 197
Barton, William E., 68
Bean example, 58–59
Beliefs, 154
Bench-Capon, Trevor, 194
Bias, 20, 55, 74, 78, 158, 187
  character judgements, 4, 75
  contextual nature of, 42
  described, 6, 41
  evidence of, 40, 75–76
  indicators of, n55
  judging, 41
  legal decision, 28
  negative, 42
  presumption of, 186
  racial, 6, 40, 75–76
  witness, 6, 186
  witness testimony, 6
Biased witness inference, 186
Blood evidence case, 12–13
Bloody knife inference, 186
Bounded rationality, 72
Bratman, Michael E., 65
Bryson, John case, 87–88, 94–95
Burden of proof, 9, 85, 161
  positive, 141
  tilted, 166
Burgoon, Michael, 99
Burning house examples, 66, 131–35, 170–74, 214
Burnyeat, Myles F., 135–37

Carberry, Sandra, 126, 147–48
Cardinal virtues, 29
Casuistry, 31, 72, 166
Challenge-response, 62, 143–44, 166, 168
Character
  assassination, 19, 28
  attack, 12, 15, 16, 98, 219
    effective, 26
    influence of, 20–21
    political, 22, 24–25
    weak, 107
  attributions, 66
  bad, 7, 40
  conclusions about, 69
  defined, 6, 8, 39–41, 63, 74
  disposition, 42
  evaluating, 29

generalizations, 8
broad, 8
inconsistencies of, 70
interpersonal concept of, 63
judgments of, 2, 17, 105, 145, 208, 214–215
flows in, 4
legal meaning of, 61
notion of, 182
quality of, 150–53, 166
rule, 7
slurs, 21
traditional definition, 3, 39
traits of, 29, 43–44
Character argument, 1, 41
misleading, 15
Character attack argument, 99
Character-based chain argument, 181
Character evidence, 27–28, 40, 186
balancing, 13
contextual basis of, 42
evaluated, 44
inadmissible, 5, 10, 14
position to know, 75
predictive, 190
prior questions, 75–76
questions about, 196
relevance of, 7, 11, 14, 34
strength of, 4–5, 33
types of, 149, 192–93
volatility of, 7
Character evidence rule, 34
Character of a witness for honesty, 30–31
Chimp experiment, 117–18
Clinton, President case, 31
Coacher, Leellen 76
Cognitive error, 14
Collingwood, Robin G., 106, 110, 150, 153, 165
theory of, 111–12, 120, 122, 140–41, 150, 163
strengthened, 122
Collins, Allan, 116
Commitments, 49, 65
active, 85, 91
altruistic, 153
determining, 84
evaluating consistency, 83
fulfilling, 91
inconsistent, 104
judged, 117
levels of, 85
living up to, 89–91
passive, 91
professed, 80, 88
retracted, 91–92, 102, 153, 155, 157
rules, 155
store, 154
testing, 92–93
Communication,
deceptive, 151
Computational dialectics, 36
Conclusions
conjectures, 130
Conditional, 141
absolute, 135
defeasible, 135
Conductive argument, 166, 168
evaluated, 144
strength of, 143
Conflict resolution, 174
Consistency, 55, 85
critical questions for, 55
Contradiction, 74, 157, 176
Conversational Principle, 52
Conviction
wrongful, 30
Corax, 142
Cragan, John F., 26
Credibility, 104
Criminal trial
stages of, 42
Critical questions
role of, 211
Crombag, Hans F.M., 54–55
Cross-examination, 156, 160
character determination in, 200
legal, 157
skill of, 157
truth determination, 158
Cutbirth, Craig W., 26

Davies, Leonard E., 158
de la Riviere, Adrien case, 31–32, 182
Deception, 81
Definition, 133

Deliberations, 111
  goal-directed, 111
  moral, 91
Delta racketeer syllogism, 13, 180
DeMorgan, Augustus, 202
Dialectical, 163
Dialogue
  critiquing, 170
  defined, 153, 167
  information-seeking, 170
  persuasion, 154
Dialogue model of explanation, 163
Discourse, political, 24–25, 99
Discussion
  critical, 41–42, 68, 75, 154, 170, 209
  goal of, 156
Dogmatism, 48, 71, 75, 119
Doxastic modal logic, 113–14
Dray, William, 111–12, 165

Election campaigns, 24
Embedding, 147
Emotional language, 160
Emotively loaded terms, 160
Emotivism, 28
Empathy, 36, 67, 109, 111, 120, 153, 207
  courtroom, 142
  degree of, 129
  spectrum of, 129
  understanding, 125
Entrapment, 11
  snares for, 162
Epistemic modal logic, 114
Ethical convictions, 102
Ethical dilemmas, 102
Ethical reflection, 150
Ethics,
  character in, 22
  commitment in 155
  study of, 28
  virtue, 24
Enthymeme, 135
  defined, 136
Euthydemus example, 188
Evidence, 189
  admissible, 10
  character-based, 189
    weakness of, 191
  circumstantial, 189
  factual, 192
  habit, 11
  inadmissible, 1
  propensity, 13
  relevant, 9, 12, 23, 139
  reputation, 149, 193
  rules of, 29–30, 192
  trace, 192
Evidence law, 2, 9, 30
  evolution of, 218
Evidential inferences, 29
Ethos, 1, 16, 62, 200
Examination, 170
Exemption, 212
Expert systems, 163
Explanation, 163–64, 167, 169
  analysis of, 164
  scientific, 165

Fallacy, 201
Fallacy of accident, 188
Fallacy of hasty conclusion, 83, 188
Fallacy of wrong conclusion, 160
Federal Rules of Evidence, 1
  Rule 401, 9, 10
  Rule 403, 10, 12
  Rule 404, 5, 7, 42–43, 218
    admissibility, 10–11, 40
    origins of, 12
  Rule 405, 11
  Rule 406, 11
  Rule 412, n11
  Rule 608, 10
  Rule 609, 10
Feedback, 47
Feigenbaum, Edward, 134
Feteris, Eveline, 156, 159
Focussing, 148
Frame problem, 126
Franklin, Stan, 50

Generalizations, 8, 135, 140, 159
  absolute, 141
  background information, 187
  common sense, 187
  defeasible, 184
  inductive, 140–41, 185

legal argumentation, 186
probabilistic, 181
qualified, 188
scientific, 187
universal, 185
Goals, 65, 194
collaborative, 154
Goldberg, Steven H., 7–8, 43–45
Goldman, Alvin I., 117
Gordon, Thomas F., 36, 118, 132, 159
Gore, Al tobacco case, 95–100, 105, 199–200, 204–207
argument analysis, 98
hypocrite, 96, 205–206
inconsistency, 205, 207
Graesser, Art, 50
Grice, Paul H., 52, 159
Gricean conversational maxims, 159
quantity, 159–60
Gricean implicature, 96–97, 100–101
Gricean notion of conversational implicature, 36
Grootendorst, Rob, 154

Hage, Jaap C., 159
Halfon, Mark S., 80–81
Hamblin, Charles L., 66, 89–90, 154, 196
Hamilton, William, sir, 135–136
Hapsfield, Nicholas, 19
Hastie, Reid, 53–54
Hasty conclusion, 14
Hasty generalization, 160
Hearsay example, 188
Hierarchy, 124
Honesty,
defined, 182
Hypocrisy, 79, 88, 175–76, 204
defined, 95
Hypothesis, 143, 167, 207

Image, 62
Impeachment, 156–57, 162, 200
Imperative, 89
Implicature, 98, 160
Inconsistency, 71, 88, 168, 170, 193, 197
allegation of, 96, 99, 203
explained, 84
practical, 96–97
pragmatic, 96
Inductive model, 183–84
Inferences
abductive, 59–60, 122, 166
chain of, 135
character-based, 178
defeasible, 149
explained, 65
leap of, 66
plausible, 128, 147
study of, 24
Inference from action to character, 182
critical questions, 194
scheme for argument, 194
Inference from character to action, 182–83
critical questions, 195
scheme for argument, 195
Inference from character to alleged criminal act, 45
Inference from dishonest character to lying, 31, 178
Inference from lying to dishonest character, 31, 178
Inference from modus operandi to alleged criminal act, 45–46
Inference from modus operandi to carrying out an action, 179
Inference linking evidence to character, 181
Inference to the best explanation, 57–59, 72, 105, 142–43, 145, 162
general rule, 57
Information dialogue
task related, 147
Information-seeking dialogue, 156
assumption of, 156
goal of, 156
Innuendo, 15–16, 160, 207
Bacon's case, 18
stain of, 18–19
unfounded, 21
Integrity, 67, 79, 92
attack on, 88
consistency, 85, 102
defined, 95
defining characteristics of, 80, 82
judged, 79–80, 91, 104

Integrity *(continued)*
  lack of, 87
  Nazi, 81
  stability of, 101
Intention, 65, 121
Isocrates, 16–17, 19
Iterated modalities, 113–114

Jennings, Nicholas R, 50–52
Jonsen, Albert R., 27
Josephson, John R., 57, 59–60, 123, 144, 166
Josephson, Susan G., 57, 59–60, 123, 144, 166

Kateb, George, 86
Key terms
  defined, 31–32
King, Martin Luther, 20
Krabbe, Erik C.W., 89, 147, 154
Kuhns, Richard B., 40–41
Kupperman, Joel, 64, 66–67, 69

Landon, James, 11–12, 42
Law
  adversarial system, 161–62
  Anglo-American, 7, 11–12, 34–35
  English, 9, 26–27, 34–35
  inquisitorial system, 161–62
  Roman, 9, 33–34
Laying a foundation, 76–77
Legal admissibility, 7
Legal examination, 157
Leonard, David P., 7–8, 9, 12, 43–45
Lincoln, Abraham, 2
  attack on character of, 24–25
  contradiction in character of, 68–71
  responses of, 25
  story about, 3
Locke, John, 196–97
Lodder, Arno R., 159
Logic, 176
Logical positivists, 112
Loui, Ron, 36
Lying, 15, 30, 49, 54, 81, 178
  defined, 31
  examples of 32
Lying witness chain of reasoning, 183

Macaulay, Thomas Babington, 18
Maieutic function, 154
Martens, Jo L., 197
Martin, Rex, 122, 165
Mathews, Nieves, 18
McBurney, Peter, 194
McCormick, Neil, 182
McFall, Lynne, 80–81
McKinnon, Christine, 33
Miller, Mark L., 116
Modus tollens, 115
Moody, James, 76
Moody-Adams, Michele, 101
Moore, Johanna, 36, 115–16, 163
  theory of explanation, 164
Motive, 5, 42, 74, 78
  relevance, 6
Multi-agent reasoning, 51, 203
  simulative, 106
Multi-agent systems, 33, 35–36, 48, 89, 145, 151, 177
  problem with, 51

Nagel, Thomas, 101
Napoleon example, 72–73
Negative ads, 99
Negative abductive character inference to a past action, 191–92
Negative campaign tactics, 24–26
Nietzsche, Friederich, 1
Norman, Timothy J., 89–90
Notion of normal patterns, 64–65
Norvig, Peter, 134
Nussbaum, Martha, 66

Open-mindedness, 41

Panegyric discourse, 19–20, 70, 160
  extremes, 28
  suspicions about, 19
Park, Roger C., 7–8, 29, 37, 43–45, 180, 183
Partial strategy, 89–90, 210

Past convictions inference, 181
Peirce, Charles.S., 56–59
Penninger, Dr. Josef case, 21
Pennington, Nancy, 53–54
Penrod, Steven D., 53
Personal attack argument, 99, 160, 197
  historical use of, 24
Persuasion, 17
PFARD system, 177, 207, 213–14
  chain of reasoning in, 215–17
Pfau, Michael, 99
Picture hanging plan, 146–48
Plans
  hierarchy, 134
Plan identification technology, 148
Plan recognition, 36, 100, 125–26, 146–47, 203–204, 207
  stages of, 126
Plato
  interpretation of Socrates, 86
Plausibility, 53, 55
Pleadings game, 159
Politics, 24
  character attack arguments in, 25–26
  image, 62
  persuasion in, 16–17
Poseidon Adventure example, 120
Positivistic deductive-nomological theory, 165
Positivists, 73, 106, 112, 125, 215
Prakken, Henry, 159
Prediction, 32, 133, 181, 185
Prejudice, 160, 188
  jury, 7, 10, 12, 17, 30, 34
Premack, David, 116
Premise
  distinct, 128
  missing, 123
Presumption, 19, 21, 49, 58, 82, 98, 122
  weight of, 200
Probability, 32, 136, 181, 184
  described, 10
Problem of dirty hands, 203
Promise, 84
Propaganda, 19, 107, 152
Propensity, 7, 11, 29, 178, 181
Propensity arguments
  nature of, 13
  relevance, 8
Proponent, 113, 153

Quantifier
  universal, 135, 140
Quarrel, 186

Reasoning
  abductive, 58, 71, 103–105, 129–130, 133, 137, 214
  chain of, 190
  autoepistemic, 114–16
  backwards, 109, 134
  case-based, 143
  chain of, 89, 137
  conductive, 143
  deductive, 49, 58, 185
  defeasible, 139
  ethical, 143
  fallacious, 14
  forward, 134
  generalization based, 187–88
  indirect, 105
  inductive, 58, 185
  interpersonal simulative, 115
  logical, 125
  nonmonotonic, 116
  means-end, 53
  plausible, 140
    basis, 141
  practical, 47, 67, 121
    chain of, 174
    critical questions for, 194
    evaluating, 209
    scheme for, 193
    sequence of, 53
  predictive, 190
  simulative, 36, 110, 112–13, 115, 118, 133, 137, 171, 204
    abductive, 119
    courtroom, 142
    critical questions, 172
    nested triple, 205
  spurious, 191
  trace, 184
Redmayne, Mike, 4, 14, 34, 218

Reed, Chris, 89–90
Reenactment, 106, 110–11, 123
  described, 124
Reflexivity, 130
Relativism, 28
Relevance
  defined, 10
  logical, 7
Reputation, 2, 152
  attacked, 15
  described, 61–62
  evidence of, 44
  good character, 17
  importance of, 17
  ruined, 16
Reputation management, 152
Reputation mechanisms, 151
Reputation systems, 23–24
Resource description framework, 211
Respect, 2–3
  affected by reputation, 2
Respect model, 3
Respondent, 113, 153
Retraction, 58, 92, 153, 155, 208
Retrodiction, 133
Rewa, Michael P., 19
Rigidity, 103
Role models, 20, 70
Routine, 123–24
Rule (see also Federal Rules), 81
  commitment, 154
  general, 58
  locution, 154
  structural, 154
  win and loss, 154
Rumor, 15–16, 19, 21–22, 192
Russell, Stuart J., 134

Sanchirico, Chris, 14
Schank, Roger C., 129, 163, 165
Schmidt, Charles F., 127, 146
Scientific investigation
  discovery stage, 56
Scripts, 105, 122, 128, 145, 163, 209
  restaurant, 122
Secundum quid (See Hasty generalization, fallacy of)
Shared plan theory, 146
Shoe print example, 189–90
Sidgwick, Alfred, 186
Simpson, Orenthal J. case, 5–7, 34, 42
  racism in, 40, 75
Simulation, 112
  defined, 116
Simulation theory, 116
Simulative practical reasoning,
  autoepistemic, 130
  characteristics of, 128–29
Sincerity, 114
Sinclair, Michael B.W., 157, 159
Singh, Munindar P., 151
Situationism, 14
Slander, 207
Smith, William Kennedy case, 7, 8
Smoking case, 83, 201–203
Socrates, 81–82, 114–15, 188
  commitment of, 86
Sophists, 141–42
Spedding, James, 18
Speech acts, 148
Sportsman's rejoinder, 202–203
Stereotypes, 188
Stevenson, Adlai E., 26, 137
Stone, Julius, 22, 61–62
STRIPS planner, 126
Subjectivism, 28
Supposition, 58
Swift, Eleanor, 40–41
Sycara, Katya, 36
Syllogism, 135, 180
  practical, 47
  proper, 47
  valid, 136

Tactics
  negative campaign, 1, 4, 24
  police, 6
  sleazy smear tactics, 101
Taking out the garbage example, 89–90
Testimonial evidence, 186
Testimonial opinion medium, 62
Theory-theory, 117
Tidmarsch case, 57–58, 60
Tillers, Peter, 14–15

Tisias, 142
Toulmin, Stephen, 27
  warrant, 159
TRACK, 147–48
  explained, 148
Trait theory, 14
Trust rating, 152
Tweety case, 141
Twining, William, 160, 187–88

Ultimate *probandum*, 193
Understanding, 164
Uviller, Richard H., 12–13, 149, 180, 192

van Eemeren, Frans H., 154
Verheij, Bart, 211
Verstehen, 122
Virtues
  ethical, 33
von Koppen, Peter J., 54–55
von Wright, Georg, 165

Wagenaar, Willem A., 54–55
Walton, Douglas, 89, 147, 154
Walton, Sir Izaak, 19
Warnock, Eleanor H., 116
Warrant
  described, 52
Wellman, Carl, 48, 143–44, 168
Why-questions, 165
Wigmore, John H., 9, 185
Witness
  credibility, 201
  described, 52
Witness's character for truthfulness case, 76–77
Witness testimony, 52, 161, 193
  bias, 6
  credibility, 5, 10
  evaluated, 158
  examination of, 164
  fallibility, 54, 156
  reproducibility, 55
  story form of, 71, 119
Woodruff, Guy, 116
Wooldridge, Michael, 50–52, 151

Yearley, Lee H., 66
Yu, Bin, 151

Zealot, 80

MIX
Papier aus verantwortungsvollen Quellen
Paper from responsible sources
FSC® C105338

If you have any concerns about our products,
you can contact us on
ProductSafety@springernature.com

In case Publisher is established outside the EU,
the EU authorized representative is:
Springer Nature Customer Service Center GmbH
Europaplatz 3, 69115 Heidelberg, Germany

Printed by Libri Plureos GmbH
in Hamburg, Germany